CREATIVE
HOMEOWNER®

BRICK
• STONE
• STUCCO
• MASONRY
HOME PLANS

CREATIVE HOMEOWNER®, Upper Saddle River, New Jersey

COPYRIGHT © 2006

CRE▲TIVE
HOMEOWNER®

A Division of Federal Marketing Corp.
Upper Saddle River, NJ

VP/Publisher: Brian H. Toolan
VP/Editorial Director: Timothy O. Bakke
Production Manager: Kimberly H. Vivas

Home Plans Editor: Kenneth D. Stuts
Home Plans Designer Liaison: Maureen Mulligan

Design and Layout: Arrowhead Direct (David Kroha, Cindy DiPierdomenico, Judith Kroha)

Cover Design: David Geer

Printed in China

Current Printing (last digit)
10 9 8 7 6 5 4 3 2 1

Brick Home Plans, First Edition
Library of Congress Control Number: 2005909004
ISBN-10: 1-58011-302-8
ISBN-13: 978-1-58011-302-1

CREATIVE HOMEOWNER®
A Division of Federal Marketing Corp.
24 Park Way
Upper Saddle River, NJ 07458
www.creativehomeowner.com

Note: The homes as shown in the photographs and renderings in this book may differ from the actual blueprints. When studying the house of your choice, please check the floor plans carefully.

PHOTO CREDITS

Front Cover: *main* plan 321051, page 220; *insets left to right* plan 151529, page 11; plan 441014, page 274; plan 441024, pages 298–299; plan 121073, page 257
Back cover: *top main* plan 121062, page 292; *bottom main* plan 161101, page 340; *insets left to right* plan 161101, page 340; plan 161101, page 340; plan 161104, page 339
Page 1: plan 121082, page 246
Page 3: *top to bottom* plan 101005, page 94; plan 161093, Pages 334-335; plan 441024, pages 298-299
Page 4: plan 111003
Page 5: plan 331005, page 320
Page 6: *top* plan 141028; *bottom* plan 161002, page 117
Page 7: plan 221022, page 321
Pages 60–63: *all* John Parsekian/CH
Page 64: *left* H. Armstrong Roberts; *right* Jessie Walker
Page 65: *both* Charles Mann
Page 66: Tim Street-Porter/Beateworks, architect: Paul Williams
Page 122: *all* John Parsekian/CH
Page 123: *top* John Parsekian/CH; *bottom both* courtesy of Prosoco
Pages 124–126: *all* John Parsekian/CH
Page 127: *top left, top right, center left & bottom left* John Parsekian/CH; *bottom right* carolynbates.com
Page 202: John Parsekian/CH
Page 204: Jerry Pavia
Page 205: *all* John Parsekian/CH
Page 206–207: *top right* Tim Street-Porter/Beateworks; *bottom sequence* John Parsekian/CH
Pages 208–209: John Parsekian/CH
Page 210: Jerry Pavia
Page 211: *both* John Parsekian/CH
Page 280: Michael Thompson, design: Sarah Robertson
Page 281: *top* Camerique/H. Armstrong Roberts; *center* courtesy of Cultured Stone Corporation; *bottom* courtesy of The Brick Industry
Page 282: Brad Simmons Photography
Page 283: *top right & bottom* Tim Street-Porter/Beateworks; *center left* Brad Simmons Photography; *top left* Richard Felber
Page 284: Richard Felber
Page 285: *top* Brad Simmons Photography; *bottom left* Elizabeth Whiting Associates; *bottom right* Creative Homeowner
Page 341: plan 291016, page 227
Page 350-351: plan 111031, page 264

Contents

Getting Started

Maybe you can't wait to bang the first nail. Or you may be just as happy leaving town until the windows are cleaned. The extent of your involvement with the construction phase is up to you. Your time, interests, and abilities can help you decide how to get the project from lines on paper to reality. But building a house requires more than putting pieces together. Whoever is in charge of the process must competently manage people as well as supplies, materials, and construction. He or she will have to

- Make a project schedule to plan the orderly progress of the work. This can be a bar chart that shows the time period of activity by each trade.
- Establish a budget for each category of work, such as foundation, framing, and finish carpentry.
- Arrange for a source of construction financing.
- Get a building permit and post it conspicuously at the construction site.
- Line up supply sources and order materials.
- Find subcontractors and negotiate their contracts.
- Coordinate the work so that it progresses smoothly with the fewest conflicts.
- Notify inspectors at the appropriate milestones.
- Make payments to suppliers and subcontractors.

You as the Builder

You'll have to take care of every logistical detail yourself if you decide to act as your own builder or general contractor. But along with the responsibilities of managing the project, you gain the flexibility to do as much of your own work as you want and subcontract out the rest. Before taking this path, however, be sure you have the time and capabilities. Do you also have the

time and ability to schedule the work, hire and coordinate subs, order materials, and keep ahead of the accounting required to manage the project successfully? If you do, you stand to save the amount that a general contractor would charge to take on these responsibilities, normally 15 to 30 percent of the construction cost. If you take this responsibility on but mismanage the project, the potential savings will erode and may even cost you more than if you had hired a builder in the first place. A subcontractor might charge extra for hav-

Acting as the builder, above, requires the ability to hire and manage subcontractors.

Building a home, opposite, includes the need to schedule building inspections at the appropriate milestones.

ing to return to the site to complete work that was originally scheduled for an earlier date. Or perhaps because you didn't order the windows at the beginning, you now have to pay for a recent cost increase. (If you had hired a builder in the first place he or she would absorb the increase.)

Hiring a Builder to Handle Construction

A builder or general contractor will manage every aspect of the construction process. Your role after signing the construction contract will be to make regular progress payments and ensure that the work for which you are paying has been completed. You will also consult with the builder and agree to any changes that may have to be made along the way.

Leads for finding builders might come from friends or neighbors who have had contractors build, remodel, or add to their homes. Real-estate agents and bankers may have some names handy but are more likely familiar with the builder's ability to complete projects on time and budget than the quality of the work itself.

The next step is to narrow your list of candidates to three or four who you think can do a quality job and work harmoniously with you. Phone each builder to see whether he or she is interested in being considered for your project. If so, invite the builder to an interview at your home. The meeting will serve two purposes. You'll be able to ask the candidate about his or her experience, and you'll be able to see whether or not your personalities are compatible. Go over the plans with the builder to make certain that he or she understands the scope of the project. Ask if they have constructed similar houses. Get references, and check the builder's standing with the Better Business Bureau. Develop a short list of builders, say three, and ask them to submit bids for the project.

Contracts

Lump-Sum Contracts

A lump-sum, or fixed-fee, contract lets you know from the beginning just what the project will cost, barring any changes made because of your requests or unforeseen conditions. This form works well for projects that promise few surprises and are well defined from the outset by a complete set of contract documents. You can enter into a fixed-price contract by negotiating with a single builder on your short list or by obtaining bids from three or four builders. If you go the latter route, give each bidder a set of documents and allow at least two weeks for them to submit their bids. When you get the bids, decide who you want and call the others to thank them for their efforts. You don't have to accept the lowest bid, but it probably makes sense to do so since you have already honed the list to builders you trust. Inform this builder of your intentions to finalize a contract.

Cost-Plus-Fee Contracts

Under a cost-plus-fee contract, you agree to pay the builder for the costs of labor and materials, as verified by receipts, plus a fee that represents the builder's overhead and profit. This arrangement is sometimes referred to as "time and materials." The fee can range between 15 and 30 percent of the incurred costs. Because you ultimately pick up the tab—whatever the costs—the contractor is never at risk, as he is with a lump-sum contract. You won't know the final total cost of a cost-plus-fee contract until the project is built and paid for. If you can live with that uncertainty, there are offsetting advantages. First, this form allows you to accommodate unknown conditions much more easily than does a lump-sum contract. And rather than being tied down by the project documents, you will be free to make changes at any point along the way. This can be a trap, though. Watching the project take shape will spark the desire to add something or do something differently. Each change costs more, and the accumulation can easily exceed your budget. Because of the uncertainty of the final tab and the built-in advantage to the contractor, you should think twice before entering into this form of contract.

Contract Content

The conditions of your agreement should be spelled out thoroughly in writing and signed by both parties, whatever contractual arrangement you make with your builder. Your contract should include provisions for the following:

- The names and addresses of the owner and builder.
- A description of the work to be included ("As described in the plans and specifications dated . . .").
- The date that the work will be completed if time is of the essence.
- The contract price for lump-sum contracts and the builder's allowed profit and overhead costs for changes.
- The builder's fee for cost-plus-fee contracts and the method of accounting and requesting payment.
- The criteria for progress payments (monthly, by project milestones) and the conditions of final payment.
- A list of each drawing and specification section that is to be included as part of the contract.
- Requirements for guarantees. (One year is the standard period for which contractors guarantee the entire project, but you may require specific guarantees on

When submitting bids, all of the builders should base their estimates on the same specifications. Once the work begins, communicate with your builder to keep the work proceeding smoothly.

Inspect your newly built home, if possible, before the builder closes it up and finishes it.

certain parts of the project, such as a 20-year guarantee on the roofing.)
- Provisions for insurance.
- A description of how changes in the work orders will be handled.

The builder may have a standard contract that you can tailor to the specifics of your project. These contain complete specific conditions with blanks that you can fill in to fit your project and a set of "general conditions" that cover a host of issues from insurance to termination provisions. It's always a good idea to have an attorney review the draft of your completed contract before signing it.

Working with Your Builder

The construction phase officially begins when you have a signed copy of the contract and copies of any insurance required from the builder. It's not unheard of for a builder to request an initial payment of 10 to 20 percent of the total cost to cover mobilization costs, those costs associated with obtaining permits and getting set up to begin the actual construction. If you agree to this, keep a careful eye on the progress of the work to ensure that the total paid out at any one time doesn't get too far out of sync with the actual work completed.

What about changes? From here on, it's up to you and your builder to proceed in good faith and to keep the channels of communication open. Even so, changes of one sort or another beset every project, and they usually add to its cost.

Light at the End of the Tunnel.

The builder's request for a final inspection marks the end of the construction phase—almost. At the final inspection meeting, you and the builder will inspect the work, noting any defects or incomplete items on a "punch list." When the builder tidies up the punch list items, you should reinspect. Sometimes, builders go on to another job and take forever to clean up the last few details, so only after all items on the list have been completed satisfactorily should you release the final payment, which often accounts for the builder's profit.

Some Final Words

Having a positive attitude is important when undertaking a project as large as building a home. A positive attitude can help you ride out the rigors and stress of the construction process.

Stay Flexible. Expect problems, because they certainly will occur. Weather can upset the schedule you have established for subcontractors. A supplier may get behind on deliveries, which also affects the schedule. An unexpected pipe may surprise you during excavation. Just as certain, every problem that comes along has a solution if you are open to it.

Be Patient. The extra days it may take to resolve a construction problem will be forgotten once the project is completed.

Express Yourself. If what you see isn't exactly what you thought you were getting, don't be afraid to look into changing it. Or you may spot an unforeseen opportunity for an improvement. Changes usually cost more money, though, so don't make frivolous decisions.

Finally, watching your home go up is exciting, so stay upbeat. Get away from your project from time to time. Dine out. Take time to relax. A positive attitude will make for smoother relations with your builder. An optimistic outlook will yield better-quality work if you are doing your own construction. And though the project might seem endless while it is under way, keep in mind that all the planning and construction will fade to a faint memory at some time in the future, and you will be getting a lifetime of pleasure from a home that is just right for you.

Plan #181224

Dimensions: 36' W x 39'8" D

Levels: 2

Square Footage: 1,727

Main Level Sq. Ft.: 837

Upper Level Sq. Ft.: 890

Bedrooms: 3

Bathrooms: 2

Foundation: Basement

Material List Available: Yes

Price Category: C

Images provided by designer/architect.

This elegant home occupies a small footprint.

Features:

• Living Room: This two-story gathering place features a cozy fireplace and tall windows, which flood the room with natural light.

• Kitchen: This island kitchen has plenty of cabinet and counter space. It is open to the breakfast room.

• Upper Level: On this level you will find a balcony that overlooks the living room. Also, there are three bedrooms and a large bathroom.

• Garage: This one-car garage has room for a car plus some storage area.

Main Level Floor Plan

11'-0" X 13'-8"
3,30 X 4,10

10'-4" X 11'-8"
3,10 X 3,50

12'-0" X 15'-8"
3,60 X 4,70

12'-0" X 24'-0"
3,60 X 7,20

39'-8"
11,9 m

36'-0"
10,8 m

Copyright by designer/architect.

Upper Level Floor Plan

13'-0" X 12'-0"
3,90 X 3,60

12'-4" X 12'-0"
3,70 X 3,60

9'-8" X 9'-4"
2,90 X 2,80

Front View

Kitchen

Dining Room/Living Room

Master Bath

Master Bath

Plan #321057

Dimensions: 38' W x 39'4" D
Levels: 2
Square Footage: 1,524
Main Level Sq. Ft.: 951
Upper Level Sq. Ft.: 573
Bedrooms: 3
Bathrooms: 2½
Foundation: Basement
Materials List Available: Yes
Price Category: C

You'll love the comfort you'll find in this compact home, which also sports a practical design.

Features:

- Entry: This two-story entry is lit by a lovely oval window on the second-floor level.

- Living Room: A masonry fireplace sets a gracious tone, and the large windows and sliding door leading to the patio give natural lighting.

- Dining Room: The bay window here makes a perfect spot to place a table in this room.

- Kitchen: Situated between the living and dining rooms for convenience, the kitchen is designed as an efficient work area.

- Master Suite: A large walk-in closet and sliding doors to the patio are highlights of the bedroom, and the private bath features a double vanity.

- Upper Level: You'll find two walk-in closets in one bedroom and one in the other.

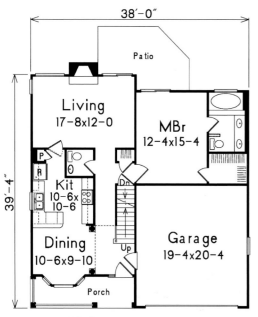

Main Level Floor Plan

Upper Level Floor Plan

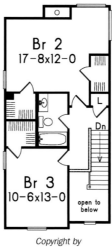

Copyright by designer/architect.

Front View

Plan #151529

Dimensions: 43' W x 66'6" D
Levels: 1
Square Footage: 1,474
Bedrooms: 2
Bathrooms: 2
Foundation: Crawl space or slab
CompleteCost List Available: Yes
Price Category: B

This elegant design is reflective of the Arts and Crafts era. Copper roofing and carriage style garage doors warmly welcome guests into this split-bedroom plan.

Features:

- Great Room: With access to the grilling porch as a bonus, this large gathering area features a 10-ft.-high ceiling and a beautiful fireplace.

- Kitchen: This fully equipped island kitchen has a raised bar and a built-in pantry. The area is open to the great room and dining room, giving an open and airy feeling to the home.

- Master Suite: Located on the opposite side of the home from the secondary bedroom, this retreat offers a large sleeping area and two large closets. The master bath features a spa tub, a separate shower, and dual vanities.

- Bedroom: This secondary bedroom has a large closet and access to the full bathroom in the hallway.

Images provided by designer/architect.

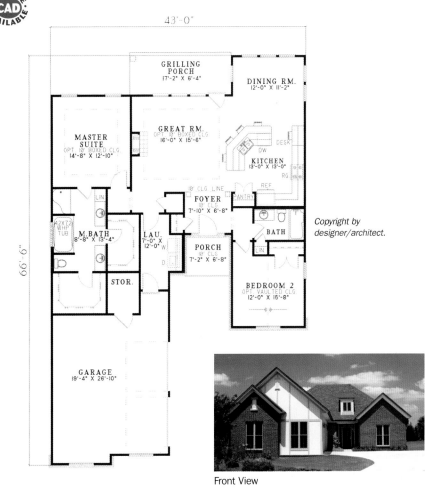

Copyright by designer/architect.

Front View

Plan #121056

Dimensions: 48' W x 50' D

Levels: 1

Square Footage: 1,479

Bedrooms: 2

Bathrooms: 2

Foundation: Basement

Materials List Available: Yes

Price Category: B

This home is ideal if the size of your live-in family is increasing with the addition of a baby, or if it's decreasing as children leave the nest.

Features:

- Entry: This entry gives you a long view into the great room that it opens into.

- Great Room: An 11-ft. ceiling and a fireplace framed by transom-topped windows make this room comfortable in every season and any time of day or night.

- Den: French doors open to this den, with its picturesque window. This room would also make a lovely third bedroom.

- Kitchen: This kitchen has an island that can double as a snack bar, a pantry, and a door into the backyard.

- Master Suite: A large walk-in closet gives a practical touch; you'll find a sunlit whirlpool tub, dual lavatories, and a separate shower in the bath.

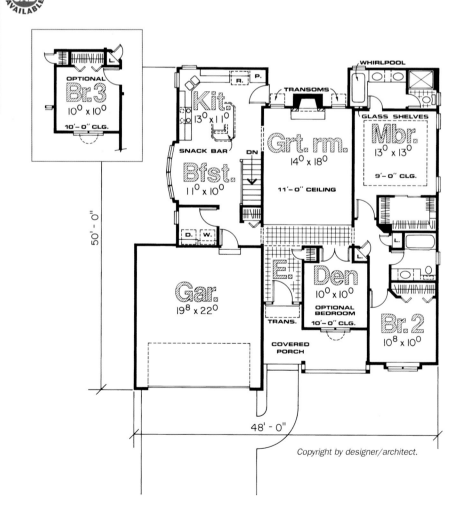

Plan #391008

Dimensions: 50' W x 40' D

Levels: 1

Square Footage: 1,312

Bedrooms: 3

Bathrooms: 2

Foundation: Crawl space, slab, or basement

Materials List Available: Yes

Price Category: B

Here's the sum of brains and beauty, which will please all types of families, from starters and nearly empty nesters to those going golden.

Features:

- Entry: This restful fresh-air porch and formal foyer bring you graciously toward the great room, with its fireplace and vaulted ceiling.

- Dining Room: This adjacent dining room features sliding doors to the deck and smooth open access to the U-shaped kitchen.

- Laundry Room: The laundry area has its own separate landing from the garage, so it's conveniently out of the way.

- Master Suite: This master suite with tray ceilings features nearly "limitless" closet space, a private bath, and large hall linen closet.

- Bedrooms: The two secondary bedrooms, also with roomy closets, share a full bath. Bedroom 3 easily becomes a home office with direct foyer access and a window overlooking the porch.

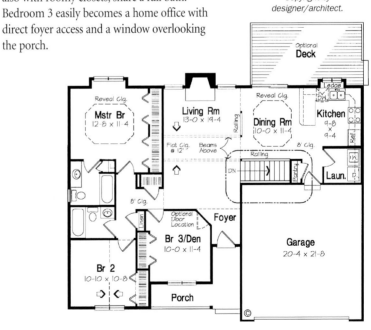

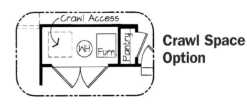

Crawl Space Option

Plan #151010

Dimensions: 38'4" W x 68'6" D

Levels: 1

Square Footage: 1,379

Bedrooms: 3

Bathrooms: 2

Foundation: Crawl space, slab

CompleteCost List Available: Yes

Price Category: B

Images provided by designer/architect.

This French Country home has a spacious great room for friends and family to gather, but you can sneak away to the covered rear porch or patio off the master suite for cozy tête-à-têtes.

Features:

- Entry: Take advantage of the marvelous 10-ft. ceilings to hang groups of potted flowering plants.

- Great Room: This spacious room, with an optional 10-ft. boxed ceiling, is the place to curl up by the gas fireplace on a cold winter night.

- Kitchen: The kitchen includes a bar for casual meals, and is open to the breakfast room.

- Rear Porch: Enjoy leisurely meals on the covered rear porch that you can access from both the master suite and the breakfast room.

- Master Suite: The 10-ft. boxed ceiling in the bedroom and the master bath with a whirlpool tub and separate shower make this suite a luxurious place to end a long day.

Copyright by designer/architect.

Plan #181215

Dimensions: 30' W x 32' D
Levels: 1
Square Footage: 929
Bedrooms: 2
Bathrooms: 1
Foundation: Basement
Materials List Available: Yes
Price Category: A

Images provided by designer/architect.

Whether just starting out or wrapping it up for the Golden Years, this generous one-level is perfect for two-plus. A peaked roofline, Palladian window, and covered front porch are a visual delight.

Features:

• Entry: An open interior branches out from the entry hall to the family room, where a cathedral ceiling soars to 10'-6¾".

• Dining Room: This room, which adjoins the family room, also embraces openness.

• Kitchen: This cordial kitchen features a breakfast counter for two and sprawling space for food preparation.

• Bedrooms: A full bathroom is nestled between two large bedrooms. Bedroom 1 enjoys a front and side view. Bedroom 2 has an intimate backyard vista.

Copyright by designer/architect.

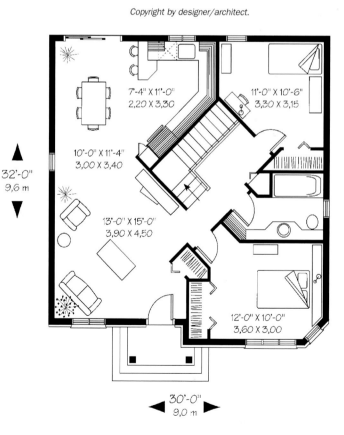

7'-4" X 11'-0"
2,20 X 3,30

11'-0" X 10'-6"
3,30 X 3,15

10'-0" X 11'-4"
3,00 X 3,40

13'-0" X 15'-0"
3,90 X 4,50

12'-0" X 10'-0"
3,60 X 3,00

32'-0"
9,6 m

30'-0"
9,0 m

Plan #151336

Dimensions: 39'4" W x 63'2" D

Levels: 1

Square Footage: 1,480

Bedrooms: 3

Bathrooms: 2

Foundation: Crawl space or slab

CompleteCost List Available: Yes

Price Category: B

Images provided by designer/architect.

This brick ranch has room for everyone.

Features:

- Great Room: At the heart of the home is this impressive room, with its 10-ft.-high ceilings and peninsula fireplace.

- Kitchen: Off the great room, your family will enjoy meals together any time of day in this expansive kitchen. It features an island, open eating bar, and breakfast nook complete with bay windows; you won't hear any excuses for not finding time to eat.

- Master Suite: This private space features a large sleeping area and access to the rear porch. The master bath boasts a large closet, dual vanities, a whirlpool tub, and a compartmentalized toilet area.

- Bedrooms: Two additional bedrooms have large closets and share a common bathroom.

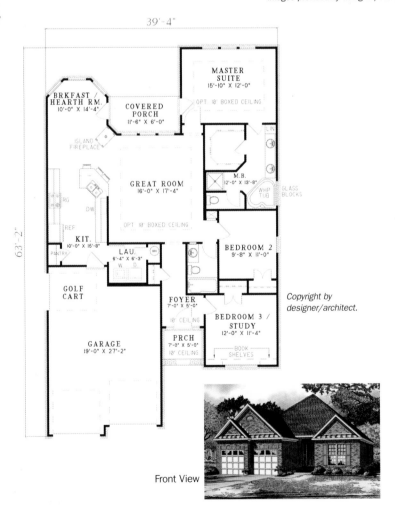

Copyright by designer/architect.

Front View

Plan #161001

Dimensions: 67'2" W x 47' D

Levels: 1

Square Footage: 1,782

Bedrooms: 3

Bathrooms: 2

Foundation: Basement

Materials List Available: Yes

Price Category: C

An all-brick exterior displays the solid strength that characterizes this gracious home.

Features:

- Great Room: A feeling of spaciousness permeates the gathering area created by the foyer, great room, and dining room. Multiple windows provide natural light that dances along a sloped ceiling, spilling onto decorative columns and a fireplace.

- Breakfast Area: A continuation of the sloped ceiling leads to the breakfast area where French doors open to a screened porch.

- Kitchen: An abundance of cabinets and counter space are the hallmarks of this large kitchen with its easy access to a spacious laundry room and storage area.

- Master Suite: A tray ceiling and spacious walk-in closet in the master bedroom, along with a whirlpool tub and double-bowl vanity in the bathroom, enable you to pamper yourself.

Images provided by designer/architect.

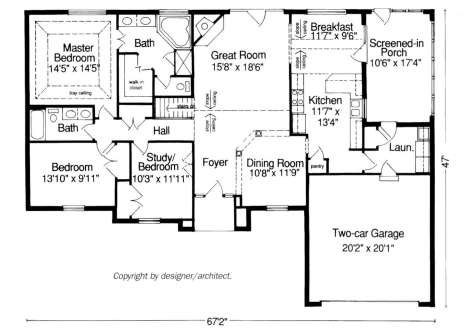

Copyright by designer/architect.

67'2"

Great Room/Foyer

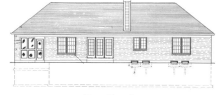

Rear Elevation

Plan #101004

Dimensions: 55'8" W x 56'6" D

Levels: 1

Square Footage: 1,787

Bedrooms: 3

Bathrooms: 2

Foundation: Crawl space, slab, or basement

Materials List Available: Yes

Price Category: C

This carefully designed ranch provides the feel and features of a much larger home.

Features:

- Ceiling Height: 9 ft. unless otherwise noted.

- Foyer: Guests will step up onto the inviting front porch and into this foyer, with its impressive 11-ft. ceiling.

- Dining Room: Open to the entry and to its left is this elegant dining room, perfect for entertaining or informal family gatherings.

- Family Room: This family gathering place features an 11-ft. ceiling to enhance its sense of spaciousness.

- Kitchen: This intelligently designed kitchen has an open plan. A breakfast bar and a serving bar are features that add to its convenience.

- Master Suite: This suite is loaded with amenities, including a double-step tray ceiling, direct access to the screened porch, a sitting room, deluxe bath, and his and her walk-in closets.

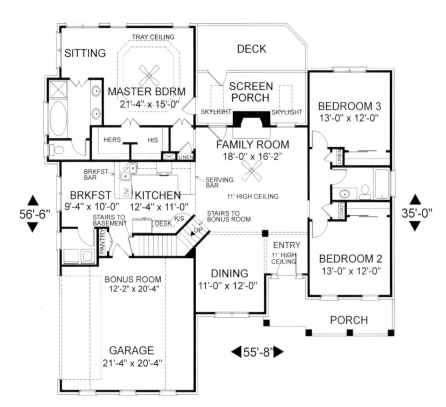

Copyright by designer/architect.

Kitchen

Family Room

Dining Room

Master Bath

Bedroom

Master Bedroom

Plan #161015

Dimensions: 55'4" W x 40'4" D
Levels: 2
Square Footage: 1,768
Main Level Sq. Ft.: 960
Upper Level Sq. Ft.: 808
Bedrooms: 3
Bathrooms: 2½
Foundation: Basement
Materials List Available: Yes
Price Category: C

Images provided by designer/architect.

One look at this dramatic exterior—a 12-ft. high entry with a transom and sidelights, multiple gables, and an impressive box window—you'll fall in love with this home.

Features:

- **Foyer:** This 2-story area announces the grace of this home to everyone who enters it.

- **Great Room:** A natural gathering spot, this room is sunken to set it off from the rest of the house. The 12-ft. ceiling adds a spacious feeling, and the access to the rear porch makes it ideal for friends and family.

- **Kitchen:** The kids will enjoy the snack bar and you'll love the adjoining breakfast room with its access to the rear porch.

- **Master Suite:** A whirlpool in the master bath and walk-in closets in the bedroom spell luxury.

- **Laundry Area:** Two large closets are so handy that you'll wonder how you ever did without them.

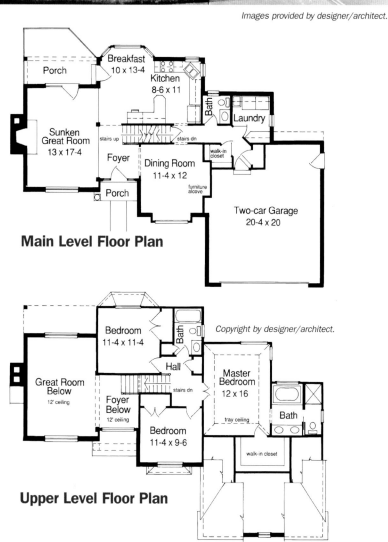

Main Level Floor Plan

Copyright by designer/architect.

Upper Level Floor Plan

Plan #441003

Dimensions: 50' W x 48' D
Levels: 1
Square Footage: 1,580
Bedrooms: 3
Bathrooms: 2½
Foundation: Crawl space;
slab or basement available for fee
Materials List Available: No
Price Category: C

Images provided by designer/architect.

Craftsman styling with modern floor planning—that's the advantage of this cozy design. Covered porches at front and back enhance both the look and the livability of the plan.

Features:

- Great Room: This vaulted entertaining area boasts a corner fireplace and a built-in media center. The area is open to the kitchen and the dining area.

- Kitchen: This large, open island kitchen will please the chef in the family. The raised bar is open to the dining area and the great room.

- Master Suite: Look for luxurious amenities such as double sinks and a separate tub and shower in the master bath. The master bedroom has a vaulted ceiling and a walk-in closet with built-in shelves.

- Bedrooms: Two secondary bedrooms are located away from the master suite. Each has a large closet and access to a common bathroom.

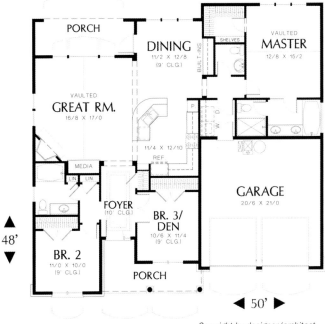

Copyright by designer/architect.

Rear Elevation

Plan #151016

Dimensions: 60'2" W x 39'10" D
Levels: 2
Square Footage: 1,783;
2,107 with bonus
Main Level Sq. Ft.: 1,124
Upper Level Sq. Ft.: 659
Bonus Room Sq. Ft.: 324
Bedrooms: 3
Bathrooms: 2½
Foundation: Crawl space, slab,
or basement
CompleteCost List Available: Yes
Price Category: C

Images provided by designer/architect.

Features:

- Great Room: Enjoy the fireplace in this spacious, versatile room.

- Dining Room: Entertaining is easy, thanks to the open design with the kitchen.

- Master Suite: Luxury surrounds you in this suite, with its large walk-in closet, double vanities, and a bathroom with a whirlpool tub and separate shower.

- Upper Bedrooms: Window seats make wonderful spots for reading or relaxing, and a nook between the windows of these rooms is a ready-made play area.

- Bonus Area: Located over the garage, this space could be converted to a home office, a studio, or a game room for the kids.

- Attic: There's plenty of storage space here.

An open design characterizes this spacious home built for family life and entertaining.

Bonus Room Above Garage

Copyright by designer/architect.

Main Level Floor Plan

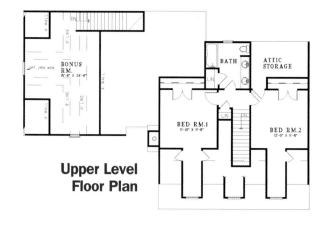

Upper Level Floor Plan

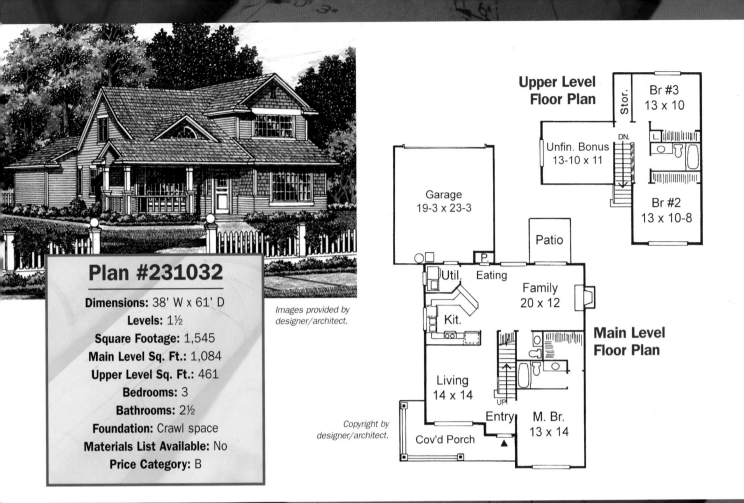

Plan #231032

Dimensions: 38' W x 61' D

Levels: 1½

Square Footage: 1,545

Main Level Sq. Ft.: 1,084

Upper Level Sq. Ft.: 461

Bedrooms: 3

Bathrooms: 2½

Foundation: Crawl space

Materials List Available: No

Price Category: B

Images provided by designer/architect.

Upper Level Floor Plan

Stor.

Br #3 13 x 10

Unfin. Bonus 13-10 x 11

DN.

L.

Br #2 13 x 10-8

Garage 19-3 x 23-3

P.

Patio

Main Level Floor Plan

Util.

Eating

Family 20 x 12

Kit.

Living 14 x 14

UP

M. Br. 13 x 14

Entry

Cov'd Porch

Copyright by designer/architect.

Plan #211153

Dimensions: 40' W x 34' D

Levels: 1

Square Footage: 848

Bedrooms: 1

Bathrooms: 1

Foundation: Crawl space

Material List Available: No

Price Category: A

Images provided by designer/architect.

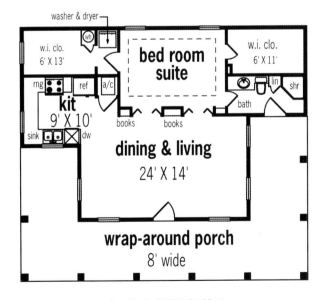

washer & dryer

w.i. clo. 6' X 13'

wh

bed room suite

w.i. clo. 6' X 11'

rng

ref

a/c

lin

shr

bath

kit 9' X 10'

sink

dw

books

books

dining & living 24' X 14'

wrap-around porch 8' wide

Copyright by designer/architect.

Plan #131014

Dimensions: 48' W x 43'4" D
Levels: 1
Square Footage: 1,380
Bedrooms: 3
Bathrooms: 2
Foundation: Crawl space, slab, or basement
Materials List Available: Yes
Price Category: B

Images provided by designer/architect.

The exterior of this home looks formal, thanks to its twin dormers, gables, and the bay windows that flank the columned porch, but the inside is contemporary in both design and features.

Features:

- **Great Room:** Centrally located, this great room has a 10-ft. ceiling. A fireplace, built-in cabinets, and windows that overlook the rear covered porch make it as practical as it is attractive.

- **Dining Room:** A bay window adds to the charm of this versatile room.

- **Kitchen:** This U-shaped room is designed to make cooking and cleaning jobs efficient.

- **Master Suite:** With a bay window, a walk-in closet, and a private bath with an oval tub, the master suite may be your favorite area.

- **Additional Bedrooms:** Located on the opposite side of the house from the master suite, these rooms share a full bath in the hall.

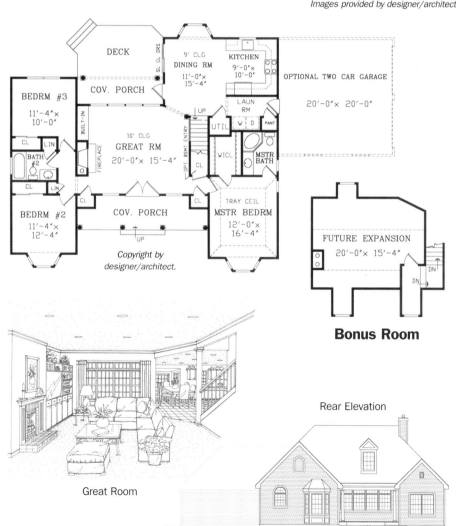

Bonus Room

Great Room

Rear Elevation

Plan #151281

Dimensions: 48'6" W x 48'4" D

Levels: 1

Square Footage: 1,461

Bedrooms: 3

Bathrooms: 2

Foundation: Walkout basement

CompleteCost List Available: Yes

Price Category: B

Images provided by designer/architect.

This brick ranch is the perfect home in which to raise your family.

Features:

- Great Room: Just off the entry is this large room, with its cozy fireplace and access to the rear porch.

- Kitchen: This fully equipped kitchen has a raised bar and is open to the great room and dining area.

- Master Suite: Located in the rear of the home, this suite has a large walk-in closet and a private bath with his and her vanities.

- Bedrooms: The two secondary bedrooms have large closets and share a hall bathroom.

- Garage: This front-loading two-car garage has plenty of room for cars and storage.

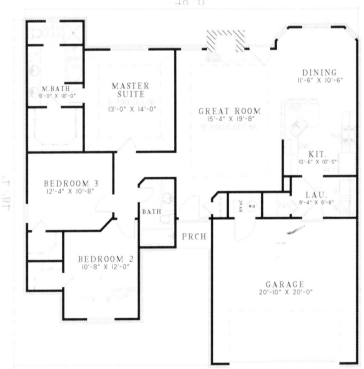

Copyright by designer/architect.

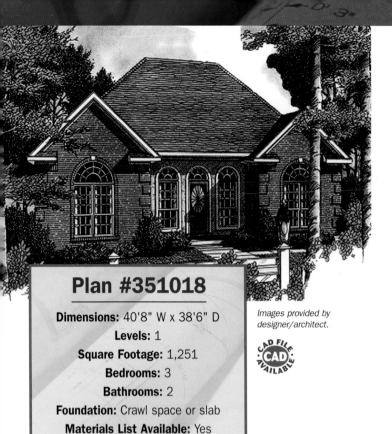

Plan #351018

Dimensions: 40'8" W x 38'6" D

Levels: 1

Square Footage: 1,251

Bedrooms: 3

Bathrooms: 2

Foundation: Crawl space or slab

Materials List Available: Yes

Price Category: B

Images provided by designer/architect.

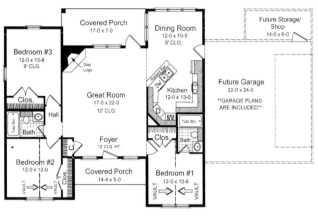

Copyright by designer/architect.

Plan #131039

Dimensions: 50' W x 37' D

Levels: 2

Square Footage: 1,149

Main Level Sq. Ft.: 1,029

Lower Level Sq. Ft.: 120

Lower Level: Optional bonus area

Bedrooms: 1

Bathrooms: 1

Foundation: Crawl space, slab, or basement

Materials List Available: Yes

Price Category: C

Images provided by designer/architect.

Copyright by designer/architect.

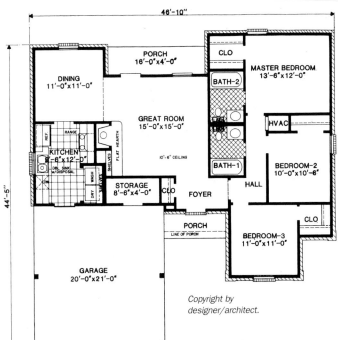

Plan #201013

Dimensions: 46'10" W x 44'5" D

Levels: 1

Square Footage: 1,211

Bedrooms: 3

Bathrooms: 2

Foundation: Crawl space, slab

Materials List Available: Yes

Price Category: B

Images provided by designer/architect.

Copyright by designer/architect.

Plan #201015

Dimensions: 63'10" W x 38'10" D

Levels: 1

Square Footage: 1,271

Bedrooms: 3

Bathrooms: 2

Foundation: Crawl space, slab

Materials List Available: Yes

Price Category: B

Images provided by designer/architect.

SMARTtip

Basic Triangle-Kitchens

Draw up your kitchen plan in this order: sink, range, refrigerator. Once you have the basic triangle located, add the other appliances, such as wall ovens and a dishwasher, and then the cabinets, counters, and eating areas.

Copyright by designer/architect.

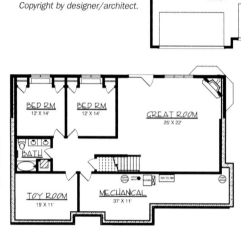

Copyright by designer/architect.

Images provided by designer/architect.

Plan #271059

Dimensions: 67' W x 57' D

Levels: 1

Square Footage: 1,790

Bedrooms: 1-3

Bathrooms: 1½-2½

Foundation: Daylight basement

Materials List Available: No

Price Category: C

Optional Basement Level Floor Plan

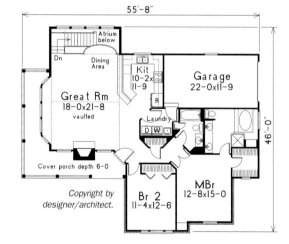

Copyright by designer/architect.

Images provided by designer/architect.

Rear View

Optional Basement Level Floor Plan

Plan #321035

Dimensions: 55'8" W x 46' D

Levels: 1

Square Footage: 1,384

Bedrooms: 2

Bathrooms: 2

Foundation: Walkout

Materials List Available: Yes

Price Category: B

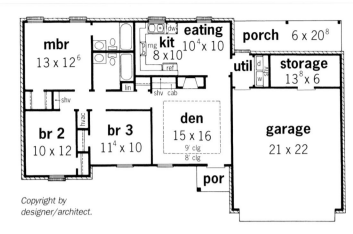

mbr 13 x 12⁶

eating 10⁴ x 10

porch 6 x 20⁸

kit 8 x 10

util

storage 13⁸ x 6

br 2 10 x 12

br 3 11⁴ x 10

den 15 x 16
9' clg
8' clg

garage 21 x 22

por

Plan #201004

Dimensions: 60'10" W x 34'10" D

Levels: 1

Square Footage: 1,121

Bedrooms: 3

Bathrooms: 2

Foundation: Crawl space, slab (basement option for fee)

Materials List Available: Yes

Price Category: B

Images provided by designer/architect.

SMARTtip

Color Basics

Use color effectively to enhance the perception of the space itself. Make a large room feel cozy with warm colors, which tend to advance. Conversely, open up a small room with cool colors or neutrals, which tend to recede.

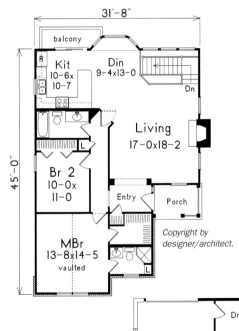

31'-8"

balcony

Kit 10-6x 10-7

Din 9-4x13-0

Dn

45'-0"

Living 17-0x18-2

Br 2 10-0x 11-0

Entry

Porch

MBr 13-8x14-5 vaulted

Plan #321039

Dimensions: 31'8" W x 45' D

Levels: 1

Square Footage: 1,231

Bedrooms: 2

Bathrooms: 2

Foundation: Basement

Materials List Available: Yes

Price Category: B

Images provided by designer/architect.

Optional Basement Level Floor Plan

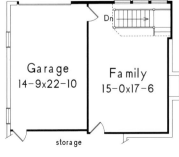

Dn

Garage 14-9x22-10

Family 15-0x17-6

storage

Plan #121031

Dimensions: 52' W x 51'4" D

Levels: 2

Square Footage: 1,772

Main Level Sq. Ft.: 1,314

Upper Level Sq. Ft.: 458

Bedrooms: 3

Bathrooms: 2½

Foundation: Basement

Materials List Available: Yes

Price Category: C

Images provided by designer/architect.

This home features architectural details reminiscence of earlier fine homes.

Features:

- Ceiling Height: 8 ft. unless otherwise noted.

- Foyer: This grand entry soars two-stories high. The U-shaped staircase with window leads to a second-story balcony.

- Great Room: You'll be drawn to the impressive views through the triple-arch

windows at the front and rear of this room.

- Kitchen: Designed for maximum efficiency, this kitchen is a pleasure to be in. It features a center island, a full pantry, and a desk for added convenience.

- Breakfast Area: This area adjoins the kitchen. Both rooms are flooded with sunlight streaming from a shared bay window.

- Master Suite: The stylish bedroom includes a walk-in closet. Luxuriate in the whirlpool tub at the end of a long day .

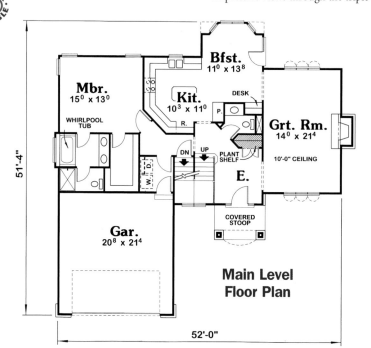

Main Level Floor Plan

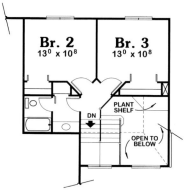

Copyright by designer/architect.

Upper Level Floor Plan

Images provided by designer/architect.

Plan #161090

Dimensions: 69'4" W x 42'4" D
Levels: 1
Square Footage: 1,563
Bedrooms: 3
Bathrooms: 2
Foundation: Basement
Materials List Available: Yes
Price Category: C

This charming ranch with stone accents is a great starter home.

Features:

- Great Room: This large entertaining area has a sloped ceiling, a gas fireplace, and a view of the backyard.

- Kitchen: This peninsula kitchen is open to the dining area and is just a few steps away from the laundry area and the garage.

- Master Suite: This suite has a raised ceiling and a large walk-in closet. The master bath has an oversized tub.

- Bedrooms: The two secondary bedrooms have large closets and share a hall bathroom.

- Garage: This front-loading two-car garage has room for cars or any needed extra storage place.

Copyright by designer/architect.

Plan #271033

Dimensions: 40' W x 41'4" D
Levels: 2
Square Footage: 1,516
Main Level Sq. Ft.: 817
Upper Level Sq. Ft.: 699
Bedrooms: 3
Bathrooms: 2½
Foundation: Basement
Materials List Available: Yes
Price Category: C

Images provided by designer/architect.

A pronounced roofline and a pleasing mix of brick and lap siding give a sunny disposition to this charming home.

Features:

• Great Room: Introduced by the sidelighted entry, this large space offers tall corner windows for natural light and a cheery corner fireplace for warmth.

• Dining Room: Joined to the great room only by air, this formal dining room basks in the glow from a broad window.

• Kitchen: Plenty of open space allows this kitchen to include ample counter space and incorporate an eating area into it. From here, a door leads to the backyard.

• Family Room: Flowing directly from the kitchen, this large family room allows passage to a backyard deck via sliding glass doors.

• Master Suite: Secluded to the upper floor, the master bedroom offers a private bath with a walk-in closet beyond.

Main Level Floor Plan

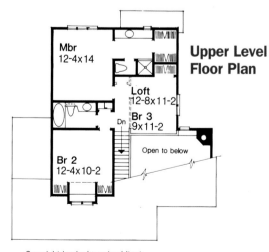

Upper Level Floor Plan

Copyright by designer/architect.

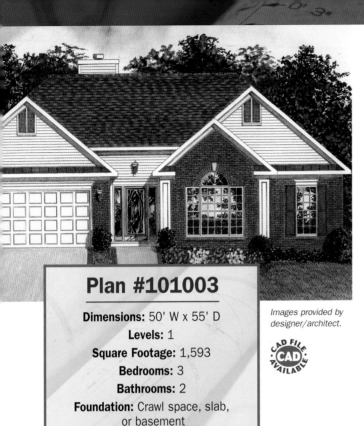

Plan #101003

Dimensions: 50' W x 55' D

Levels: 1

Square Footage: 1,593

Bedrooms: 3

Bathrooms: 2

Foundation: Crawl space, slab, or basement

Materials List Available: Yes

Price Category: C

Images provided by designer/architect.

CAD FILE AVAILABLE

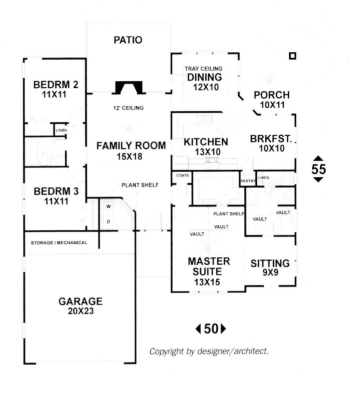

Copyright by designer/architect.

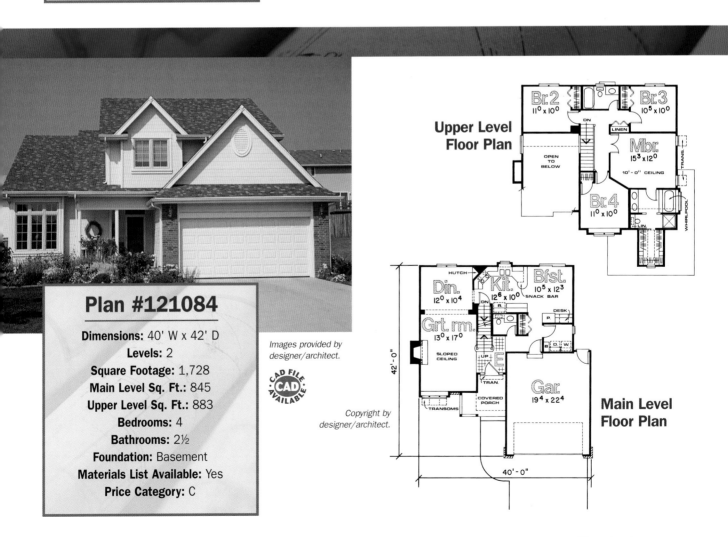

Plan #121084

Dimensions: 40' W x 42' D

Levels: 2

Square Footage: 1,728

Main Level Sq. Ft.: 845

Upper Level Sq. Ft.: 883

Bedrooms: 4

Bathrooms: 2½

Foundation: Basement

Materials List Available: Yes

Price Category: C

Images provided by designer/architect.

CAD FILE AVAILABLE

Copyright by designer/architect.

Upper Level Floor Plan

Main Level Floor Plan

Plan #101002

Dimensions: 46' W x 42' D
Levels: 1
Square Footage: 1,296
Bedrooms: 3
Bathrooms: 2
Foundation: Crawl space, slab, basement
Materials List Available: No
Price Category: B

Images provided by designer/architect.

CAD FILE AVAILABLE

Copyright by designer/architect.

SMARTtip

Preparing Walls for Paint

Poor surface preparation is the number-one cause of paint failure. Preparing surfaces properly—including removing loose paint and thoroughly sanding—may be tedious, but it's important for a good-looking and long-lasting finish.

Plan #211029

Dimensions: 68' W x 60' D
Levels: 1
Square Footage: 1,672
Bedrooms: 3
Bathrooms: 2
Foundation: Crawl space
Materials List Available: Yes
Price Category: C

Images provided by designer/architect.

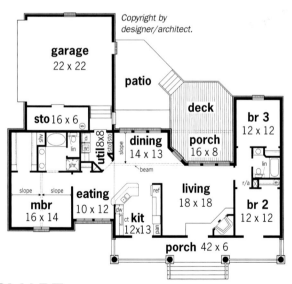

Copyright by designer/architect.

SMARTtip

Ponds

If a pond or small body of water already exists on your property, arrange your garden elements to take advantage of it. Build a bridge over it to connect it to other areas of the garden. If there's a dock already in place, make use of it for an instant midday picnic for one.

Plan #121002

Dimensions: 42' W x 54' D
Levels: 1
Square Footage: 1,347
Bedrooms: 3
Bathrooms: 2
Foundation: Basement
Materials List Available: Yes
Price Category: B

This home's convenient single level and luxury amenities are a recipe for gracious living.

Features:

- Ceiling Height: 8 ft. except as noted.

- Great Room: The entry enjoys a long view into this great room where a pair of transom-topped windows flanks the fireplace and a 10-ft. ceiling visually expands the space.

- Snack Bar: This special feature adjoins the great room, making it a real plus for informal entertaining, as well as the perfect spot for family get-togethers.

- Kitchen: An island is the centerpiece of this well-designed convenient kitchen that features a door to the backyard, a pantry, and convenient access to the laundry room.

- Master Suite: Located at the back of the home for extra privacy, the master suite feels like its own world. It features a tiered ceiling and sunlit corner whirlpool.

Images provided by designer/architect.

This home, as shown in the photograph, may differ from the actual blueprints. For more detailed information, please check the floor plans carefully.

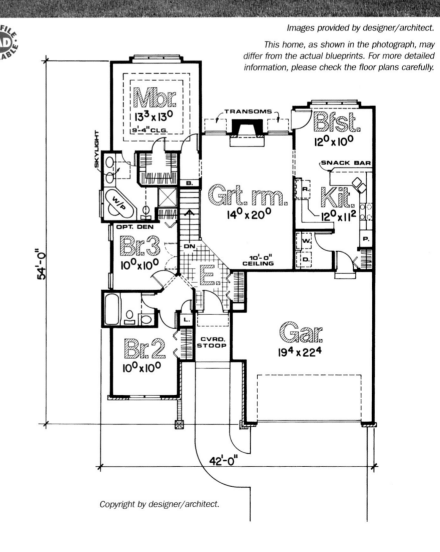

Copyright by designer/architect.

Plan #441004

Dimensions: 55' W x 48' D

Levels: 1

Square Footage: 1,728

Bedrooms: 2

Bathrooms: 2

Foundation: Crawl space; slab or basement available for fee

Materials List Available: No

Price Category: C

Empty nesters and first-time homeowners will adore the comfort within this charming home. Rooms benefit from the many windows, which welcome light into the home.

Features:

• Great Room: This vaulted room is equipped with a media center and fireplace. Windows span across the back of the room and the adjoining dining room, extending the perceived area and offering access to the covered patio.

• Kitchen: Taking advantage of corner space, this kitchen provides ample cabinets and countertops to store goods and prepare meals. Every chef will appreciate the extra space afforded by the pantry.

• Master Suite: This luxurious escape has a large sleeping area with views of the backyard. The master bath features a spa tub, dual vanities, and a walk-in closet.

• Garage: This front-loading two-car garage has a shop area located in the rear.

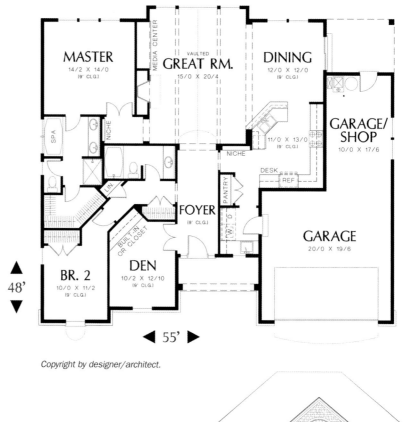

Copyright by designer/architect.

Rear Elevation

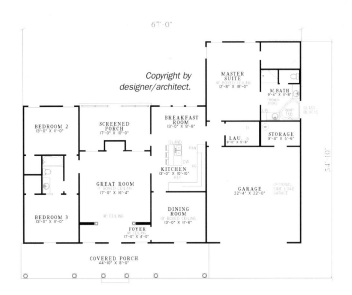

Copyright by designer/architect.

Plan #151054

Dimensions: 67' W x 54'10" D
Levels: 1
Square Footage: 1,746
Bedrooms: 3
Bathrooms: 2
Foundation: Crawl space or slab
(basement option for fee)
CompleteCost List Available: Yes
Price Category: C

Images provided by designer/architect.

CAD FILE AVAILABLE

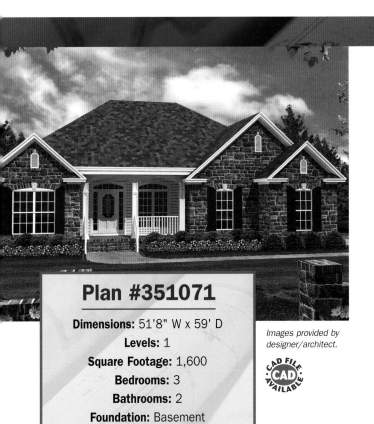

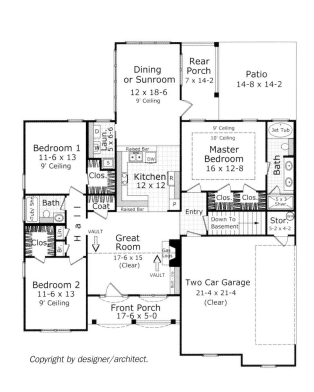

Plan #351071

Dimensions: 51'8" W x 59' D
Levels: 1
Square Footage: 1,600
Bedrooms: 3
Bathrooms: 2
Foundation: Basement
Materials List Available: No
Price Category: D

Images provided by designer/architect.

CAD FILE AVAILABLE

Copyright by designer/architect.

Plan #151528

Dimensions: 41'4" W x 84'2" D
Levels: 1
Square Footage: 1,747
Bedrooms: 2
Bathrooms: 2
Foundation: Crawl space or slab
CompleteCost List Available: Yes
Price Category: C

Images provided by designer/architect.

This Craftsman-inspired design combines a rustic exterior with an elegant interior. The 10-ft.-high ceilings and abundance of windows enhance the family areas with plenty of natural lighting.

Features:

- **Great Room:** Featuring a fireplace and built-in computer center, this central gathering area is open to the breakfast room and has access to the rear covered porch.

- **Kitchen:** This combination kitchen and breakfast room enjoys a bar counter for additional seating. Note the large laundry room with pantry, which is located between the kitchen and the garage.

- **Master Suite:** You'll spend many luxurious hours in this beautiful suite, with its 10-ft.-high boxed ceiling, his and her walk-in closets, and large bath with glass shower, whirlpool tub, and double vanity.

- **Bedrooms:** On the same side of the home as the master suite are these two other bedrooms, which have large closets and an adjoining bathroom between them.

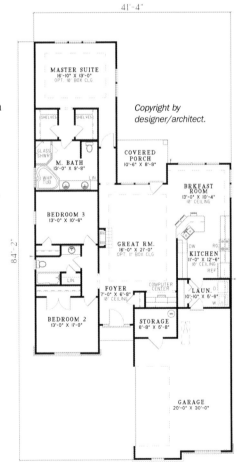

Copyright by designer/architect.

Front View

Plan #441021

Dimensions: 50' W x 44'6" D

Levels: 2

Square Footage: 1,760

Main Level Sq. Ft.: 941

Upper Level Sq. Ft.: 819

Bedrooms: 4

Bathrooms: 3

Foundation: Crawl space; slab or basement available for fee

Material List Available: No

Price Category: C

Add French country charm to any neighborhood with this great two-story home. A tall arched entry is adorned with stone. Varied window shapes add character to the façade.

Features:

• Great Room: Equipped with a fireplace, this vaulted room is a great place for the family to relax.

• Kitchen: This centralized kitchen features an island complete with a breakfast bar and sink. The spacious L-shape provides plenty of space for storage.

• Master Suite: Located upstairs, this suite features full amenities, with its spa bath, dual sinks, and a walk-in closet.

• Utility area: This laundry room—and more—is located on the second floor, eliminating trips up and down the stairs with laundry.

Images provided by designer/architect.

Copyright by designer/architect.

Main Level Floor Plan

DINING
11/6 X 11/6
(9' CLG.)

DEN/BR. 4
10/8 X 10/0
(9' CLG.)

GARAGE
11/0 X 17/0

VAULTED
GREAT RM.
17/2 X 15/0
(TO ISLAND)

GARAGE
21/0 X 22/0

FOYER

UP

44'-6"

50'

Upper Level Floor Plan

VAULTED
MASTER
12/2 X 14/10

BONUS / BR.3
17/6 X 12/6

LINEN

DN

BR. 2
11/2 X 11/6

D. W.

Rear Elevation

Plan #211002

Dimensions: 68' W x 62' D
Levels: 1
Square Footage: 1,792
Bedrooms: 3
Bathrooms: 2
Foundation: Crawl space
Materials List Available: Yes
Price Category: C

Arched windows on the front of this home give it a European style that you're sure to love.

SMARTtip

Water Features

Water features create the ambiance of a soothing oasis on a deck. A water-filled urn becomes a mirror that reflects the sky— making a small deck look larger. Fish flashing in an ornamental pool add color and act as a focal point for a deck with no view.

A water fountain introduces a pleasant rhythmical sound that helps drown out the background noises of traffic and nearby neighbors.

Images provided by designer/architect.

Features:

- Living Room: The 12-ft. ceiling in this large, open room enhances its spacious feeling. A fireplace adds warmth on chilly days and cool evenings.

- Dining Room: Decorate to accentuate the 12-ft. ceiling and formal feeling of this room.

- Kitchen: Designed for comfort and efficiency, this room also has a 12-ft. ceiling. The cozy breakfast bar is a natural gathering spot for friends and family.

- Master Suite: A split design guarantees privacy here. A sloped cathedral ceiling adds elegance, and a walk-in closet makes it practical. The bath has two vanities, a tub, and a walk-in shower.

- Garage: Park two cars here, and use the balance of this 520 sq. ft. area as a handy storage area.

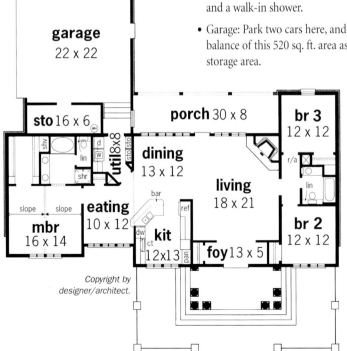

Plan #161007

Dimensions: 66'4" W x 43'10" D

Levels: 1

Square Footage: 1,611

Bedrooms: 3

Bathrooms: 2

Foundation: Basement, optional crawl space for no additional charge

Materials List Available: Yes

Price Category: C

A lovely front porch and an entry with side-lights invite you to experience the impressive amenities offered in this exceptional ranch home.

Features:

- **Great Room:** Grand openings, featuring columns from the foyer to this great room and continuing to the bayed dining area, convey an open, spacious feel. The fireplace and matching windows on the rear wall of the great room enhance this effect.

- **Kitchen:** This well-designed kitchen offers convenient access to the laundry and garage. It also features an angled counter with ample space and an abundance of cabinets.

- **Master Suite:** This deluxe master suite contains many exciting amenities, including a lavishly appointed dressing room and a large walk-in closet.

- **Porch:** Sliding doors lead to this delightful screened porch for relaxing summer interludes.

Images provided by designer/architect.

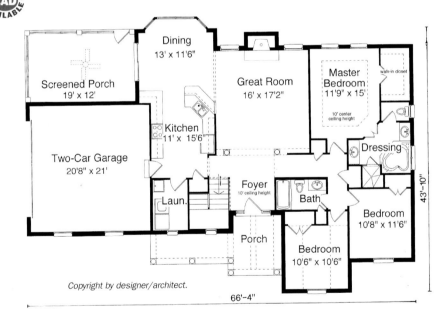

Copyright by designer/architect.

Rear Elevation

Plan #151026

Dimensions: 34' W x 66'8" D

Levels: 2

Square Footage: 1,574

Main Level Sq. Ft.: 1,131

Upper Level Sq. Ft.: 443

Bedrooms: 3

Bathrooms: 2½

Foundation: Crawl space, slab; optional full basement plan available for extra fee

CompleteCost List Available: Yes

Price Category: C

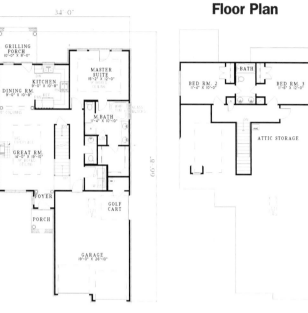

Main Level Floor Plan

Upper Level Floor Plan

Images provided by designer/architect.

CAD FILE AVAILABLE

Copyright by designer/architect.

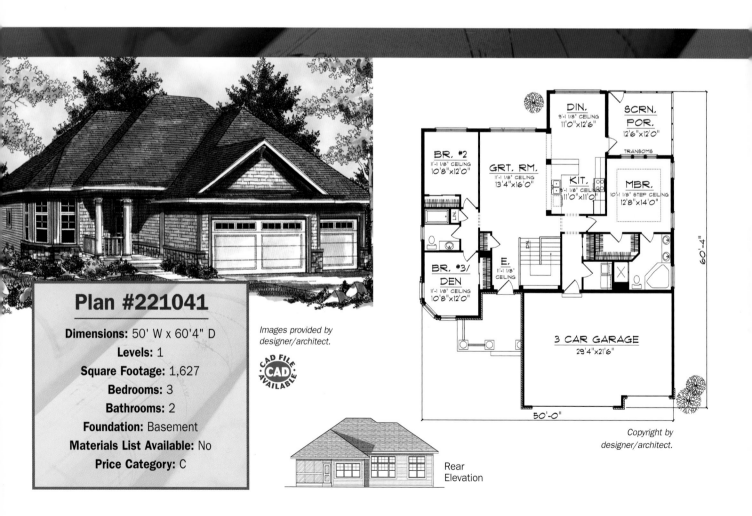

Plan #221041

Dimensions: 50' W x 60'4" D

Levels: 1

Square Footage: 1,627

Bedrooms: 3

Bathrooms: 2

Foundation: Basement

Materials List Available: No

Price Category: C

Images provided by designer/architect.

CAD FILE AVAILABLE

Copyright by designer/architect.

Rear Elevation

Plan #271036

Dimensions: 43'4" W x 50' D

Levels: 2

Square Footage: 1,602

Main Level Sq. Ft.: 1,112

Upper Level Sq. Ft.: 490

Bedrooms: 3

Bathrooms: 2½

Foundation: Basement

Materials List Available: No

Price Category: C

Images provided by designer/architect.

Main Level Floor Plan

43'-4"

Patio

Kit/Brk 10-8x14

Master 12x13-8

Dining 11x10-6 vaulted

DN

Living 17x15 vaulted

UP

50'-0"

Garage 19-4x19-4

Br 2 10-6x13-8

Br 3 10x10

DN

open to below

unfinished storage

Plant Shelf

Upper Level Floor Plan

Copyright by designer/architect.

Plan #321033

Dimensions: 38' W x 46' D

Levels: 1

Square Footage: 1,268

Bedrooms: 3

Bathrooms: 2

Foundation: Basement

Materials List Available: Yes

Price Category: B

Images provided by designer/architect.

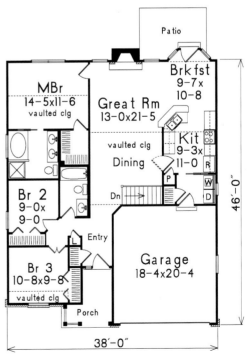

Patio

MBr 14-5x11-6 vaulted clg

Great Rm 13-0x21-5

Brkfst 9-7x 10-8

vaulted clg

Dining

Kit 9-3x 11-0

R

Br 2 9-0x 9-0

Dn

P

W D

Entry

46'-0"

Br 3 10-8x9-8 vaulted clg

Garage 18-4x20-4

Porch

38'-0"

Copyright by designer/architect.

Plan #151007

Dimensions: 54'2" W x 56'2" D
Levels: 1
Square Footage: 1,787
Bedrooms: 3
Bathrooms: 2
Foundation: Crawl space, slab, basement, or walkout
CompleteCost List Available: Yes
Price Category: C

Images provided by designer/architect.

This compact, well-designed home is graced with amenities usually reserved for larger houses.

Features:

- Foyer: A 10-ft. ceiling creates unity between the foyer and the dining room just beyond it.

- Dining Room: 8-in. boxed columns welcome you to this dining room, with its 10-ft. ceilings.

- Great Room: The 9-ft. boxed ceiling suits the spacious design. Enjoy the fireplace in the winter and the rear-grilling porch in the summer.

- Breakfast Room: This bright room is a lovely spot for any time of day.

- Master Suite: Double vanities and a large walk-in closet add practicality to this quiet room with a 9-ft. pan ceiling. The master bath includes whirlpool tub with glass block and a separate shower.

- Bedrooms: Bedroom 2 features a bay window, and both rooms are convenient to the bathroom.

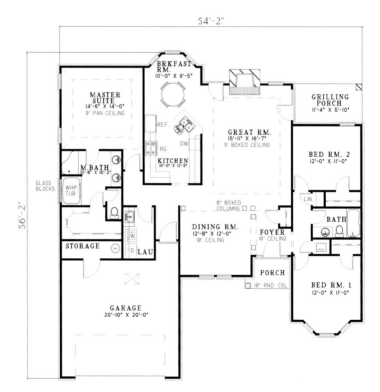

Copyright by designer/architect.

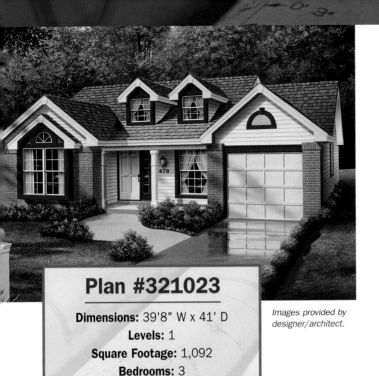

Plan #321023

Dimensions: 39'8" W x 41' D

Levels: 1

Square Footage: 1,092

Bedrooms: 3

Bathrooms: 1½

Foundation: Basement

Materials List Available: Yes

Price Category: B

Images provided by designer/architect.

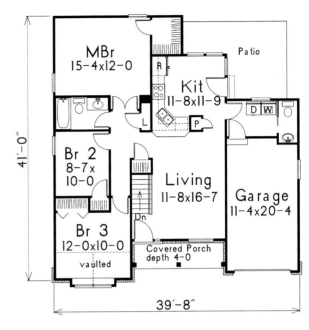

Copyright by designer/architect.

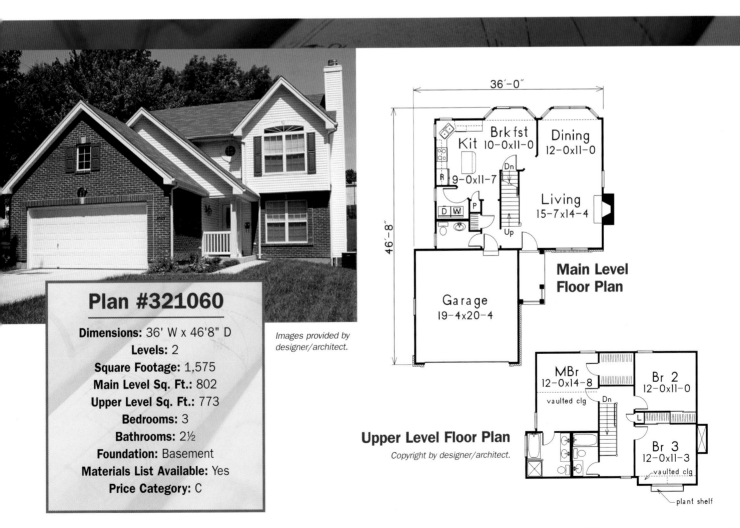

Plan #321060

Dimensions: 36' W x 46'8" D

Levels: 2

Square Footage: 1,575

Main Level Sq. Ft.: 802

Upper Level Sq. Ft.: 773

Bedrooms: 3

Bathrooms: 2½

Foundation: Basement

Materials List Available: Yes

Price Category: C

Images provided by designer/architect.

Main Level Floor Plan

Upper Level Floor Plan

Copyright by designer/architect.

Alternate Floor Plan

10'-8" X 12'-0"
3,20 X 3,60

11'-8" X 13'-0"
3,50 X 3,90

12'-4" X 22'-4"
3,70 X 6,70

12'-4" X 13'-8"
3,70 X 4,10

14'-0" X 13'-0"
4,20 X 3,90

11'-0" X 12'-0"
3,30 X 3,60

13'-8" X 16'-0"
4,10 X 4,80

12'-4" X 22'-4"
3,70 X 6,70

45'-0"
13,5 m

39'-0"
11,7 m

Images provided by designer/architect.

Copyright by designer/architect.

Plan #181018

Dimensions: 39' W x 45' D
Levels: 1
Square Footage: 1,231
Bedrooms: 2
Bathrooms: 1
Foundation: Basement
Materials List Available: Yes
Price Category: B

CAD FILE AVAILABLE

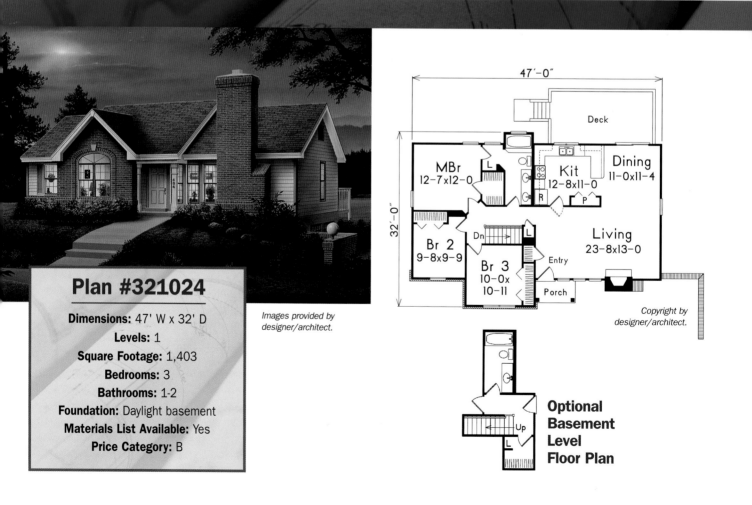

47'-0"

Deck

MBr
12-7x12-0

Kit
12-8x11-0

Dining
11-0x11-4

Living
23-8x13-0

Br 2
9-8x9-9

Br 3
10-0x
10-11

Entry

Porch

32'-0"

Copyright by designer/architect.

Optional Basement Level Floor Plan

Up

Plan #321024

Dimensions: 47' W x 32' D
Levels: 1
Square Footage: 1,403
Bedrooms: 3
Bathrooms: 1-2
Foundation: Daylight basement
Materials List Available: Yes
Price Category: B

Images provided by designer/architect.

Plan #151548

Dimensions: 55'10" W x 52' D

Levels: 1

Square Footage: 1,763

Bedrooms: 3

Bathrooms: 2

Foundation: Crawl space or slab

CompleteCost List Available: Yes

Price Category: C

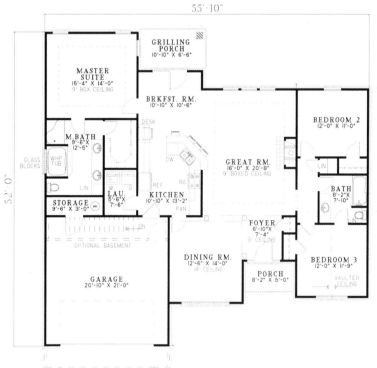

Round-top windows and a sleek roofline provide a sense of elegance in this plan.

Features:

- Entertaining: A spacious great room with a fireplace and a backyard view blends with the kitchen and breakfast room, which has access to the grilling porch, creating the perfect area for entertaining.

- Master Suite: Indulge yourself in this private suite. The bath has a relaxing whirlpool tub, with a privacy glass-block window above, as well as a walk-in closet and split vanities.

- Garage: This front-loading two-car garage has extra storage space.

Plan #151009

Dimensions: 44' W x 86'2" D
Levels: 1
Square Footage: 1,601
Bedrooms: 3
Bathrooms: 2
Foundation: Crawl space, slab
CompleteCost List Available: Yes
Price Category: C

This can be the perfect home for a site with views you can enjoy in all seasons and at all times.

Features:

- **Porches:** Enjoy the front porch with its 10-ft. ceiling and the more private back porch where you can set up a grill or just get away from it all.

- **Foyer:** With a 10-ft. ceiling, this foyer opens to the great room for a warm welcome.

- **Great Room:** Your family will love the media center and the easy access to the rear porch.

- **Kitchen:** This well-designed kitchen is open to the dining room and the breakfast nook, which also opens to the rear porch.

- **Master Suite:** The bedroom has a 10-ft. boxed ceiling and a door to the rear. The bath includes a corner whirlpool tub with glass block windows.

- **Bedrooms:** Bedroom 2 has a vaulted ceiling, while bedroom 3 features a built-in desk.

Images provided by designer/architect.

Copyright by designer/architect.

SMARTtip
Fertilizing Your Grass

Fertilizers contain nutrients balanced for different kinds of growth. The ratio of nutrients is indicated on the package by three numbers (for example, 10-10-10). The first specifies nitrogen content; the second, phosphorus; and the third, potash.

Nitrogen helps grass blades to grow and improves the quality and thickness of the turf. Fertilizers contain up to 30 percent nitrogen.

Phosphorus helps grass to develop a healthy root system. It also speeds up the maturation process of the plant.

Potash helps grass stay healthy by providing amino acids and proteins to the plants.

Plan #161087

Dimensions: 48'10" W x 53'4" D

Levels: 1

Square Footage: 1,664

Bedrooms: 3

Bathrooms: 2

Foundation: Walkout basement

Materials List Available: Yes

Price Category: C

A brick-and-stone facade with cedar shakes, a large front porch, arches, and a double gable decorate the exterior of this charming cottage-style home.

Features:

- **Great Room:** This area has plenty of space for entertaining or just relaxing. It features a gas fireplace and access to the rear deck.

- **Kitchen:** This well equipped cooking center has everything the chef in the family could want. It is open to the dining room and great room.

- **Master Suite:** This private space boasts a large sleeping area with a bath that has two vanities.

- **Expansion:** The lower level can be finished to add an additional bedroom, bathroom, and recreation room.

Images provided by designer/architect.

Plan #101036

Dimensions: 50' W x 60' D

Levels: 1

Square Footage: 1,343

Bedrooms: 3

Bathrooms: 2

Foundation: Basement

Materials List Available: No

Price Category: B

Images provided by designer/architect.

This lovely three-bedroom brick home with an attached two-car garage is perfect for any family.

Features:

- Family Room: This room with 12-ft.-high ceiling is open to the dining room.

- Kitchen: This kitchen boasts a built-in pantry, access to the garage, and a peninsula reaching into the family room.

- Master Bedroom: This main bedroom features a 12-ft.-high ceiling and its own private screened in porch.

- Master Bath: This bath features a walk-in closet, double vanity, and separate shower area.

- Bedrooms: Two additional bedrooms share a full bathroom located in the hallway.

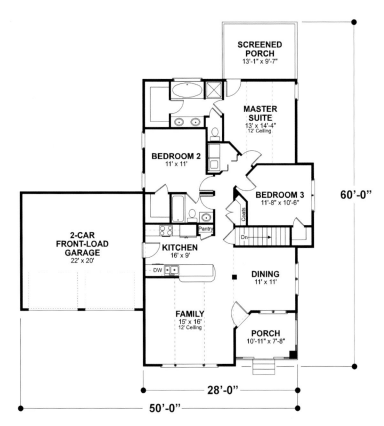

Copyright by designer/architect.

Plan #161110

Dimensions: 75' W x 39'1" D

Levels: 1

Square Footage: 1,623

Bedrooms: 3

Bathrooms: 2

Foundation: Crawl space, slab, or basement; walkout for fee

Materials List Available: Yes

Price Category: C

Images provided by designer/architect.

This three-bedroom ranch packs a lot of home into a small footprint.

Features:

- **Great Room:** This large entertaining area features a raised ceiling and a beautiful fireplace. Sliding glass doors allow access to the rear yard.

- **Kitchen:** This island kitchen has a raised bar and is open to the dining and great rooms. There is also a raised ceiling, which extends into the dining room and gives an open and airy feeling to this space.

- **Master Suite:** This retreat has a large sleeping area with a view of the backyard. The master bath features a large walk-in closet and dual vanities.

- **Bedrooms:** The two secondary bedrooms have large closets and share a common bathroom.

Copyright by designer/architect.

Plan #121008

Dimensions: 62' W x 56' D
Levels: 1
Square Footage: 1,651
Bedrooms: 2
Bathrooms: 2
Foundation: Basement
Materials List Available: Yes
Price Category: C

This elegant home is packed with amenities that belie its compact size.

Features:

- Ceiling Height: 8 ft.

- Dining Room: The foyer opens into a view of the dining room, with its distinctive boxed ceiling.

- Great Room: The whole family will want to gather around the fireplace and enjoy the views and sunlight streaming through the transom-topped window.

- Breakfast Area: Next to the great room and sharing the transom-topped windows, this cozy area invites you to linger over morning coffee.

- Covered Porch: When the weather is nice, take your coffee through the door in the breakfast area and enjoy this large covered porch.

- Master Suite: French doors lead to this comfortable suite featuring a walk-in. Enjoy long, luxurious soaks in the corner whirlpool accented with boxed windows.

Images provided by designer/architect.

CAD FILE AVAILABLE

Optional Bedroom

Br.3
10² x 10⁰

WHIRLPOOL
LIN.
Mbr.
14⁰ x 13⁰
9'-0" CEILING
TRANSOMS
TRANSOMS
COVERED PORCH
Grt. rm.
17⁰ x 17⁰
10'-0" CEILING
Bfst.
11⁰ x 11⁰
10'-0" CEILING
SNACK BAR
Den
10² x 10⁰
OPTIONAL BEDROOM
WET BAR
SERVERY
Kit.
13⁰ x 11⁸
Din.
12⁰ x 11⁰
9'-0" CEILING
Gar.
30⁰ x 20⁸
Br. 2
11⁰ x 10⁰
10'-0" CLG.
COVERED PORCH
56'-0"
62'-0"

Copyright by designer/architect.

SMARTtip

Finishing Your Fireplace with Tile

An excellent finishing material for a fireplace is tile. Luckily, there are reproductions of art tiles today. Most showrooms carry examples of Arts and Crafts, Art Nouveau, California, Delft, and other European tiles. Granite, limestone, and marble tiles are affordable alternatives to custom stone slabs.

Plan #341049

Dimensions: 58'9" W x 53'2" D

Levels: 1.5

Square Footage: 1,494

Bedrooms: 3

Bathrooms: 2

Foundation: Crawl space

Material List Available: Yes

Price Category: B

Images provided by designer/architect.

This distinguished home design incorporates classic elements with desired features for contemporary living. An unfinished recreation room over the garage is also included in the plan.

Features:

- **Entry:** A porch shelters this front entry, which is accented with a sidelight and a transom window.

- **Living Room:** A vaulted ceiling and a fireplace make this room inviting. The triple windows and decorative columns enhance the transitions at the foyer and dining room.

- **Dining Room:** This room has French doors to the rear screened porch and deck.

- **Master Suite:** This suite has a master bedroom with walk-in closet and a private full bath with garden tub/shower.

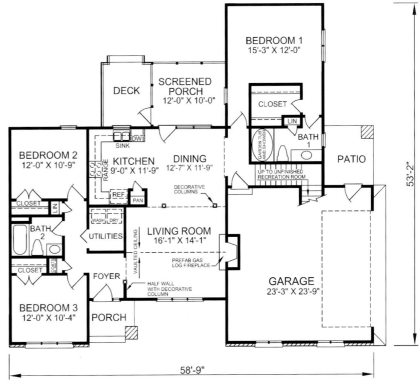

Copyright by designer/architect.

Plan #271060

Dimensions: 72' W x 52' D

Levels: 1

Square Footage: 1,726

Bedrooms: 2-4

Bathrooms: 2½-3½

Foundation: Daylight basement

Materials List Available: No

Price Category: C

Images provided by designer/architect.

CAD FILE AVAILABLE

Copyright by designer/architect.

Optional Basement Level Floor Plan

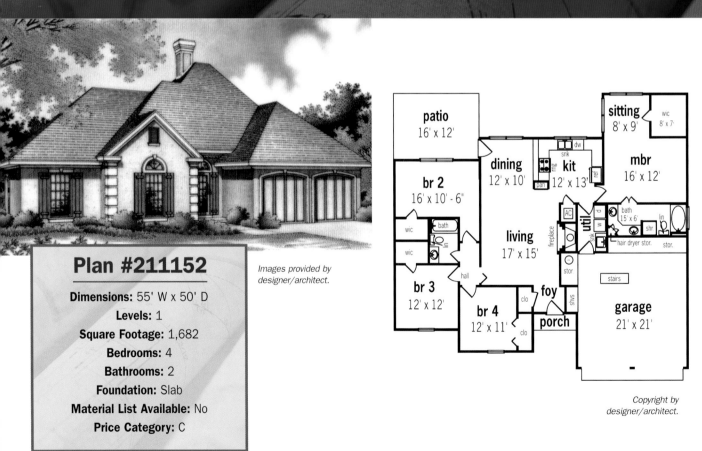

Plan #211152

Dimensions: 55' W x 50' D

Levels: 1

Square Footage: 1,682

Bedrooms: 4

Bathrooms: 2

Foundation: Slab

Material List Available: No

Price Category: C

Images provided by designer/architect.

Copyright by designer/architect.

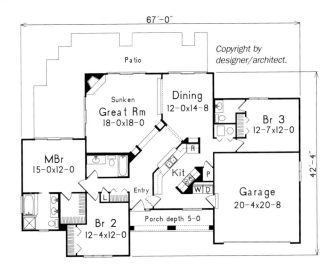

Copyright by designer/architect.

Plan #321026

Dimensions: 67' W x 42'4" D

Levels: 1

Square Footage: 1,712

Bedrooms: 3

Bathrooms: 2½

Foundation: Crawl space

Materials List Available: Yes

Price Category: C

Images provided by designer/architect.

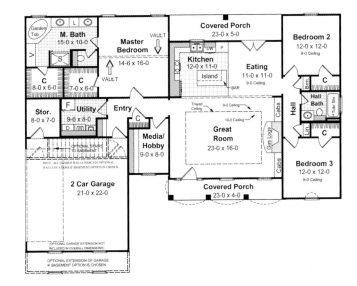

Plan #351003

Dimensions: 64' W x 45'10" D

Levels: 1

Square Footage: 1,751

Bedrooms: 3

Bathrooms: 2

Foundation: Crawl space, slab, or basement

Materials List Available: Yes

Price Category: C

Images provided by designer/architect.

Copyright by designer/architect.

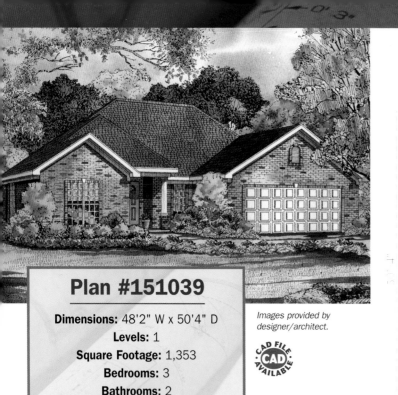

Plan #151039

Dimensions: 48'2" W x 50'4" D

Levels: 1

Square Footage: 1,353

Bedrooms: 3

Bathrooms: 2

Foundation: Crawl space, slab

CompleteCost List Available: Yes

Price Category: B

Images provided by designer/architect.

Copyright by designer/architect.

Plan #341057

Dimensions: 35' W x 44'4" D

Levels: 2

Square Footage: 1,642

Main Level Sq. Ft.: 762

Upper Level Sq. Ft.: 880

Bedrooms: 3

Bathrooms: 2½

Foundation: Crawl space

Materials List Available: Yes

Price Category: C

Images provided by designer/architect.

Main Level Floor Plan

Upper Level Floor Plan

Copyright by designer/architect.

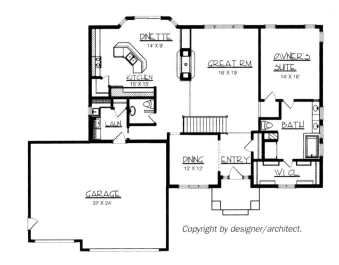

Copyright by designer/architect.

Plan #271061

Dimensions: 68' W x 52' D

Levels: 1

Square Footage: 1,750

Bedrooms: 1-3

Bathrooms: 1½-2½

Foundation: Daylight basement

Materials List Available: No

Price Category: C

Optional Basement Level Floor Plan

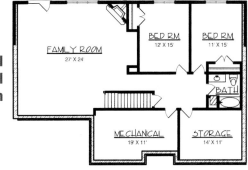

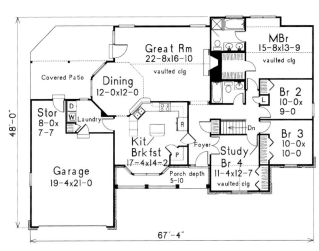

Copyright by designer/architect.

Plan #321003

Dimensions: 67'4" W x 48' D

Levels: 1

Square Footage: 1,791

Bedrooms: 4

Bathrooms: 2

Foundation: Basement

Materials List Available: Yes

Price Category: C

Plan #131041

Dimensions: 42' W x 45' D
Levels: 2
Square Footage: 1,679
Main Level Sq. Ft.: 1,134
Upper Level Sq. Ft.: 545
Bedrooms: 3
Bathrooms: 2½
Foundation: Crawl space, slab, or basement
Materials List Available: Yes
Price Category: D

Images provided by designer/architect.

This rustic-looking two-story cottage includes contemporary amenities for your total comfort.

Features:

- Great Room: With a 9-ft.-4-in.-high ceiling, this large room makes everyone feel at home. A fireplace with raised hearth and built-in niche for a TV will encourage the whole family to gather here on cool evenings, and sliding glass doors leading to

the rear covered porch make it an ideal entertaining area in mild weather.

- Kitchen: When people aren't in the great room, you're likely to find them here, because the convenient serving bar welcomes casual dining, and this room also opens to the p porch.

- Master Suite: Relax at the end of the day in this room, with its 9-ft.-4-in.-high ceiling and walk-in closet, or luxuriate in the private bath with whirlpool tub and dual-sink vanity.

- Optional Basement: This area can include a tuck-under two-car garage if you desire it.

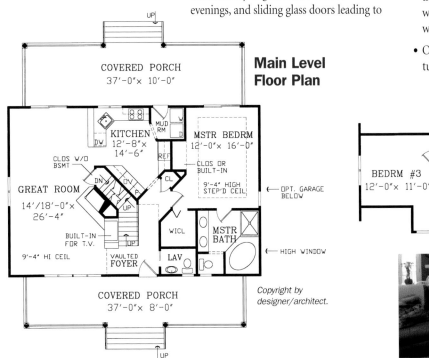

Main Level Floor Plan

Copyright by designer/architect.

Upper Level Floor Plan

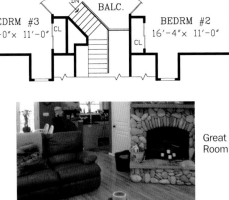

Great Room

Copyright by designer/architect.

Plan #321001

Dimensions: 83' W x 42' D

Levels: 1

Square Footage: 1,721

Bedrooms: 3

Bathrooms: 2

Foundation: Crawl space, slab, or basement

Materials List Available: Yes

Price Category: C

Images provided by designer/architect.

Rear View

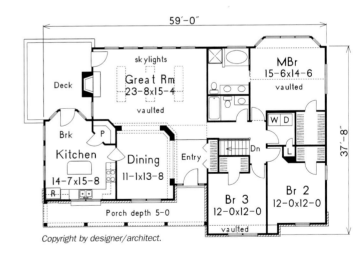

Copyright by designer/architect.

Plan #321010

Dimensions: 59' W x 37'8" D

Levels: 1

Square Footage: 1,787

Bedrooms: 3

Bathrooms: 2

Foundation: Basement

Materials List Available: Yes

Price Category: C

Images provided by designer/architect.

SMARTtip

Country Décor in Your Bathroom

Collections are often part of a country decor, even in the bathroom. All you need is three or more of anything that have size, shape, or color in common. You can mass them on walls, on shelves, on the windowsills, or even along the edge of the tub.

Brick Materials

In one form or another, brick has been used as a building material for thousands of years. It is durable, attractive, and noncombustible, among other things, and installing it is a straightforward job. The work is well suited to do-it-yourselfers because you can do it a little at a time.

Bricks are bonded together with mortar. But most projects will also require accessories such as anchors, ties, or joint reinforcements. These materials can strengthen the overall structure, will anchor masonry to existing construction, and will control expansion and contraction.

Types of Brick

Brick is made from molded clay that is fired at very high temperatures in a kiln. The clay color and firing temperature determine the brick color, although some manufacturers combine clays to produce tones from off-white to almost black. Brick textures vary too, depending on the molding process.

Brick made in the United States and Canada today is extremely dense, hard, and durable. If the bricks are shaped by extruding clay through a die, they usually have large holes through the middle. The holes make the bricks lighter and improve the mortar bond. This type of brick is most commonly used for wall construction, where the holes are not visible.

To choose brick for your project, visit a local supplier and look at sample panels. Bear in mind that bricks with a wide range of light and dark shades can be more difficult to work with than bricks of a single color.

Face Brick. A batch of face brick will be quite uniform in color, size, and texture. It comes in three types. Type FBA (architectural) brick has no limits on size variations or on the amount of chips and cracks that are permitted. This type is popular for residential work because the units resemble old brick. Type FBS (standard) and FBX (extra) have tighter limits on variations and are generally used on commercial jobs.

Bricks similar to those used in historic buildings are still produced by some manufacturers.

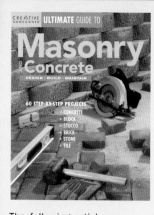

The following article was reprinted from *Ultimate Guide to Masonry and Concrete* (Creative Homeowner 2006).

Common Brick Types

Face Bricks are uniform in color and texture.

Modular Building Bricks are often rough-faced.

Locking Pavers nestle together without mortar.

Firebrick is baked at high temperature to resist heat.

Brick Pavers are strong and weatherproof.

Veneer Bricks are thin slices of real brick.

But they will absorb more water than extruded bricks. You could also work with genuine used brick, but unpredictable durability makes them risky for exterior use.

Modular Building Brick. Building bricks, or common bricks, are rougher in appearance and less expensive than face bricks, but are structurally sound. Most building bricks today are sold with interior holes that reduce weight.

Paving Brick. Paving brick is manufactured to be denser than the other bricks because in paving, the widest faces are visible. The clay is machine-pressed densely into molds and baked longer than either extruded or molded face bricks. This process reduces the amount of water that will be absorbed by the brick.

With pavers, low absorption is critical because the materials must be able to withstand repeated cycles of winter freez-

ing and thawing as well as heavy traffic. Paving brick is classified by its appearance in the same way as face brick: PA (architectural), PS (standard), and PX (extra).

Firebrick. Firebrick is made of a special clay that is baked at an extremely high temperature. It is used to line fireplaces and is generally a yellowish off-white color. You must install it with a special fireclay mortar.

Water Testing and Grading

Very dry brick absorbs much of the water in fresh mortar, weakening the bond. To test for excessive absorption, place 12 drops of water on any spot on the brick. If the water is absorbed in less than one minute, the brick is too dry, and you should wet the bricks as you install them. Overall grading is based on resistance to freeze-thaw damage. Grade MW moderate weathering) can be exposed to moisture but not freezing. Grade SW (severe weathering) is used when the bricks are likely to be frozen when saturated. Grade NW (no weathering), is for indoor use only.

Using a Brick Splitter

1 **Measure your brick** and mark the length required to fill the void, allowing for mortar joints.

2 **Line up your squared mark** with the angled cutting blades in the jaws of the brick splitter.

Layouts and Estimates

Laying out bricks is simple when you set them to a multiple of 4 inches. This multiple also applies against 8 x 8 x 16-inch concrete block. With 8-inch brick, the 4-inch module is the length of half bricks that create a staggered layout. For example, make a brick wall a multiple of 4 inches long (80 inches long rather than 78 inches). For estimating purposes, figure about seven bricks (nominally 4 x 8 inches) for every square foot of area in a wall. Estimate about 4½ bricks for every square foot when laying paving bricks broad faced, horizontally on the ground.

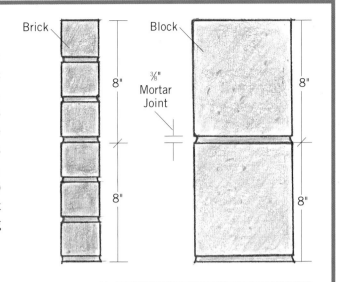

Common Brick Sizes

The basic modular unit is 3⅝ inches wide, 2¼ inches thick, and 7⅝ inches long. When laid with standard ⅜-inch mortar joints, the nominal length becomes about 8 inches. Three bricks laid on top of one another with ⅜-inch mortar joints measure 8 inches high. Paving bricks designed to butt together without mortar have a full 4 x 8-inch face. The most common are 1 inch thick for light traffic areas and 2¼ inches for heavy traffic areas, such as driveways and streets. Some suppliers offer special shapes such as copings and angled corner bricks that fit a modular system.

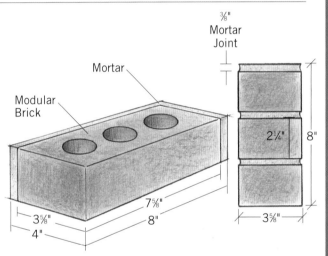

3 **Push down** slowly on the lever, compressing the upper and lower jaws until the brick snaps.

4 **The blades** of a brick splitter produce a cleaner cut than you can make with hammer and chisel.

Brick Patterns

Bricks and pavers come in so many sizes and shapes that you can create an almost endless number of patterns.

The most common bond pattern is called a running bond. In a wall with this pattern bricks are laid flat on their wide surface and run lengthwise. Each brick in a course of stretchers is offset by one-half brick from the bricks in the courses above and below.

This bond is also generally used on walks, which don't present the same structural considerations as walls do. And staggered joints tend to hold together better than joints that are aligned in a row. There are variations, such as using an offset of one-third or one-quarter brick in each course. But a running bond works well in any landscape and is easy to keep consistent, whether you are using

bricks set with mortar joints or pavers butted without mortar.

Bear in mind that any layout becomes more complicated when you introduce curves, more common in walks than in walls. You can make some adjustments in the joints to run the brick in line with the walk or set the running bond so that the bricks are all parallel with each other.

This mortared running bond curves with the walk.

This curved walk has a rigid, parallel running bond.

Paver Patterns

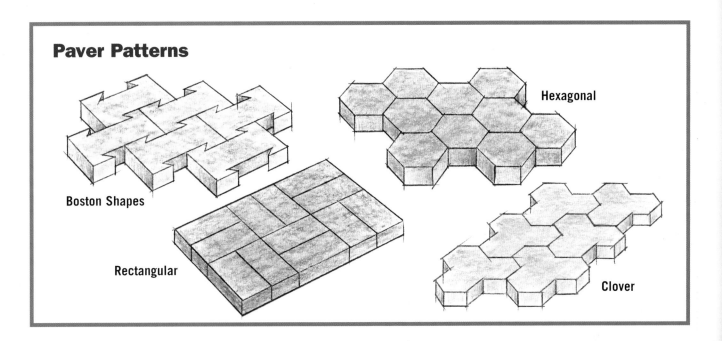

Boston Shapes

Rectangular

Hexagonal

Clover

This informal garden walk has an organic pattern.

A herringbone pattern is more complex to lay out.

When you need to turn a corner in a wall, bricks called headers are turned perpendicular to the stretcher courses. Also by alternating header and stretcher bricks in different ways, you can create a variety of patterns. And because header units help hold the two wythes, or brick widths, of a wall together, they are functional as well as decorative. A number of decorative bond patterns mimic the look of historic masonry buildings.

Other popular bond patterns include the common, or American, bond. It is similar to the running bond, except that it has courses of headers spaced every sixth course. The English bond consists of alternating courses of stretchers and headers; the headers are centered over the stretchers, and the vertical joints of all the stretcher courses align.

A stack bond lays all the bricks as either headers or stretchers with all joints aligning vertically. But the stack bond is weak structurally, and generally not permitted for load-bearing walls without reinforcement in the joints.

The Flemish bond is a complex pattern in which every course has alternating stretchers and headers. The pattern is offset by courses so that the headers center over stretchers and vice versa. Remember that more complex patterns often require more cutting.

Brick lends itself well to traditional home exteriors like this one.

Brick Patterns

RUNNING

ENGLISH

COMMON

DUTCH

GARDEN WALL

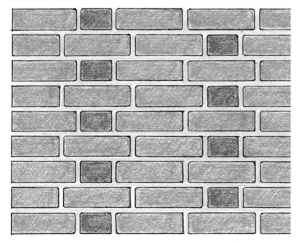

FLEMISH

Plan #151037

Dimensions: 50' W x 56' D

Levels: 1

Square Footage: 1,538

Bedrooms: 3

Bathrooms: 2

Foundation: Crawl space, slab, or basement

CompleteCost List Available: Yes

Price Category: C

Images provided by designer/architect.

You'll love this traditional-looking home, with its covered porch and interesting front windows.

Features:

- Ceiling Height: 8 ft.

- Great Room: This large room has a boxed window that emphasizes its dimensions and a fireplace where everyone will gather on chilly evenings. A door opens to the backyard.

- Dining Room: A bay window overlooking the front porch makes this room easy to decorate.

- Kitchen: This well-planned kitchen features ample counter space, a full pantry, and an eating bar that it shares with the dining room.

- Master Suite: A pan ceiling in this lovely room gives an elegant touch. The huge private bath includes two walk-in closets, a whirlpool tub, a dual-sink vanity, and a skylight in the ceiling.

- Additional Bedrooms: On the opposite side of the house, these bedrooms share a large bath, and both feature excellent closet space.

Copyright by designer/architect.

Plan #121006

Dimensions: 46' W x 58' D

Levels: 1

Square Footage: 1,762

Bedrooms: 3

Bathrooms: 2

Foundation: Slab

Materials List Available: Yes

Price Category: C

Images provided by designer/architect.

The entry has a trio of arched openings that leads you to other areas of this amenity-packed home.

Features:

- Ceiling Height: 8 ft. except as noted.

- Eating Bar: Conveniently located between the kitchen and family room, this is sure to be a favorite spot for informal entertaining and family gatherings.

- Family room: A wall of windows, a fireplace, and a vaulted ceiling stretching to 11 ft. work together to make this a bright and warm room.

- Kitchen: There's no shortage of counter space in this well-planned kitchen that features a center island in addition to the eating bar.

- Master Suite: Luxuriate at the end of the day in this large bedroom with its decorative tray ceiling and walk-in closet. Enjoy the pampering bath with its sunlit corner whirlpool flanked by vanities.

- Garage: Two bays provide room for cars and plenty of storage as well.

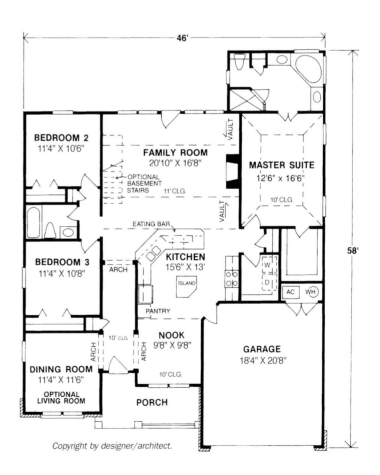

Copyright by designer/architect.

Plan #241005

Dimensions: 53' W x 55'9" D

Levels: 1

Square Footage: 1,670

Bedrooms: 3

Bathrooms: 2

Foundation: Crawl space or slab (basement for fee)

Materials List Available: No

Price Category: C

This charming starter home, in split-bedroom format, combines big-house features in a compact design.

Features:

- **Great Room:** With easy access to the formal dining room, kitchen, and breakfast area, this great room features a cozy fireplace.

- **Kitchen:** This big kitchen, with easy access to a walk-in pantry, features an island for added work space and a lovely plant shelf that separates it from the great room.

- **Master Suite:** Separated for privacy, this master suite offers a roomy bath with whirlpool tub, dual vanities, a separate shower, and a large walk-in closet.

- **Additional Rooms:** Additional rooms include a laundry/utility room—with space for a washer, dryer, and freezer—a large area above the garage, well-suited for a media or game room, and two secondary bedrooms.

Images provided by designer/architect.

Copyright by designer/architect.

Bonus Area Floor Plan

SMARTtip

Window Scarf

The best way to wrap a window scarf around a pole is as follows:

- Lay out the material on a large, clean surface. Gather the fabric at the top of each jabot, and use elastic to hold it together.

- Swing one jabot into place over the pole and, starting from there, wind the swag portion as many times as you need around the pole until you reach the elastic at the second jabot, which should have landed at the opposite pole end.

- Readjust wraps along the pole. Generally, wrapped swags just touch or slightly overlap.

- For a dramatic effect, stuff the wrapped swags with tissue paper or thin foam, depending on the translucence and weight of fabric.

- Release elastics at tops of jabots.

Plan #221028

Dimensions: 50' W x 67' D

Levels: 1

Square Footage: 1,773

Bedrooms: 2

Bathrooms: 2

Foundation: Basement

Materials List Available: No

Price Category: C

This chateau-style ranch home feels as if it belongs on a French countryside somewhere.

Features:

• Entry: This octagonal shaped space has a tray ceiling, giving a grand, open feeling to the area.

• Master Suite: This suite has a tray ceiling in the bedroom, a Jacuzzi tub in the bath, and a spacious walk-in closet with ample storage space.

• Bedroom: This second bedroom can be found at the front of the house just off the entry, along with a full bathroom for guests.

• Garage: This large front-loading three-car garage has room for cars plus storage.

Rear Elevation

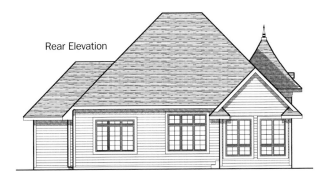

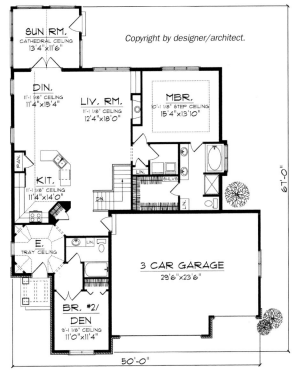

Plan #161005

Dimensions: 60' W x 48'10" D

Levels: 1

Square Footage: 1,593

Bedrooms: 3

Bathrooms: 2

Foundation: Basement

Materials List Available: Yes

Price Category: C

Images provided by designer/architect.

This delightful ranch home includes many thoughtful conveniences and a full basement to expand your living enjoyment.

Features:

- Great Room: Take pleasure in welcoming guests through a spacious foyer into the warm and friendly confines of this great room with corner fireplace, sloped ceiling, and view to the rear yard.

- Kitchen: Experience the convenience of enjoying meals while seated at the large island that separates the dining area from this well-designed kitchen. Also included is an oversized pantry with an abundance of storage.

- Master Suite: This master suite features a compartmented bath, large walk-in closet, and master bedroom that has a tray ceiling with 9-ft. center height.

- Porch: Retreat to this delightful rear porch to enjoy a relaxing evening.

Rear Elevation

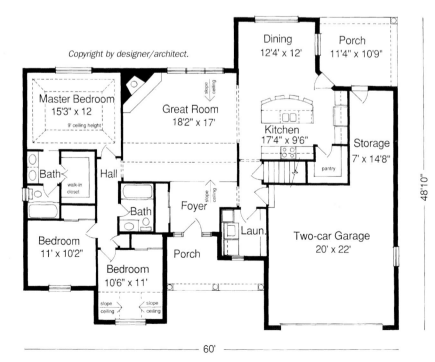

Copyright by designer/architect.

Plan #321002

Dimensions: 72' W x 28' D

Levels: 1

Square Footage: 1,400

Bedrooms: 3

Bathrooms: 2

Foundation: Crawl space, basement

Materials List Available: Yes

Price Category: B

If you're looking for a well-designed compact home with contemporary amenities, this could be the home of your dreams.

Features:

- **Porch:** Just the right size for some rockers and a swing, this porch could become your outdoor living area when the weather is fine.

- **Living Room:** A vaulted ceiling adds to the spacious feeling in this room, where friends and family are sure to gather.

- **Kitchen:** This space-saving design, in combination with the ample counter and cabinet space, makes cooking a pleasure.

- **Utility Room:** This large room is fitted with cabinets for extra storage space. You'll find storage space in the large garage, too.

- **Master Bedroom:** This room is somewhat secluded for privacy, making it an ideal place for some quiet time at the end of the day.

Images provided by designer/architect.

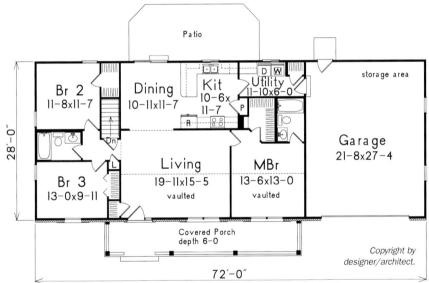

Copyright by designer/architect.

SMARTtip

Fabric Draping Ability

Test a fabric's draping ability by looking at a large piece in a fabric store. Gather at least two to three yards of material, holding one end in your hand. Check how it drapes. Does it fall into folds easily? Also look at the pattern when it is gathered. Does the design become lost in the folds? Ask a salesclerk or a friend to hold the fabric, and look at it from a few feet away.

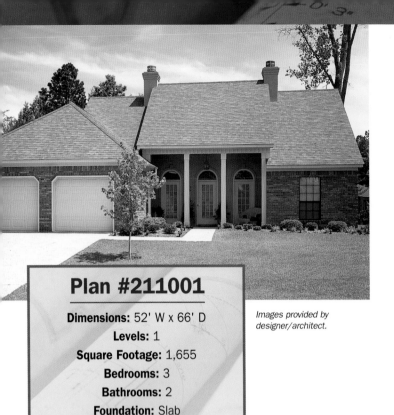

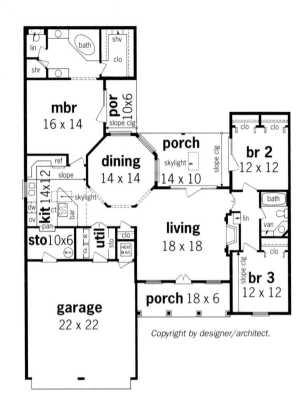

Plan #211001

Dimensions: 52' W x 66' D

Levels: 1

Square Footage: 1,655

Bedrooms: 3

Bathrooms: 2

Foundation: Slab

Materials List Available: Yes

Price Category: C

Images provided by designer/architect.

Copyright by designer/architect.

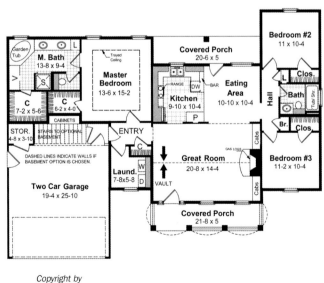

Plan #351005

Dimensions: 61' W x 47'4" D

Levels: 1

Square Footage: 1,501

Bedrooms: 3

Bathrooms: 2

Foundation: Crawl space, slab, or basement

Materials List Available: Yes

Price Category: C

Images provided by designer/architect.

CAD FILE AVAILABLE

Copyright by designer/architect.

**Bonus Area
Floor Plan**

Plan #341050

Dimensions: 50' W x 47'6" D

Levels: 1.5

Square Footage: 1,540

Bedrooms: 3

Bathrooms: 2

Foundation: Crawl space

Material List Available: Yes

Price Category: C

Images provided by designer/architect.

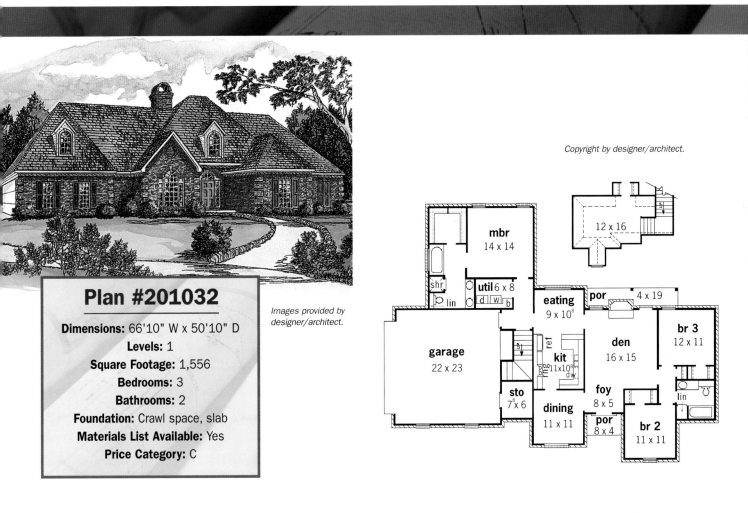

Copyright by designer/architect.

Plan #201032

Dimensions: 66'10" W x 50'10" D

Levels: 1

Square Footage: 1,556

Bedrooms: 3

Bathrooms: 2

Foundation: Crawl space, slab

Materials List Available: Yes

Price Category: C

Images provided by designer/architect.

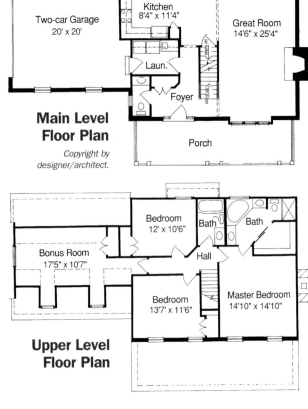

Plan #161024

Dimensions: 54'4" W x 26'8" D

Levels: 2

Square Footage: 1,698

Main Level Sq. Ft.: 868

Upper Level Sq. Ft.: 830

Bonus Space Sq. Ft.: 269

Bedrooms: 3

Bathrooms: 2½

Foundation: Basement

Materials List Available: No

Price Category: C

Images provided by designer/architect.

This home, as shown in the photograph, may differ from the actual blueprints. For more detailed information, please check the floor plans carefully.

CAD FILE AVAILABLE

Two-car Garage
20' x 20'

Kitchen
8'4" x 11'4"

Breakfast
9'6" x 14'6"

Great Room
14'6" x 25'4"

Laun.

Foyer

Main Level Floor Plan

Copyright by designer/architect.

Porch

Bedroom
12' x 10'6"

Bath

Bath

Bonus Room
17'5" x 10'7"

Hall

Bedroom
13'7" x 11'6"

Master Bedroom
14'10" x 14'10"

Upper Level Floor Plan

Plan #181116

Dimensions: 36' W x 34' D

Levels: 2

Square Footage: 1,872

Main Level Sq. Ft.: 1,078

Upper Level Sq. Ft.: 794

Bedrooms: 3

Bathrooms: 2

Foundation: Walkout basement

Materials List Available: Yes

Price Category: C

Images provided by designer/architect.

Main Level Floor Plan

Copyright by designer/architect.

13'-0" X 12'-4"
3,90 X 3,70

34'-0"
10,2 m

15'-0" X 13'-8"
4,50 X 4,10

10'-8" X 8'-8"
3,20 X 2,60

14'-0" X 10'-0"
4,20 X 3,00

36'-0"
10,8 m

CAD FILE AVAILABLE

Basement Level Floor Plan

30'-2" X 17'-3" / 13'-3"
9,05 X 5,18 / 3,98

Upper Level Floor Plan

12'-4" X 12'-4"
3,70 X 3,70

11'-8" X 15'-0"
3,50 X 4,50

14'-0" X 11'-10"
4,20 X 3,55

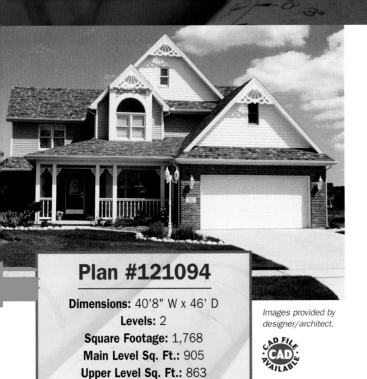

Plan #121094

Dimensions: 40'8" W x 46' D

Levels: 2

Square Footage: 1,768

Main Level Sq. Ft.: 905

Upper Level Sq. Ft.: 863

Bedrooms: 3

Bathrooms: 2½

Foundation: Basement

Materials List Available: Yes

Price Category: C

Images provided by designer/architect.

CAD FILE AVAILABLE

Main Level Floor Plan

Upper Level Floor Plan

Copyright by designer/architect.

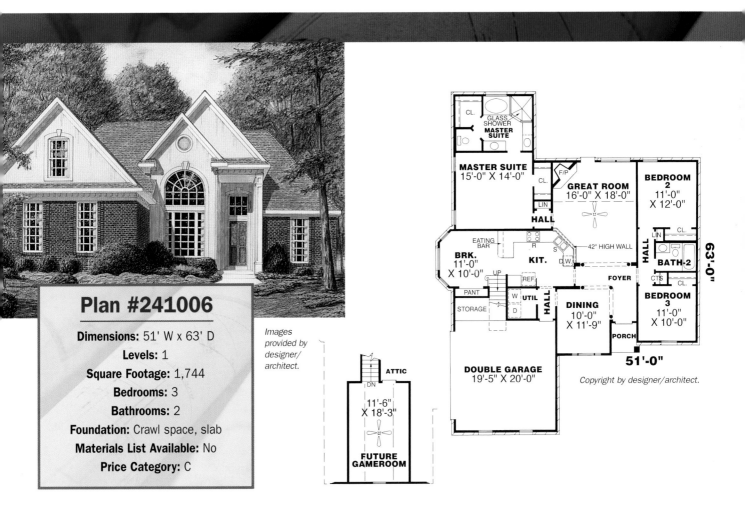

Plan #241006

Dimensions: 51' W x 63' D

Levels: 1

Square Footage: 1,744

Bedrooms: 3

Bathrooms: 2

Foundation: Crawl space, slab

Materials List Available: No

Price Category: C

Images provided by designer/architect.

Copyright by designer/architect.

Plan #211070

Dimensions: 46' W x 68' D

Levels: 2

Square Footage: 1,700

Main Level Sq. Ft.: 1,160

Upper Level Sq. Ft.: 540

Bedrooms: 3

Bathrooms: 2½

Foundation: Crawl space, optional slab, or basement

Materials List Available: Yes

Price Category: C

Images provided by designer/architect.

Upper Level Floor Plan

Main Level Floor Plan

Copyright by designer/architect.

Plan #161009

Dimensions: 60'9" W x 49' D

Levels: 1

Square Footage: 1,651

Bedrooms: 3

Bathrooms: 2

Foundation: Basement

Materials List Available: Yes

Price Category: C

Images provided by designer/architect.

Copyright by designer/architect.

Rear Elevation

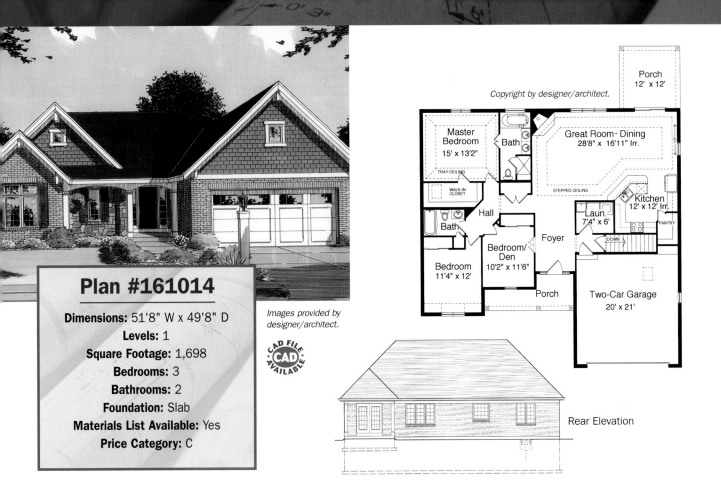

Plan #161014

Dimensions: 51'8" W x 49'8" D

Levels: 1

Square Footage: 1,698

Bedrooms: 3

Bathrooms: 2

Foundation: Slab

Materials List Available: Yes

Price Category: C

Images provided by designer/architect.

CAD FILE AVAILABLE

Copyright by designer/architect.

Rear Elevation

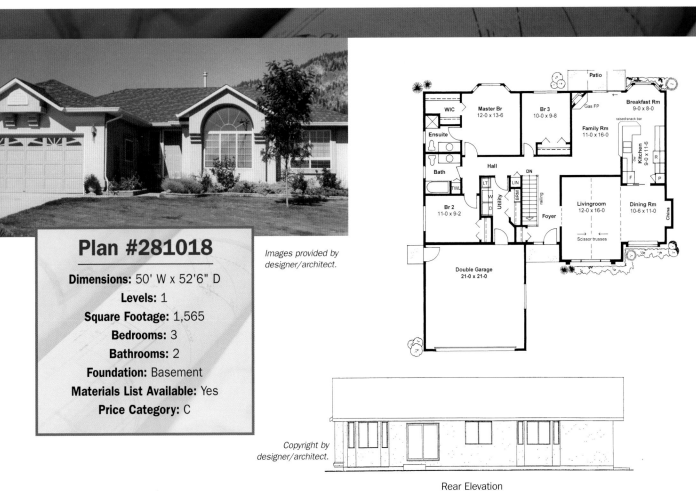

Plan #281018

Dimensions: 50' W x 52'6" D

Levels: 1

Square Footage: 1,565

Bedrooms: 3

Bathrooms: 2

Foundation: Basement

Materials List Available: Yes

Price Category: C

Images provided by designer/architect.

Copyright by designer/architect.

Rear Elevation

Plan #391034

Dimensions: 72'4" W x 43' D

Levels: 1

Square Footage: 1,737

Bedrooms: 3

Bathrooms: 2

Foundation: Crawl space, slab, or basement

Materials List Available: Yes

Price Category: C

Images provided by designer/architect.

This lovely home brings together traditional single-level architectural elements, current features, and just the right amount of living space.

Features:

- Entry: A demure covered porch and well-mannered foyer deliver all the important rooms.

- Dining Room: This formal room features exquisite vaulted ceilings.

- Kitchen: This close-knit kitchen with pantry embraces a cheerful breakfast nook with sliding doors to the deck.

- Master Suite: This suite is a visual treat, with its own vaulted ceiling as well as a skylight over the master bathtub and shower area.

- Bedrooms: The two secondary bedrooms are pampered with good closeting, proximity to a shared bath with double sink vanities, and wonderful windows that enhance the spacious atmosphere.

Rear Elevation

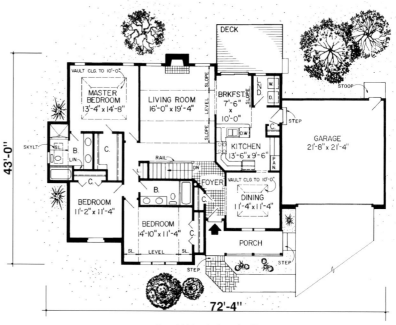

Copyright by designer/architect.

Plan #221044

Dimensions: 60'4" W x 55' D

Levels: 1

Square Footage: 1,781

Bedrooms: 3

Bathrooms: 2

Foundation: Basement

Materials List Available: No

Price Category: C

This adorable ranch home, with its blend of stone, shutters, and shingle siding is sure to capture your attention.

Features:

• Great Room: This spacious room shares a see-through fireplace with the den and features an 11-ft.-high ceiling.

• Kitchen: This island kitchen boasts a walk-in pantry and is open to the dining area. Just off the kitchen is a mudroom and then the garage.

• Master Suite: This suite features a large walk-in closet, spacious bath with Jacuzzi tub, and stepped ceiling in the bedroom.

• Bedrooms: On the other side of the home you'll find two additional bedrooms, one of which has a cathedral ceiling.

Images provided by designer/architect.

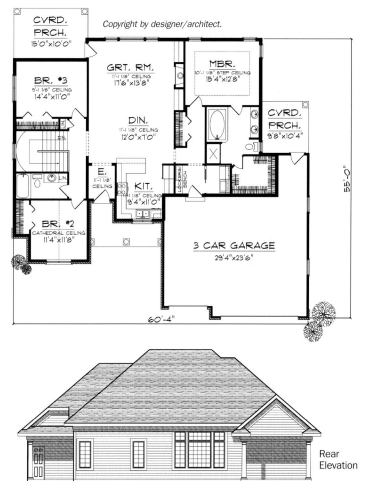

Rear Elevation

Plan #351002

Dimensions: 64' W x 45'10" D

Levels: 1

Square Footage: 1,751

Bedrooms: 3

Bathrooms: 2

Foundation: Crawl space, slab, or basement

Materials List Available: Yes

Price Category: C

This is a beautiful classic traditional home with a European touch.

Features:

- **Great Room:** This gathering area has a gas log fireplace that is flanked by two built-in cabinets. The area has a 10-ft.-tall tray ceiling.

- **Kitchen:** This L-shaped island kitchen has a raised bar and is open to the eating area and great room. The three open spaces work together as one large room.

- **Master Suite:** Located on the opposite side of the home from the secondary bedrooms, this suite has a vaulted ceiling. The master bath has dual vanities and a garden tub.

- **Bedrooms:** The two secondary bedrooms share a hall bathroom and have ample closet space.

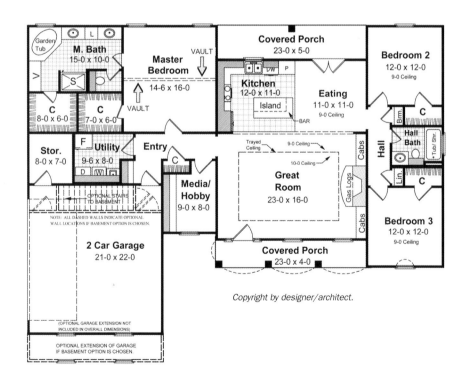

Plan #221004

Dimensions: 67'8" W x 43' D

Levels: 1

Square Footage: 1,763

Bedrooms: 3

Bathrooms: 2

Foundation: Basement

Materials List Available: No

Price Category: C

Images provided by designer/architect.

Rear Elevation

You'll love the spacious feeling provided by the open design of this traditional ranch.

Features:

- Ceiling Height: 8 ft.

- Dining Room: This formal room is perfect for entertaining groups both large and small, and the open design makes it easy to serve.

- Living Room: The vaulted ceiling here and in the dining room adds to the elegance of these rooms. Use window treatments that emphasize these ceilings for a truly sumptuous look.

- Kitchen: Designed for practicality and efficiency, this kitchen will thrill all the cooks in the family. An attached dining nook makes a natural gathering place for friends and family.

- Master Suite: The private bath in this suite features a double vanity and whirlpool tub. You'll find a walk-in closet in the bedroom.

- Garage: You'll love the extra storage space in this two-car garage.

Copyright by designer/architect.

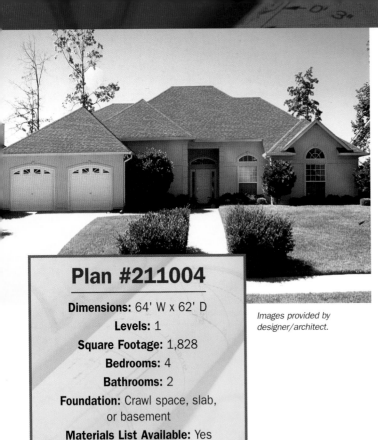

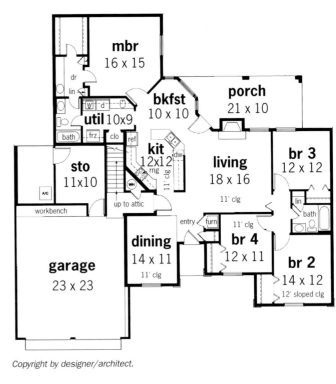

Plan #211004

Dimensions: 64' W x 62' D

Levels: 1

Square Footage: 1,828

Bedrooms: 4

Bathrooms: 2

Foundation: Crawl space, slab, or basement

Materials List Available: Yes

Price Category: D

Images provided by designer/architect.

Copyright by designer/architect.

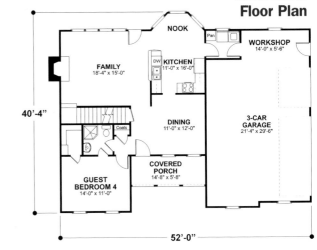

Main Level Floor Plan

Plan #101031

Dimensions: 52' W x 40'4" D

Levels: 2

Square Footage: 1,932

Main Level Sq. Ft.: 1,012

Upper Level Sq. Ft.: 920

Bedrooms: 4

Bathrooms: 3

Foundation: Basement

Material List Available: No

Price Category: D

Images provided by designer/architect.

CAD FILE AVAILABLE

Upper Level Floor Plan

Copyright by designer/architect.

Main Level Floor Plan

Plan #451148

Dimensions: 48'6" W x 42' D

Levels: 2

Square Footage: 1,889

Main Level Sq. Ft.: 1,103

Upper Level Sq. Ft.: 786

Bedrooms: 3

Bathrooms: 2½

Foundation: Walkout basement

Material List Available: No

Price Category: D

Images provided by designer/architect.

Upper Level Floor Plan

Basement Level Floor Plan

Copyright by designer/architect.

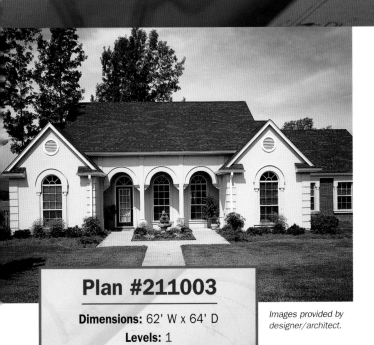

Plan #211003

Dimensions: 62' W x 64' D

Levels: 1

Square Footage: 1,865

Bedrooms: 3

Bathrooms: 2

Foundation: Slab

Materials List Available: Yes

Price Category: D

Images provided by designer/architect.

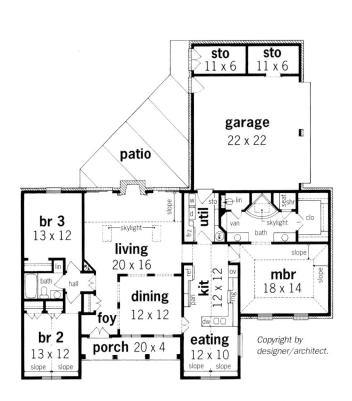

Copyright by designer/architect.

Plan #441005

Dimensions: 50' W x 59' D

Levels: 1

Square Footage: 1,800

Bedrooms: 3

Bathrooms: 2

Foundation: Crawl space

Materials List Available: No

Price Category: D

Images provided by designer/architect.

This home looks as if it's a quaint little abode—with its board-and-batten siding, cedar shingle detailing, and column-covered porch—but even a quick peek inside will prove that there is much more to this plan than meets the eye.

CAD FILE AVAILABLE

Features:

• **Foyer:** This entry area rises to a 9-ft.-high ceiling. On one side is a washer-dryer alcove with a closet across the way; on the other is another large storage area. Just down the hallway is a third closet.

• **Kitchen:** This kitchen features a center island, built-in desk/work center, and pantry. This area and the dining area also boast 9-ft.-high ceilings and are open to a vaulted great room with corner fireplace.

• **Dining Room:** Sliding doors in this area lead to a covered side porch, so you can enjoy outside dining.

• **Master Suite:** This suite has a vaulted ceiling. The master bath is wonderfully appointed with a separate shower, spa tub, and dual sinks.

• **Bedrooms:** Three bedrooms (or two plus an office) are found on the right side of the plan.

Rear Elevation

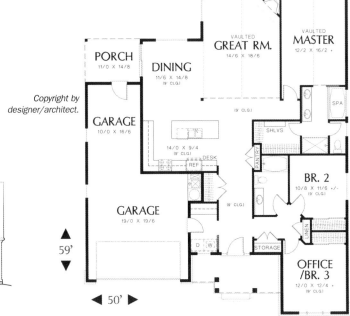

Copyright by designer/architect.

Plan #121051

Dimensions: 64' W x 44' D
Levels: 1
Square Footage: 1,808
Bedrooms: 3
Bathrooms: 2½
Foundation: Basement
Materials List Available: Yes
Price Category: D

Images provided by designer/architect.

You'll love the way that natural light pours into this home from the gorgeous windows you'll find in room after room.

Features:

- Great Room: You'll notice the bayed, transom-topped window in the great room as soon as you step into this lovely home. A wet-bar makes this great room a natural place for entertaining, and the see-through fireplace makes it cozy on chilly days and winter evenings.

- Kitchen: This well-designed kitchen will be a delight for everyone who cooks here, not only because of the ample counter and cabinet space but also because of its location in the home.

- Master Suite: Angled ceilings in both the bedroom and the bathroom of this suite make it feel luxurious, and the picturesque window in the bedroom gives it character. The bath includes a corner whirlpool tub where you'll love to relax at the end of the day.

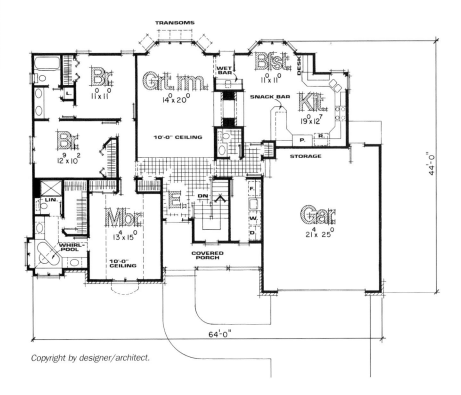

Copyright by designer/architect.

Plan #351070

Dimensions: 63'4" W x 53' D

Levels: 1

Square Footage: 1,818

Bedrooms: 3

Bathrooms: 3

Foundation: Basement

Materials List Available: No

Price Category: D

Images provided by designer/architect.

This charming farmhouse has everything, including three bedrooms, three bathrooms and a two-car garage.

Features:

• Great Room: Enjoy the vaulted ceiling, gas log fireplace, and built-ins in this expansive room.

• Flex Space: This space is provided for uses such as an office/media center, half bathroom, hobby room, or winter-wear closet.

• Master Suite: This suite has a tray ceiling, a large closet for him and her, a jetted tub, an oversized shower, and a large vanity next to her closet.

• Bedrooms: All bedrooms feature walk-in closets with their own private bathroom. Bedroom 2 could be used as an in-law suite.

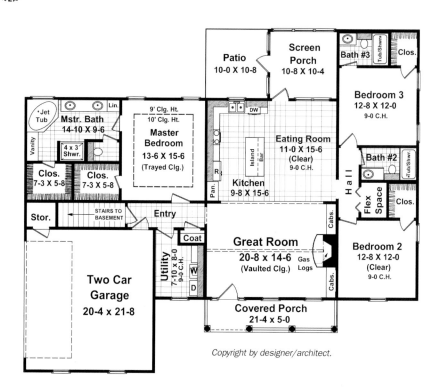

Copyright by designer/architect.

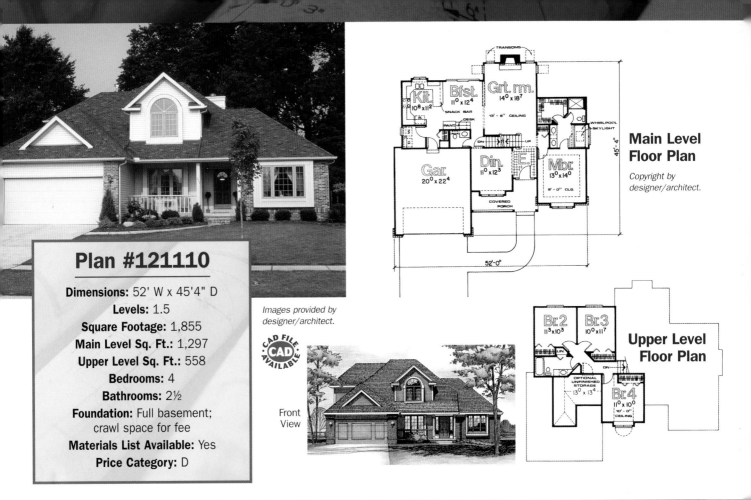

Plan #121110

Dimensions: 52' W x 45'4" D

Levels: 1.5

Square Footage: 1,855

Main Level Sq. Ft.: 1,297

Upper Level Sq. Ft.: 558

Bedrooms: 4

Bathrooms: 2½

Foundation: Full basement; crawl space for fee

Materials List Available: Yes

Price Category: D

Images provided by designer/architect.

Main Level Floor Plan

Copyright by designer/architect.

Upper Level Floor Plan

Front View

Plan #271030

Dimensions: 55'8" W x 45' D

Levels: 2

Square Footage: 1,926

Main Level Sq. Ft.: 1,490

Upper Level Sq. Ft.: 436

Bedrooms: 3

Bathrooms: 2½

Foundation: Basement

Materials List Available: Yes

Price Category: D

Images provided by designer/architect.

Main Level Floor Plan

Copyright by designer/architect.

Upper Level Floor Plan

Plan #221040

Dimensions: 50' W x 66' D

Levels: 1

Square Footage: 1,822

Bedrooms: 2

Bathrooms: 2

Foundation: Basement

Materials List Available: No

Price Category: D

This narrow ranch home has timeless curb appeal with its perfect combination of stone and shingle siding.

CAD FILE AVAILABLE

Features:

• Kitchen: This kitchen features a breakfast bar that overlooks both the dining room and great room, all with 11-ft.-high ceilings.

• Master Suite: This suite is sure to please, with its stepped ceiling, large walk-in closet, and spacious bath with Jacuzzi tub.

• Bedroom: The second bedroom and another full bathroom can be found at the front of the home, away from the master, for maximum privacy.

• Garage: This three-bay garage provides ample storage and makes the narrow home attractive for today's economically minded buyer.

Images provided by designer/architect.

Rear Elevation

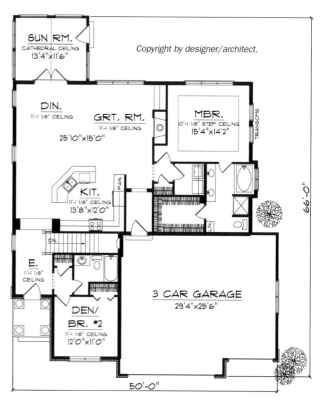

Copyright by designer/architect.

Plan #121001

Dimensions: 56' W x 58' D
Levels: 1
Square Footage: 1,911
Bedrooms: 3
Bathrooms: 2
Foundation: Basement
Materials List Available: Yes
Price Category: D

Detailed, soaring ceilings and top-notch amenities set this distinctive home apart.

Features:

- Ceiling Height: 8 ft. except as noted.

- Great Room: A soaring ceiling and six tall transom-topped windows make this a light and airy spot for entertaining.

- Formal Dining Room: The entry enjoys a pleasing view of this dining room's detailed 12-ft. ceiling and picture window.

- Great Room: At the back of the home, a see-through fireplace in this great room is joined by a built-in entertainment center.

- Hearth Room: This bayed room shares the see-through fireplace with the great room.

- Master Suite: Enjoy the stars and the sun in the private bath's whirlpool and separate shower. The bath features the same decorative ceiling as the dining room.

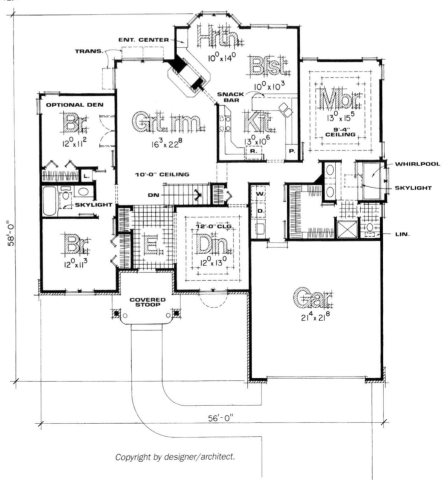

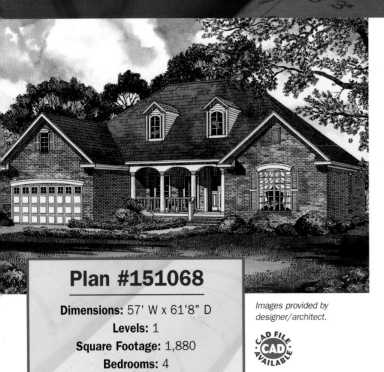

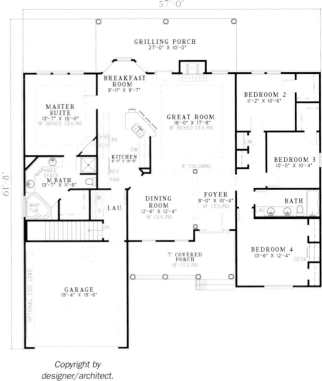

Plan #151068

Dimensions: 57' W x 61'8" D

Levels: 1

Square Footage: 1,880

Bedrooms: 4

Bathrooms: 2

Foundation: Crawl space, slab, or basement

CompleteCost List Available: Yes

Price Category: D

Images provided by designer/architect.

CAD FILE AVAILABLE

Copyright by designer/architect.

Plan #271078

Dimensions: 83' W x 52' D

Levels: 1

Square Footage: 1,855

Bedrooms: 1-2

Bathrooms: 1½-2½

Foundation: Daylight basement

Materials List Available: No

Price Category: D

Images provided by designer/architect.

CAD FILE AVAILABLE

Optional Basement Level Floor Plan

Copyright by designer/architect.

Plan #221056

Dimensions: 54' W x 58' D

Levels: 1

Square Footage: 1,917

Bedrooms: 2

Bathrooms: 2

Foundation: Basement

Materials List Available: No

Price Category: D

Images provided by designer/architect.

You'll think this home was built many years ago because of its perfect blend of shingle siding and stone. With an open floor plan, this ranch home packs a lot of amenities in a small footprint.

Features:

- **Open Plan:** From the breakfast bar that overlooks the nook and great room, to the 10-ft.-high ceilings throughout, this home feels spacious and roomy enough for any size family.

- **Great Room:** This gathering area has a cozy fireplace, a built-in cabinet, and views of the backyard.

- **Master Suite:** This master suite features a stepped ceiling, a Jacuzzi tub in the bath, and a spacious walk-in closet.

- **Bedrooms:** Two additional bedrooms are located on the opposite side of the home, allowing for plenty of privacy for mom and dad.

NOOK
10'-1 1/8" CEILING
13'4"x10'0"

GRT. RM.
10'-1 1/8" CEILING
14'8"x18'0"

MBR.
10'-1 1/8" STEP CEILING
15'8"x14'0"

KIT.
10'-1 1/8" CEILING
13'4"x11'4"

DIN./DEN/BR. #3
10'-1 1/8" CEILING
13'4"x11'4"

E.
10'-1 1/8" CEILING

BR. #2
10'-1 1/8" CEILING
12'0"x12'0"

3 CAR GARAGE
30'8"x24'0"

54'-0"

58'-0"

BR. #3/DEN
10'-1 1/8" CEILING
11'8"x11'4"

**Dining Room
Den
Bedroom 3
Optional
Floor Plan**

Copyright by designer/architect.

Rear Elevation

Plan #101005

Dimensions: 63' W x 57'2" D

Levels: 1

Square Footage: 1,992

Bedrooms: 3

Bathrooms: 2½

Foundation: Crawl space, slab, or basement

Materials List Available: Yes

Price Category: D

Images provided by designer/architect.

Rear View

This midsized ranch is accented with Palladian windows and inviting front porch.

Features:

- Ceiling Height: 9 ft. unless otherwise noted.

- Special Ceilings: Tray or vaulted ceilings adorn the living room, family room, dining room, and master suite.

- Kitchen: This bright and airy kitchen is designed to be a pleasure in which to work. It shares a big bay window with the contiguous breakfast room.

- Breakfast Room: The light streaming in from the bay window makes this the perfect place to linger with coffee and the Sunday paper.

- Master Suite: This lovely suite is exceptional, with its sitting area and direct access to the deck, as well as a full-featured bath, and spacious walk-in closet.

- Secondary Bedrooms: The other bedrooms each measure about 13 ft. x 11 ft. They have walk-in closets and share a "Jack-and-Jill" bath.

Copyright by designer/architect.

Plan #151170

Dimensions: 57' W x 64'4" D

Levels: 1

Square Footage: 1,965

Bedrooms: 4

Bathrooms: 2

Foundation: Crawl space, slab (basement or daylight basement option for fee)

CompleteCost List Available: Yes

Price Category: D

The clean lines of the open floor plan and high ceilings match the classic good looks of this home's exterior.

Features:

- Foyer: The 10-ft. ceiling here sets the stage for the open, airy feeling of this lovely home.

- Dining Room: Set off by columns from the foyer and great room, this area is ideal for entertaining.

- Great Room: Open to the breakfast room beyond, this great room features a masonry fireplace and a door to the rear grilling porch.

- Breakfast Room: A deep bay overlooking the porch is the focal point here.

- Kitchen: Planned for efficiency, the kitchen has an angled island with storage and snack bar.

- Master Suite: A boxed ceiling adds elegance to the bedroom, and the bath features a whirlpool tub, double vanity, and separate shower.

Images provided by designer/architect.

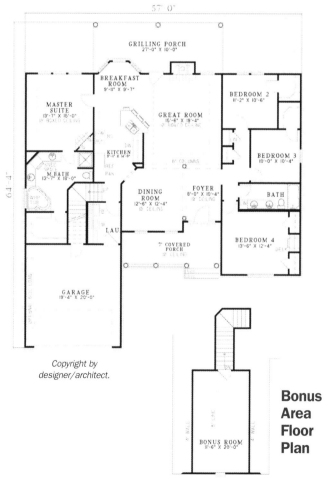

Copyright by designer/architect.

Bonus Area Floor Plan

Plan #321006

Dimensions: 76' W x 45' D

Levels: 1, optional lower

Square Footage: 1,977

Optional Basement Level Sq. Ft.: 1,416

Bedrooms: 4

Bathrooms: 2½

Foundation: Basement

Materials List Available: Yes

Price Category: D

Images provided by designer/architect.

This design is ideal if you're looking for a home with space to finish as your family and your budget grow.

Features:

- Great Room: A vaulted ceiling in this room sets an elegant tone that the gorgeous atrium windows pick up and amplify.

- Atrium: Elegance marks the staircase here that leads to the optional lower level.

- Kitchen: Both experienced cooks and beginners will appreciate the care that went into the design of this step-saving kitchen, with its ample counter space and generous cabinets.

- Master Suite: Enjoy the luxuries you'll find in this suite, and revel in the quiet that the bedroom can provide.

- Lower Level: Finish the 1,416 sq. ft. here to create a family room, two bedrooms, two bathrooms, and a study.

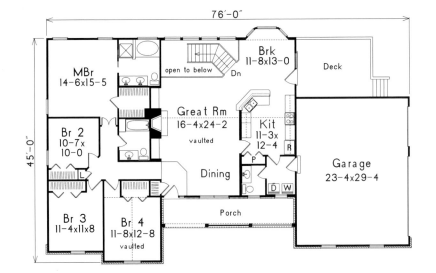

Optional Basement Level Floor Plan

Copyright by designer/architect.

Plan #131015

Dimensions: 57'4" W x 56'10" D

Levels: 1

Square Footage: 1,860

Bedrooms: 3

Bathrooms: 2

Foundation: Crawl space, slab, or basement

Materials List Available: Yes

Price Category: E

Images provided by designer/architect.

The mixture of country charm and formal elegance is sure to thrill any family looking for a distinctive and comfortable home.

Features:

• Great Room: Separated from the dining room by a columned arch, this spacious room has a stepped ceiling, a built-in media center, and a fireplace. French doors within a rear bay lead to the large backyard patio at the rear of the house.

• Dining Room: Graced by a bay window, this formal room has an impressive 11-ft. 6-in.-high stepped ceiling.

• Breakfast Room: With a 12-ft. sloped ceiling, this room shares an eating bar with the kitchen.

• Master Bedroom: The 10-ft. tray ceiling and bay window contribute elegance, and the walk-in closet and bath with a bayed nook, whirlpool tub, and separate shower make it practical.

Copyright by designer/architect.

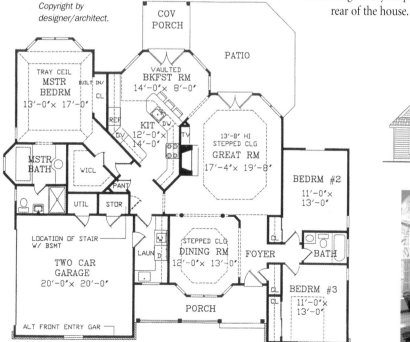

Rear Elevation

Great Room

Images provided by designer/architect.

Copyright by designer/architect.

Plan #321020

Dimensions: 58' W x 47'6" D

Levels: 1

Square Footage: 1,882

Bedrooms: 4

Bathrooms: 2

Foundation: Basement

Materials List Available: Yes

Price Category: D

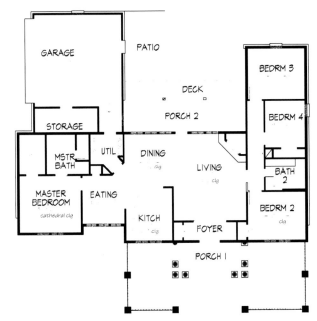

Images provided by designer/architect.

CAD FILE AVAILABLE

Plan #271082

Dimensions: 71' W x 62' D

Levels: 1

Square Footage: 2,074

Bedrooms: 4

Bathrooms: 2

Foundation: Crawl space or slab

Materials List Available: No

Price Category: D

Copyright by designer/architect.

Plan #151104

Dimensions: 43' W x 55' D

Levels: 1

Square Footage: 1,860

Bedrooms: 3

Bathrooms: 2

Foundation: Crawl space or slab; basement for fee

CompleteCost List Available: Yes

Price Category: D

If you're just starting a family or the children have left the nest, this is the ideal home for you.

CAD FILE AVAILABLE

Features:

- **Great Room:** Set off by 8-in. columns, this gathering area features a fireplace and access to the backyard.

- **Kitchen:** This U-shaped kitchen has a raised bar that's open to the breakfast room. The built-in computer desk will be a great asset to today's family.

- **Master Suite:** This private retreat offers a large sleeping area with access to the rear yard. The master bath features dual vanities and a whirlpool tub.

- **Garage:** This front-loading two-car garage has room for cars plus storage.

Main Level Floor Plan

Bonus Area Floor Plan

Copyright by designer/architect.

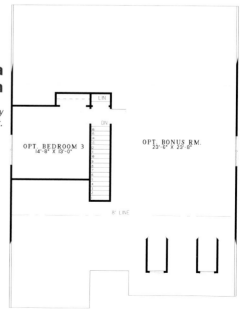

Plan #441001

Dimensions: 44' W x 68' D
Levels: 1
Square Footage: 1,850
Bedrooms: 3
Bathrooms: 2
Foundation: Crawl space
Materials List Available: No
Price Category: D

Images provided by designer/architect.

With all the tantalizing elements of a cottage and the comfortable space of a family-sized home, this Arts and Crafts-style one-story design is the best of both worlds. Exterior accents such as stone wainscot, cedar shingles under the gable ends, and mission-style windows just add to the effect.

Features:

- **Great Room:** A warm hearth lights this room—right next to a built-in media center.

- **Dining Room:** This area features a sliding glass door to the rear patio for a breath of fresh air.

- **Den:** This quiet area has a window seat and a vaulted ceiling, giving the feeling of openness and letting your mind wander.

- **Kitchen:** This open corner kitchen features a 42-in. snack bar and a giant walk-in pantry.

- **Master Suite:** This suite boasts a tray ceiling and a large walk-in closet.

Rear Elevation

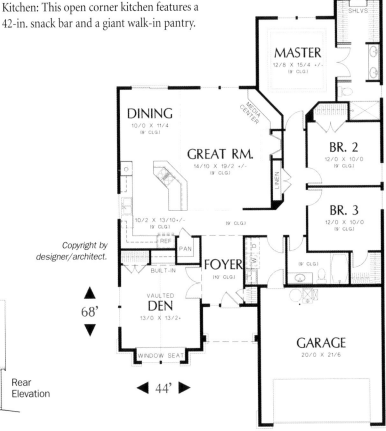

Copyright by designer/architect.

68'

44'

Plan #121050

Dimensions: 64' W x 50' D
Levels: 1
Square Footage: 1,996
Bedrooms: 2
Bathrooms: 2
Foundation: Basement
Materials List Available: Yes
Price Category: D

Images provided by designer/architect.

This compact design includes features usually reserved for larger homes and has styling that is typical of more-exclusive home designs.

Features:

- **Entry:** As you enter this home, you'll see the formal living and dining rooms—both with special ceiling detailing—on either side.

- **Great Room:** Located in the rear of the home for convenience, this great room is likely to be your favorite spot. The fireplace is framed by transom-topped windows, so you'll love curling up here, no matter what the weather or time of day.

- **Kitchen:** Ample counter and cabinet space make this kitchen a dream in which to work.

- **Master Suite:** A tray ceiling and lovely corner windows create an elegant feeling in the bedroom, and two walk-in closets make it easy to keep this space tidy and organized. The private bath has a skylight, corner whirlpool tub, and two separate vanities.

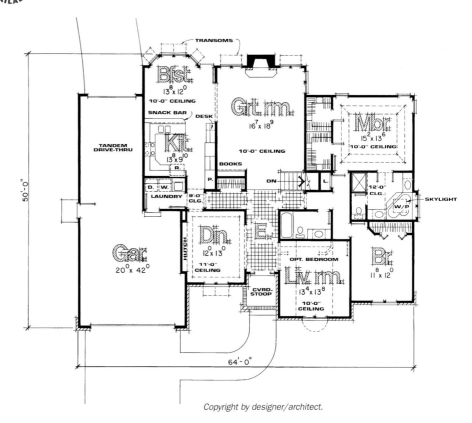

Copyright by designer/architect.

Plan #331001

Dimensions: 57' W x 45' D

Levels: 2

Square Footage: 1,846

Main Level Sq. Ft.: 1,156

Upper Level Sq. Ft.: 690

Bedrooms: 3

Bathrooms: 2½

Foundation: Crawl space, slab, or basement

Materials List Available: No

Price Category: D

Images provided by designer/architect.

Main Level Floor Plan

Upper Level Floor Plan

Copyright by designer/architect.

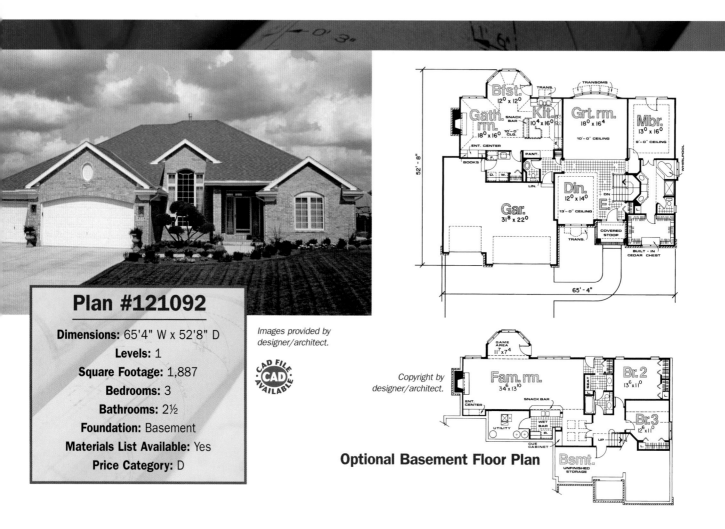

Plan #121092

Dimensions: 65'4" W x 52'8" D

Levels: 1

Square Footage: 1,887

Bedrooms: 3

Bathrooms: 2½

Foundation: Basement

Materials List Available: Yes

Price Category: D

Images provided by designer/architect.

CAD FILE AVAILABLE

Copyright by designer/architect.

Optional Basement Floor Plan

Plan #151490

Dimensions: 52' W x 69'6" D
Levels: 1
Square Footage: 1,869
Bedrooms: 3
Bathrooms: 2
Foundation: Crawl space or slab
CompleteCost List Available: Yes
Price Category: D

Beautiful brick and wood siding impart warmth to this French Country design.

Features:

- **Open Plan:** Elegance is achieved in this home by using boxed columns and 10-ft.-high ceilings. The foyer and dining room are lined with columns and adjoin the great room, all with high ceilings.

- **Kitchen:** This combined kitchen and breakfast room is great for entertaining and has access to the grilling porch.

- **Master Suite:** The split-bedroom plan features this suite, with its large walk-in closet, whirlpool tub, shower, and private area.

- **Bedrooms:** The two bedrooms and a large bathroom are located on the other side of the great room, giving privacy to the entire family.

Images provided by designer/architect.

Bonus Area Floor Plan

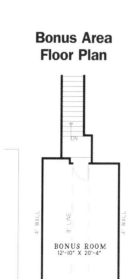

Copyright by designer/architect.

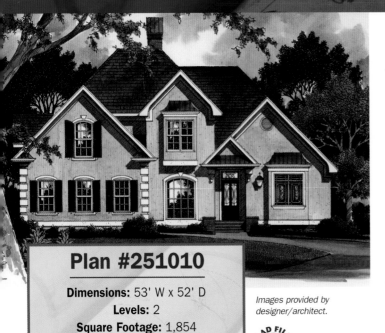

Plan #251010

Dimensions: 53' W x 52' D

Levels: 2

Square Footage: 1,854

Main Level Sq. Ft.: 1,317

Upper Level Sq. Ft.: 537

Bedrooms: 3

Bathrooms: 2½

Foundation: Basement

Materials List Available: Yes

Price Category: D

Images provided by designer/architect.

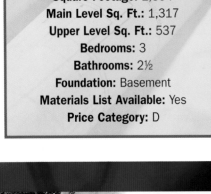

Main Level Floor Plan

Upper Level Floor Plan

Copyright by designer/architect.

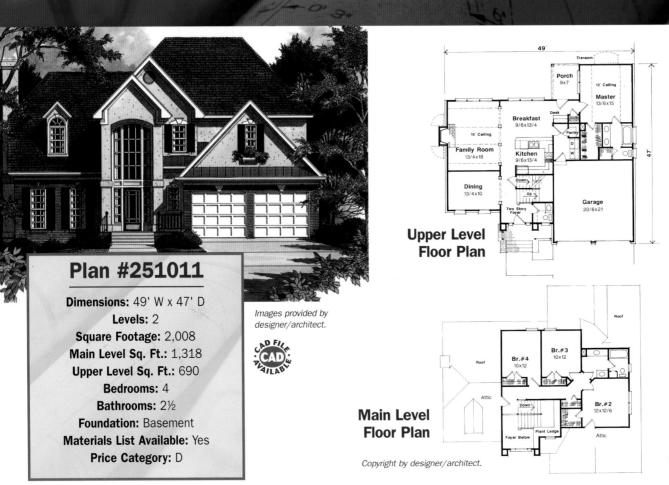

Plan #251011

Dimensions: 49' W x 47' D

Levels: 2

Square Footage: 2,008

Main Level Sq. Ft.: 1,318

Upper Level Sq. Ft.: 690

Bedrooms: 4

Bathrooms: 2½

Foundation: Basement

Materials List Available: Yes

Price Category: D

Images provided by designer/architect.

Upper Level Floor Plan

Main Level Floor Plan

Copyright by designer/architect.

Plan #121086

Dimensions: 55'4" W x 37'8" D

Levels: 2

Square Footage: 1,998

Main Level Sq. Ft.: 1,093

Upper Level Sq. Ft.: 905

Bedrooms: 3

Bathrooms: 2½

Foundation: Basement

Materials List Available: Yes

Price Category: D

Images provided by designer/architect.

Main Level Floor Plan

Upper Level Floor Plan

Copyright by designer/architect.

Plan #311016

Dimensions: 63'10" W x 64'7" D

Levels: 1

Square Footage: 2,089

Bedrooms: 3

Bathrooms: 2½

Foundation: Crawl space, slab, or basement

Materials List Available: Yes

Price Category: D

Images provided by designer/architect.

Bonus Area Floor Plan

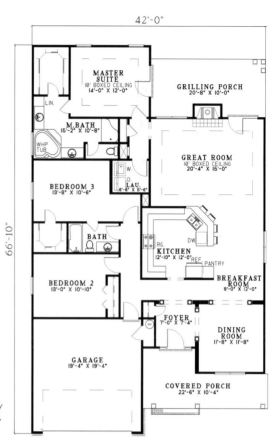

Plan #151008

Dimensions: 42' W x 66'10" D

Levels: 1

Square Footage: 1,892

Bedrooms: 3

Bathrooms: 2

Foundation: Crawl space, slab, basement, or daylight basement

CompleteCost List Available: Yes

Price Category: D

Images provided by designer/architect.

This home, as shown in the photograph, may differ from the actual blueprints. For more detailed information, please check the floor plans carefully.

Copyright by designer/architect.

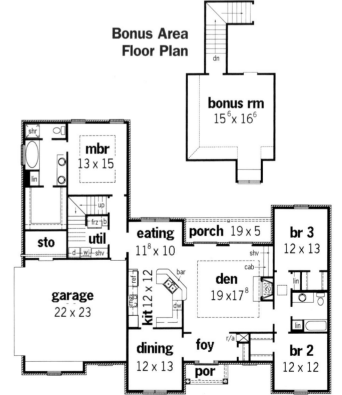

Plan #201081

Dimensions: 65'10" W x 55'10" D

Levels: 1

Square Footage: 1,940

Bedrooms: 3

Bathrooms: 2

Foundation: Crawl space, slab

Materials List Available: Yes

Price Category: D

Images provided by designer/architect.

Copyright by designer/architect.

Plan #211039

Dimensions: 62' W x 64' D
Levels: 1
Square Footage: 1,868
Bedrooms: 3
Bathrooms: 2
Foundation: Slab
Materials List Available: Yes
Price Category: D

Images provided by designer/architect.

This home exudes traditional charm, but its layout and amenities are thoroughly modern.

Features:

- Formal Dining Room: This elegant room is perfect for dinner parties of any size.

- Kitchen: If you love to cook, you will love this kitchen. It's U-shaped for maximum efficiency, and it boasts a built-in desk for making menus and shopping lists, as well as a handy pantry closet. The kitchen has access to the carport, so groceries make a short trip to the counter.

- Eating Area: Just off the kitchen you'll find this informal eating area designed for quick meals on the go.

- Master Suite: Here is the perfect place to unwind after a long day. This generous bedroom hosts a lavish master bath with a spa tub, separate shower, and his and hers dressing areas.

- Secondary Bedrooms: Located across the home from the master suite, the two secondary bedrooms share another full bath.

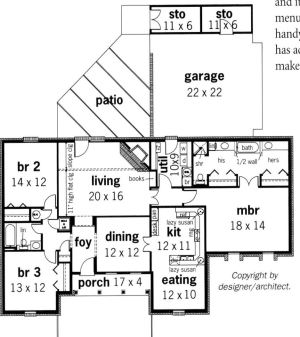

Copyright by designer/architect.

SMARTtip
Kitchen Wallpapering

For wrapping outside corners, measure from the last piece to the corner, and add ½ inch to the measurement. Cut the paper to size, and place it in position, but before wrapping it around the corner, make small slits in the waste portions of the paper near the ceiling and the baseboard. The cuts will allow you to turn the corner without wrinkling or tearing the paper. Hang the other part of the cut sheet so that it overlaps the first portion.

Plan #181063

Dimensions: 55' W x 41' D
Levels: 2
Square Footage: 2,037
Main Level Sq. Ft.: 1,347
Upper Level Sq. Ft.: 690
Bedrooms: 4
Bathrooms: 2
Foundation: Full basement
Materials List Available: Yes
Price Category: D

Quaint brick and stone, plus deeply pitched rooflines, create the storybook aura folks fall for when they see this home, but it's the serenely versatile interior layout that captures their hearts.

Features:

• Family Room: The floor plan is configured to bring a panoramic view to nearly every room, beginning with this room, with its fireplace and towering cathedral ceiling.

• Kitchen: This kitchen, with its crowd-pleasing island, has an eye on the outdoors. It also has all the counter and storage space a cook would want, plus a lunch counter with comfy seats and multiple windows to bring in the breeze.

• Bedrooms: Downstairs, you'll find the master bedroom, with its adjoining master bath. Upstairs, three uniquely shaped bedrooms, styled with clever nooks and windows to dream by, easily share a large bathroom.

• Mezzanine: This sweeping mezzanine overlooks the open living and dining rooms.

CAD FILE AVAILABLE

Images provided by designer/architect.
This home, as shown in the photograph, may differ from the actual blueprints. For more detailed information, please check the floor plans carefully.

Front View

Rear View

41'-0"
12,3 m

19'-0" X 20'-0"
5,70 X 6,00

12'-0" X 14'-8"
3,60 X 4,40

13'-0" X 19'-0"
3,90 X 5,70

16'-0" X 15'-0"
4,80 X 4,50

11'-8" X 12'-8"
3,50 X 3,80

55'-0"
16,5 m

**Main Level
Floor Plan**

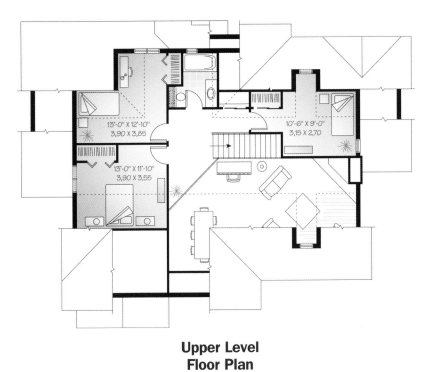

13'-0" X 12'-10"
3,90 X 3,85

10'-6" X 9'-0"
3,15 X 2,70

13'-0" X 11'-10"
3,90 X 3,55

**Upper Level
Floor Plan**

Living Room

Master Bath

Kitchen

Plan #151386

Dimensions: 64'2" W x 49' D

Levels: 1

Square Footage: 1,989

Bedrooms: 4

Bathrooms: 3

Foundation: Crawl space, slab, basement, or walkout

CompleteCost List Available: Yes

Price Category: D

Images provided by designer/architect.

An interesting roofline gives this ranch home a unique look.

Features:

- **Dining Room:** Enjoy a nice dinner as the beautiful boxed columns frame this regal room.

- **Great Room:** You will enjoy the openness of this room, which has a fireplace and access to the rear covered porch.

- **Kitchen:** Mornings bring a new day, and preparing breakfast will be enjoyable in this spacious kitchen with breakfast room.

- **Master Suite:** A beautiful tray ceiling adorns this suite, while the bath is complete with a huge walk-in closet, whirlpool tub, and corner glass shower.

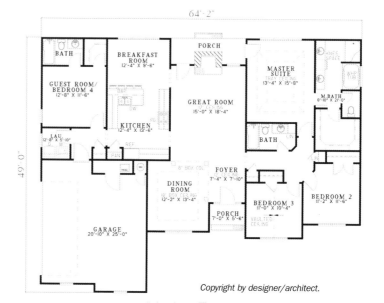

Copyright by designer/architect.

Plan #151117

Dimensions: 66' W x 55' D

Levels: 1

Square Footage: 1,957

Bedrooms: 3

Bathrooms: 3

Foundation: Crawl space, slab, or basement

CompleteCost List Available: Yes

Price Category: D

Images provided by designer/architect.

You'll love this home if you have a family-centered lifestyle and enjoy an active social life.

Features:

- Foyer: A 10-ft. ceiling sets the tone for this home.

- Great Room: A 10-ft. boxed ceiling and fireplace are the highlights of this room, which also has a door leading to the rear covered porch.

- Dining Room: Columns mark the entry from the foyer to this lovely formal dining room.

- Study: Add the French doors from the foyer to transform bedroom 3, with its vaulted ceiling, into a quiet study.

- Kitchen: This large kitchen includes a pantry and shares an eating bar with the adjoining, bayed breakfast room.

- Master Suite: You'll love the access to the rear porch, as well as the bath with every amenity, in this suite.

Copyright by designer/architect.

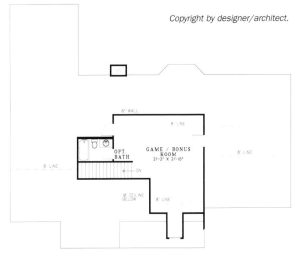

Bonus Area Floor Plan

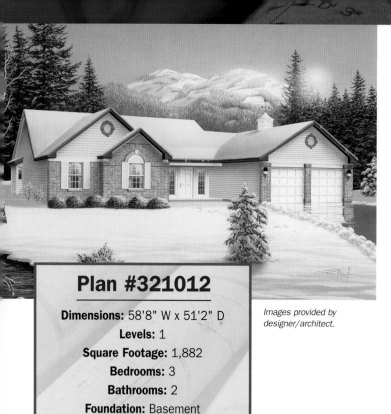

Images provided by designer/architect.

Plan #321012

Dimensions: 58'8" W x 51'2" D

Levels: 1

Square Footage: 1,882

Bedrooms: 3

Bathrooms: 2

Foundation: Basement

Materials List Available: Yes

Price Category: D

Copyright by designer/architect.

Images provided by designer/architect.

Plan #151005

Dimensions: 58' W x 54'10" D

Levels: 1

Square Footage: 1,940

Bedrooms: 4

Bathrooms: 2

Foundation: Crawl space, slab, or basement

CompleteCost List Available: Yes

Price Category: D

Copyright by designer/architect.

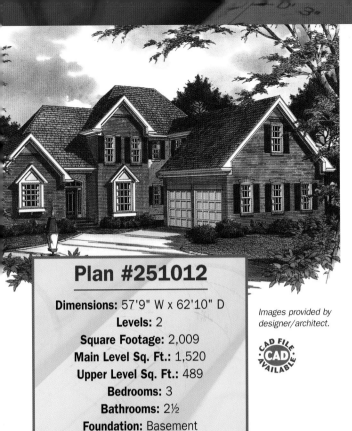

Plan #251012

Dimensions: 57'9" W x 62'10" D
Levels: 2
Square Footage: 2,009
Main Level Sq. Ft.: 1,520
Upper Level Sq. Ft.: 489
Bedrooms: 3
Bathrooms: 2½
Foundation: Basement
Materials List Available: Yes
Price Category: D

Images provided by designer/architect.

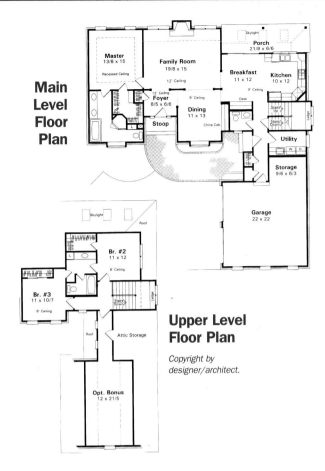

Main Level Floor Plan

Upper Level Floor Plan

Copyright by designer/architect.

Plan #251013

Dimensions: 58' W x 44' D
Levels: 2
Square Footage: 2,073
Main Level Sq. Ft.: 1,441
Upper Level Sq. Ft.: 632
Bedrooms: 4
Bathrooms: 2½
Foundation: Basement
Materials List Available: Yes
Price Category: D

Images provided by designer/architect.

Main Level Floor Plan

Upper Level Floor Plan

Copyright by designer/architect.

Plan #351001

Dimensions: 72'8" W x 51' D

Levels: 1

Square Footage: 1,855

Bedrooms: 3

Bathrooms: 2½

Foundation: Crawl space, slab, or basement

Materials List Available: Yes

Price Category: D

From the lovely arched windows on the front to the front and back covered porches, this home is as comfortable as it is beautiful.

Features:

- Great Room: Come into this room with 12-ft. ceilings, and you're sure to admire the corner gas fireplace and three windows overlooking the porch.

- Dining Room: Set off from the open design, this room is designed to be used formally or not.

- Kitchen: You'll love the practical walk-in pantry, broom closet, and angled snack bar here.

- Breakfast Room: Brightly lit and leading to the covered porch, this room will be a favorite spot.

- Bonus Room: Develop a playroom or study in this area.

- Master Suite: The large bedroom is complemented by the private bath with garden tub, separate shower, double vanity, and spacious walk-in closet.

Images provided by designer/architect.

Copyright by designer/architect.

Master Bedroom 14-0 x 17-0 9-0 Ceiling

M. Bath 10-0 x 13-6

Garden Tub / Shr.

Closet 10-0 x 8-0

Stor. 8-4 x 4-4

Entry

Stor.

OUTLINE OF STAIRS

OPTIONAL STAIRS TO BASEMENT

Covered Porch 17 x 8

Breakfast 12-0 x 11-0 9-0 Ceiling

Clos.

Bath

HVAC

Bedroom 3 12-0 x 12-0 9-0 Ceiling

Gas Logs

Great Room 17-0 x 22-0 12-0 Ceiling

Kitchen 12-0 x 15-0

Utility 8-0 x 9-0

Bar

DW

P

W D

Two Car Garage 24-0 x 22-0

Clos.

Bath

Tub/Shr.

Hall

Bedroom 2 12-0 x 12-0 9-0 Ceiling

Clos.

C.

Covered Porch 14-4 x 5

Dining 12-0 x 12-0 9-0 Ceiling

Br

EXTENSION OF GARAGE IF BASEMENT FOUNDATION IS CHOSEN

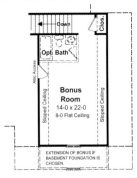

Kitchen/Great Room

Bonus Area Floor Plan

Down

Closet

Opt. Bath

Attic Access

Sloped Ceiling

Bonus Room 14-0 x 22-0 8-0 Flat Ceiling

Sloped Ceiling

EXTENSION OF BONUS IF BASEMENT FOUNDATION IS CHOSEN

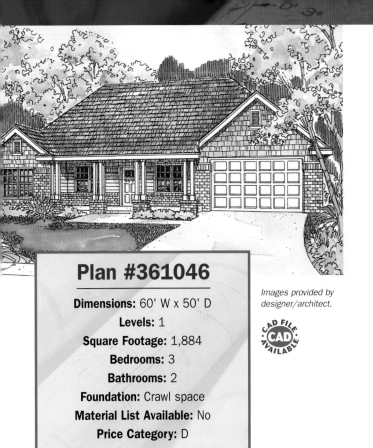

Plan #361046

Dimensions: 60' W x 50' D

Levels: 1

Square Footage: 1,884

Bedrooms: 3

Bathrooms: 2

Foundation: Crawl space

Material List Available: No

Price Category: D

Images provided by designer/architect.

CAD FILE AVAILABLE

Copyright by designer/architect.

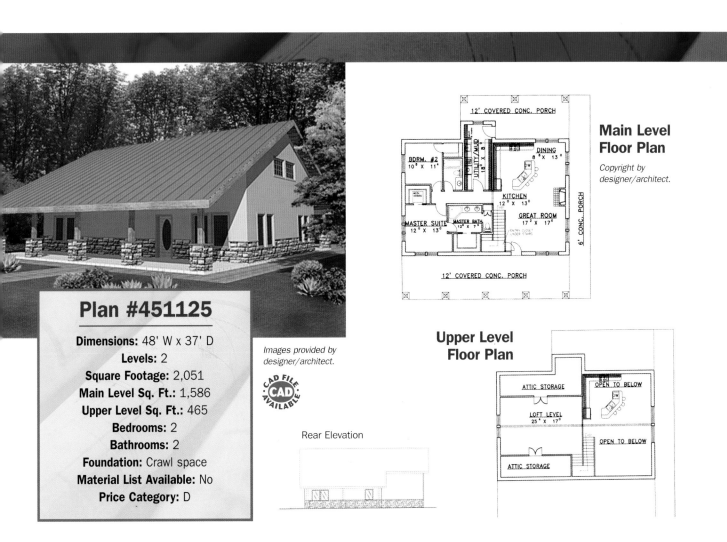

Plan #451125

Dimensions: 48' W x 37' D

Levels: 2

Square Footage: 2,051

Main Level Sq. Ft.: 1,586

Upper Level Sq. Ft.: 465

Bedrooms: 2

Bathrooms: 2

Foundation: Crawl space

Material List Available: No

Price Category: D

Images provided by designer/architect.

CAD FILE AVAILABLE

Main Level Floor Plan

Copyright by designer/architect.

Upper Level Floor Plan

Rear Elevation

Plan #151684

Dimensions: 65'2" W x 63' D

Levels: 1

Square Footage: 1,994

Bedrooms: 3

Bathrooms: 2

Foundation: Crawl space, slab, basement, or walkout

CompleteCost List Available: Yes

Price Category: D

CAD FILE AVAILABLE

Enter the brick arched entry, and prepare for the perfect home.

Features:

- Great Room: This inviting room, with its romantic fireplace, is a comfortable gathering space, while a formal dining room allows for elegant entertaining.

- Kitchen: This kitchen adjoins the large breakfast room, which has an atrium door leading to the rear grilling porch.

- Master Suite: This suite features a private office and has the ultimate master bath. The corner whirlpool tub is framed by columns and has a large walk-in closet, shower, and private toilet.

- Bedrooms: The two secondary bedrooms feature large closets and share a hall bathroom.

Plan #161002

Dimensions: 64'2" W x 44'2" D
Levels: 1
Square Footage: 1,860
Bedrooms: 3
Bathrooms: 2
Foundation: Basement
Materials List Available: Yes
Price Category: D

Images provided by designer/architect.

The brick, stone, and cedar shake facade provides color and texture to the exterior, while the unique nooks and angles inside this delightful one-level home give it character.

Features:

- **Great Room/Dining Room:** This spacious great room is furnished with a wood-burning fireplace, a high ceiling, and French doors. Wide entrances to the breakfast room and dining room expand its space to comfortably hold large gatherings.

- **Kitchen:** The breakfast bar offers additional seating. The covered porch lets you enjoy a view of the landscape and is conveniently located for outdoor meals off this kitchen and breakfast area.

- **Master Bedroom:** The master bedroom is a private retreat. An alcove creates a comfortable sitting area, and an angled entry leads to the bath with whirlpool and a double-bowl vanity.

Great Room/Foyer

Rear Elevation

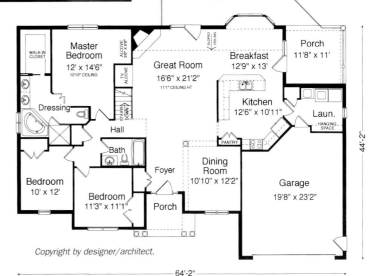

Copyright by designer/architect.

Plan #441006

Dimensions: 48' W x 64' D

Levels: 1

Square Footage: 1,891

Bedrooms: 3

Bathrooms: 2

Foundation: Crawl space

Materials List Available: No

Price Category: D

If you prefer the look of Craftsman homes, you'll love the details this plan includes. Wide-based columns across the front porch, Mission-style windows, and a balanced mixture of exterior materials add up to true good looks.

Features:

- **Great Room:** A built-in media center and a fireplace in this room make it distinctive.

- **Kitchen:** A huge skylight over an island eating counter brightens this kitchen. A private office space opens through double doors nearby.

- **Dining Room:** This room has sliding glass doors opening to the rear patio.

- **Bedrooms:** Two bedrooms with two bathrooms are located on the right side of the plan. One of the bedrooms is a master suite with a vaulted salon and a bath with a spa tub.

- **Garage:** You'll be able to reach this two-car garage via a service hallway that contains a laundry room, a walk-in pantry, and a closet.

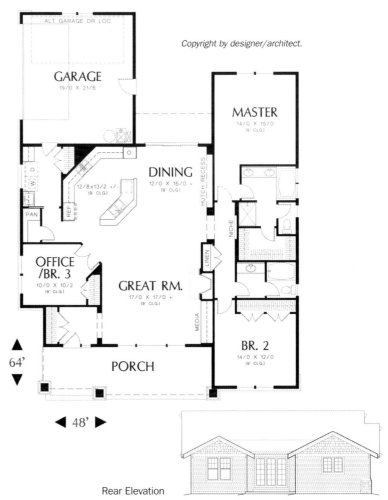

Rear Elevation

Plan #121015

Dimensions: 52' W x 47'4" D
Levels: 2
Square Footage: 1,999
Main Level Sq. Ft.: 1,421
Upper Level Sq. Ft.: 578
Bedrooms: 4
Bathrooms: 2½
Foundation: Basement
Materials List Available: Yes
Price Category: D

Hipped roofs and a trio of gables bring distinction to this plan.

Features:

- Ceiling Height: 8 ft.

- Open Floor Plan: The rooms flow into each other and are flanked by an abundance of windows. The result is a light and airy space that seems much larger than it really is.

- Formal Dining Room: Here is the perfect room for elegant entertaining.

- Breakfast Nook: This bright, bayed nook is the perfect place to start the day. It's also great for intimate get-togethers.

- Great Room: The family will enjoy gathering in this spacious area.

- Bedrooms: This large master bedroom, along with three secondary bedrooms and an extra room, provides plenty of room for a growing family.

- Attached Garage: The garage provides two bays of parking plus plenty of storage space.

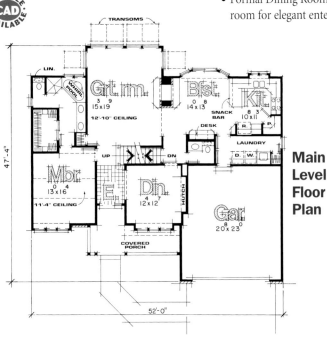

Main Level Floor Plan

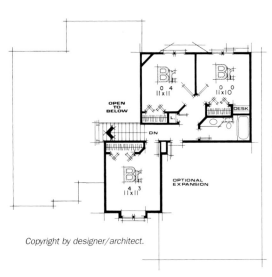

Upper Level Floor Plan

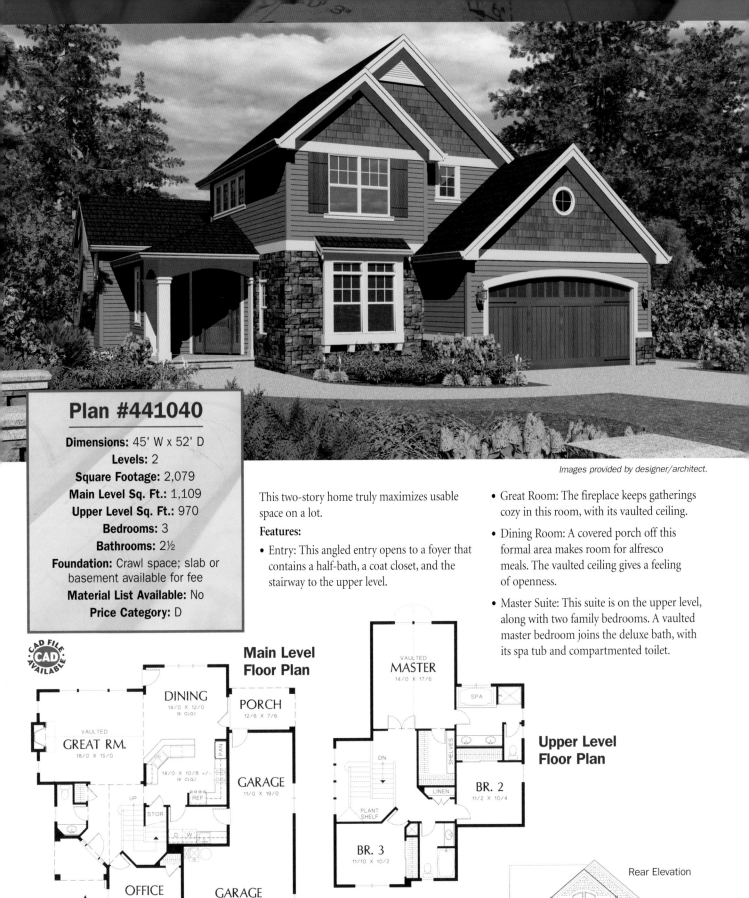

Plan #441040

Dimensions: 45' W x 52' D
Levels: 2
Square Footage: 2,079
Main Level Sq. Ft.: 1,109
Upper Level Sq. Ft.: 970
Bedrooms: 3
Bathrooms: 2½
Foundation: Crawl space; slab or basement available for fee
Material List Available: No
Price Category: D

Images provided by designer/architect.

This two-story home truly maximizes usable space on a lot.

Features:

- Entry: This angled entry opens to a foyer that contains a half-bath, a coat closet, and the stairway to the upper level.

- Great Room: The fireplace keeps gatherings cozy in this room, with its vaulted ceiling.

- Dining Room: A covered porch off this formal area makes room for alfresco meals. The vaulted ceiling gives a feeling of openness.

- Master Suite: This suite is on the upper level, along with two family bedrooms. A vaulted master bedroom joins the deluxe bath, with its spa tub and compartmented toilet.

Main Level Floor Plan

DINING
14/0 X 12/0
(9' CLG.)

PORCH
12/6 X 7/6

VAULTED
GREAT RM.
18/0 X 15/0

GARAGE
11/0 X 19/0

14/0 X 10/8 +/-
(9' CLG.)

UP

STOR

REF

D W

OFFICE
12/6 X 10/0 +
(9' CLG.)

GARAGE
19/0 X 21/0

WINDOW SEAT

52'

45'

Upper Level Floor Plan

VAULTED
MASTER
14/0 X 17/6

SPA

DN.

SHELVES

LINEN

BR. 2
11/2 X 10/4

PLANT SHELF

BR. 3
11/10 X 10/2

Copyright by designer/architect.

Rear Elevation

Plan #151050

Dimensions: 69'2" W x 74'10" D

Levels: 1

Square Footage: 2,096

Bedrooms: 3

Bathrooms: 2½

Foundation: Crawl space, slab, or basement

CompleteCost List Available: Yes

Price Category: D

Images provided by designer/architect.

You'll love this spacious home for both its elegance and its convenient design.

Features:

- Ceiling Height: 8 ft.

- Great Room: A 9-ft. boxed ceiling complements this large room, which sits just beyond the front gallery. A fireplace and door to the rear porch make it a natural gathering spot.

- Kitchen: This well-designed kitchen includes a central work island and shares an angled eating bar with the adjacent breakfast room.

- Breakfast Room: This room's bay window is gorgeous, and the door to the garage is practical.

- Master Suite: You'll love the 9-ft. boxed ceiling in the bedroom and the vaulted ceiling in the bath, which also includes two walk-in closets, a corner whirlpool tub, split vanities, a shower, and a compartmentalized toilet.

- Workshop: A huge workshop with half-bath is ideal for anyone who loves to build or repair.

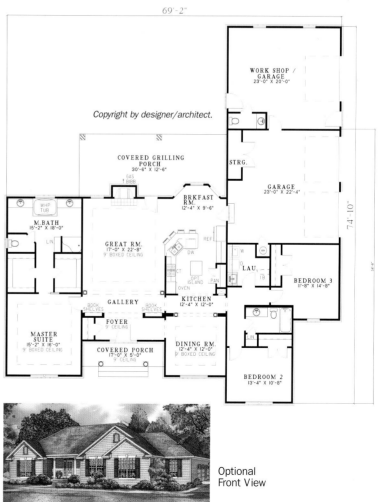

Optional
Front View

Brick Maintenance and Repair

To evaluate a brick wall, each component must be considered. Large cracks, called faults, in the overall structure are usually the most obvious problems and the most costly to repair. Most faults can be traced to uneven settling. When soil under one section settles more than under another, the foundation and the wall above can crack under the strain.

The signs of fundamental structural problems are staircase-pattern cracking in joints along many courses of brick and either large-scale convex or concave cupping of the walls. You can check for this curving, which can be difficult to detect over a large surface, by using mason's blocks and string.

Evaluating Cracks. Don't write off a wall just because it has some cracks. They may be only cosmetic or the result of settling that occurred long ago. Old,

Diagnosing Brick Problems

There are three main types of brick deterioration. The most serious is staircase-pattern cracking (below), which is often a sign of major structural problems. To correct the cracking, you may first need to correct settling problems or other weaknesses in the foundation. Eroded mortar joints (right) can let water into the wall, which can cause many types of deterioration and weaken the wall. Promptly repoint eroded mortar joints. Spalling (lower right) often occurs when freezing water causes a brick to fracture—usually the face of the brick cracks off. To fix this problem you need to replace the fractured brick.

ERODED MORTAR JOINTS

STAIRCASE CRACKING

SPALLING

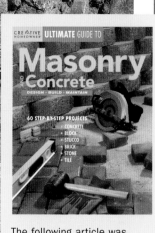

The following article was reprinted from *Ultimate Guide to Masonry and Concrete* (Creative Homeowner 2006).

stable cracks can usually be patched and sealed against the weather. They tend to look somewhat weathered and dirty and may even contain dirt, debris, or spider webs.

New, unstable cracks are usually clean, with lighter colored mortar than that on the surrounding wall, indicating that the building is still in motion. Watch such a cracked wall carefully. If it's moving quickly, the foundation is unstable and needs immediate attention.

Repairing Mortar. Maintenance on a brick wall should include a careful check of the mortar joints. Any mortar that is loose, spongy, and easily scraped away needs to be repointed. This process includes excavating the mortar to a depth that is no less than the width of the joint, cleaning away all loose dust and debris, and then refilling the joints with mortar. Without repointing, the process of deterioration accelerates, particularly in winter due to freezing and thawing. Water gets into the cracks and expands as it freezes, forcing the cracks to enlarge. You can expect to repoint brick homes built before 1900, but not because of age alone. The mortar commonly used at that time was lime-based, which is softer and very porous.

Bricks are generally more durable than the surrounding mortar, although leaks and condensation can sometimes harm them unexpectedly. Water absorption through the brick can lead to fragmentation and flaking of the brick face. To avoid the potential problems associated with this splitting action, called spalling, keep water out of your masonry walls, and repair leak-prone brick and mortar joints as soon as possible.

Cleaning Brick

Sandblasting and power washing are effective cleaning techniques. But the force could seriously erode the mortar joints (right), particularly in older buildings. Chemical cleaning (below) may produce good results with less damage. If you want to power-wash brick (bottom right), test the treatment on a small patch of wall using a low-pressure setting (under 700 pounds per square inch). In older buildings, mortar may break away under a more forceful flow. Under high pressures, even some modern brick may begin to pit. In all cases you'll need to protect nearby shrubs and flowers with drop cloths or plastic sheeting.

HIGH-PRESSURE EROSION

CHEMICAL CLEANING

POWER WASH

Cleaning and Repairing Walls

There are four basic ways to clean masonry: by sandblasting or using chemicals, steam, or water. Sandblasting takes away surface and embedded dirt—and often some of the masonry, too. Chemical- and steam-cleaning contractors can tailor their mix of chemicals to the job at hand, such as removing algae. Be careful when working with acid cleaners. Water cleaning is a job you can do yourself, either with a bucket and brush or with a pressurized sprayer (power washing).

Plant life can be destructive to brick walls. When ivy roots start growing into cracks in mortar joints, you should cut them as close to the wall as possible and treat the ends with ammonium phosphate paste to kill the plant. Mold and mildew may also take hold on masonry that is not exposed to enough sunlight. To test discoloration, drop a small amount of bleach on the area. It will whiten mildew and have no effect on dirt. To clear the mildew, scrub the area with a solution of one part bleach to one part warm water, and then rinse.

Stains from iron can be removed with a solution of oxalic acid. Mix about 1 pound of the crystals in a gallon of water with ½ pound of ammonium bifluoride. Brush the mix over the stained area, and then rinse. Brick may also become stained with asphalt and tar from a roof. Scrape off as much tar as possible and clean remaining stains with a solvent such as benzene.

Spot Repairs

Fix cracks in brick as quickly as you detect them. Even small cracks in the mortar joints will let water seep into the underlying structure, where it can eventually cause damage. Over time, water and the winter freeze-thaw cycles will turn minor cracks into major problems that are more difficult and expensive to fix.

In some cases you can add fresh mortar over the old. But you'll get better results by digging out old mortar and replacing it in a process called tuck pointing. You can chip it out with a hammer and cold chisel or use a grinder. If the

---

Removing Stains

To remove surface stains, start by trying to lift, scrape, slice or shave off the deposit. You'll find that most cleaning agents generally spread the discoloration over a larger area as they dilute stains. Eventually they may release enough material so that you can rinse or wipe away the problem. But sometimes cleaning can create more problems than it solves. To limit the work area, mix cleaners into a paste with diatomaceous earth (pool filter medium), which keeps the cleaner on the wall. The mixture can pull stains from masonry.

STAIN	SOLUTION
Oil	For brick, emulsifying agent; also try repeated passes with paper towel, blotting paper, or other absorbent agent to remove traces of oil left in the brick surface
Iron	1 lb. oxalic acid crystals, 1 gal. water, ½ lb. ammonium bifluoride
Paint	2 lbs. TSP to 1 gal. water; also try scraping or peeling deposits
Smoke	Scouring powder with bleach; paste-like mixture of trichlorethylene and talc; or alkali detergents and emulsifying agents

Tuck-Pointing Brick

TOOLS

- Power grinder (or hand scraper)
- Spray bottle
- Hawk
- Narrow jointing trowel
- Striking tool (for tooling)

MATERIALS
- Mortar mix

1 **Adjust the depth fence** on a power grinder so that the blade cuts at least ½ in. into the old mortar.

2 **Guide the grinder blade** along the mortar joints. Be sure to wear safety glasses.

3 **Spray the brick and joint** to keep the old mortar from suctioning excess water from the new mix.

4 **Set the new mortar mix** on a hawk next to the joint, and force it in with a thin trowel.

5 **Use a striking tool** to compact the mortar in a concave shape that matches the surrounding joints.

mortar is badly eroded you can simply scrape it out with a nail, hammer claw, or screwdriver.

After you clear old mortar, sweep the joints clean of debris. Then spray a little water in the cavity before forcing in fresh mortar. To minimize cleanup time, set the mortar on a board or mason's hawk, hold it directly against the brick, and push the mortar into place. When the mix starts to set up, tool the joint to match the surrounding seams.

Where the brick itself is cracked or damaged, you will need to replace it. If you shop around, you can usually find replacements for damaged bricks or facing stones that closely match the existing material. Mortar, however, is more difficult to match. You'll probably need to mix a few test batches before you arrive at one that will blend in with the rest of the house. Add powdered colorant, if necessary, to duplicate the existing mortar. Wait for the mortar mix to dry thoroughly, and view the samples

outside before making any decisions.

The first step in replacing a broken brick is to chisel it—and the surrounding mortar—out of the wall. After cleaning out the hole and spraying it with water, spread some mortar on the bottom. Then spread mortar on the top and sides of the brick, and slide it into place. Once the wall is sound, you can seal it with a clear silicon-based sealer, which helps the wall shed water and dirt and makes the surface easier to clean.

Replacing Brick

TOOLS

- Work gloves
- 2-1b. hammer
- Cold chisel
- Wire brush
- Trowel
- Striking tool

MATERIALS

- Mortar
- Replacement brick

1 **Any broken** or otherwise damaged bricks will need to be replaced with new ones.

3 **Break away** remaining chunks of mortar, and then wire-brush the surfaces to remove debris.

4 **Mix enough mortar** to thoroughly coat the mating surfaces of the replacement brick.

Surface Deposits

Efflorescence (left) is a powdery residue caused by water moving through the wall and bringing salts to the surface. But some paints are formulated to shed dirt as the surface breaks down into a powder (right) and washes away slightly with each rainfall. Do not use these chalking paints on siding above a brick wall.

2 **Use a cold chisel** and hammer to chip away the damaged brick, working from the joints in.

5 **Force more mortar** into the joints as needed. Then tool the seams to blend in the repair.

Offset bricks create decorative patterns around fireplaces.

Plan #101022

Dimensions: 66'2" W x 62' D

Levels: 1

Square Footage: 1,992

Bedrooms: 3

Bathrooms: 3

Foundation: Crawl space, slab, or basement

Materials List Available: Yes

Price Category: D

Images provided by designer/architect.

The exterior of this lovely home is traditional, but the unusually shaped rooms and amenities are contemporary.

Features:

- **Foyer:** This two-story foyer is open to the family room, but columns divide it from the dining room.

- **Family Room:** A gas fireplace and TV niche, flanked by doors to the covered porch, sit at the rear of this seven-sided, spacious room.

- **Breakfast Room:** Set off from the family room by columns, this area shares a snack bar with the kitchen and has windows looking over the porch.

- **Bedroom 3:** Use this room as a living room if you wish, and transform the guestroom to a media room or a family bedroom.

- **Master Suite:** The bedroom features a tray ceiling, has his and her dressing areas, and opens to the porch. The bath has a large corner tub, separate shower, linen closet, and two vanities.

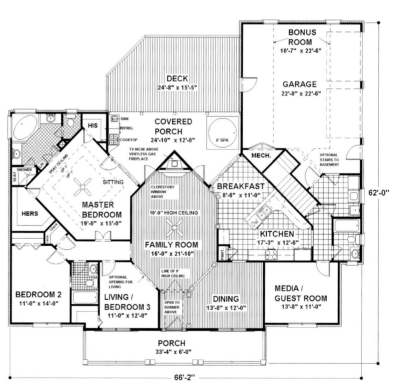

Copyright by designer/architect.

Kitchen

Living Room

Dining Room

Family Room

Master Bedroom

Master Bath

Plan #161095

Dimensions: 59' W x 49'8" D
Levels: 1
Square Footage: 3,620
Main Level Sq. Ft.: 2,068
Basement Level Sq. Ft.: 1,552
Bedrooms: 3
Bathrooms: 3
Foundation: Walkout basement
Material List Available: No
Price Category: H

Images provided by designer/architect.

This home, as shown in the photograph, may differ from the actual blueprints. For more detailed information, please check the floor plans carefully.

This elegant ranch design has everything your family could want in a home.

Features:

- Dining Room: This column-accented formal area has a sloped ceiling and is open to the great room.

- Great Room: Featuring a cozy fireplace, this large gathering area offers a view of the backyard.

- Kitchen: This fully equipped island kitchen has everything the chef in the family could want.

- Master Suite: Located on the main level for privacy, this suite has a sloped ceiling in the sleeping area. The master bath boasts a whirlpool tub, a walk-in closet, and dual vanities.

Main Level Floor Plan

Rear View

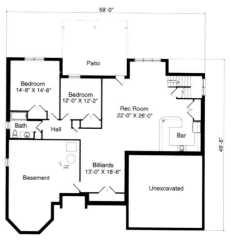

Lower Level Floor Plan

Copyright by designer/architect.

Plan #351008

Dimensions: 64'6"W x 61'4" D

Levels: 1

Square Footage: 2,002

Bedrooms: 3

Bathrooms: 2

Foundation: Crawl space or basement

Materials List Available: Yes

Price Category: E

Images provided by designer/architect.

This home has the charming appeal of a quaint cottage that you might find in an old village in the English countryside. It's a unique design that maximizes every inch of its usable space.

Features:

- **Great Room:** This room has a vaulted ceiling and built-in units on each side of the fireplace.

- **Kitchen:** This kitchen boasts a raised bar open to the breakfast area; the room is also open to the dining room.

- **Master Bedroom:** This bedroom retreat features a raised ceiling and a walk-in closet.

- **Master Bath:** This bathroom has a double vanity, large walk-in closet, and soaking tub.

- **Bedrooms:** Two bedrooms share a common bathroom and have large closets.

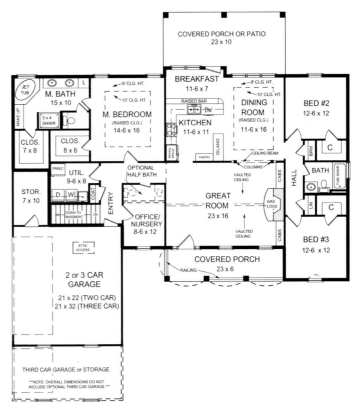

Copyright by designer/architect.

Plan #221018

Dimensions: 67' W x 53' D

Levels: 1

Square Footage: 2,007

Bedrooms: 3

Bathrooms: 2

Foundation: Basement

Materials List Available: No

Price Category: D

CAD FILE AVAILABLE

Images provided by designer/architect.

Rear Elevation

You'll love this ranch design, with its traditional stucco facade and interesting roofline.

Features:

- Ceiling Height: 9 ft.

- Great Room: A cathedral ceiling points up the large dimensions of this room, and the handsome fireplace with tall flanking windows lets you decorate for a formal or a casual feeling.

- Dining Room: A tray ceiling imparts elegance to this room, and a butler's pantry just across from the kitchen area lets you serve in style.

- Kitchen: You'll love the extensive counter space in this well-designed kitchen. The adjoining nook is large enough for a full-size dining set and features a door to the outside deck, where you can set up a third dining area.

- Master Suite: Located away from the other bedrooms for privacy, this suite includes a huge walk-in closet, windows overlooking the backyard, and a large bath with a whirlpool tub, standing shower, and dual-sink vanity.

Plan #221033

Dimensions: 63' W x 61'4" D

Levels: 1

Square Footage: 1,948

Bedrooms: 3

Bathrooms: 2

Foundation: Basement

Materials List Available: No

Price Category: D

The spacious front porch on this ranch home is perfect for a relaxing evening at home.

Features:

- Kitchen: You'll love this spacious cooking center, with its breakfast bar that overlooks the dining room.

- Great Room: Columns lead you into this room from the dining-kitchen area, and you'll be impressed as you enter by the fireplace that is flanked by built-ins.

- Master Suite: This restful area features his and her walk-in closets, a corner Jacuzzi in the bath, and a stepped ceiling in the bedroom.

- Bedrooms: Two additional bedrooms face the front of the home, along with a full bathroom.

- Garage: This three-stall garage has additional space for storage; the laundry leads you from the garage into the home so that muddy shoes stay out of sight.

Images provided by designer/architect.

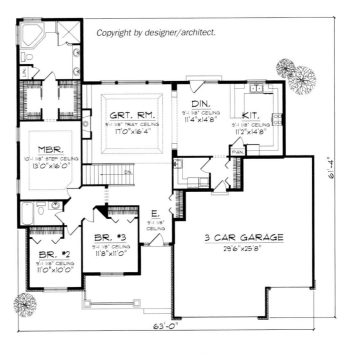

Copyright by designer/architect.

Rear Elevation

Plan #161026

Dimensions: 67'6" W x 63'6" D
Levels: 1
Square Footage: 2,041
Bedrooms: 3
Bathrooms: 2
Foundation: Basement
Materials List Available: No
Price Category: D

You'll love the special features of this home, which has been designed for efficiency and comfort.

Images provided by designer/architect.

Features:

- Foyer: This raised foyer offers a view through the great room and beyond it to the covered deck.

- Great Room: Elegant windows allow versatility — decorate casually or more formally.

- Kitchen: You'll find ample counter space and cabinets in this spacious room, which adjoins the dining room and opens onto the rear yard.

- Library: Curl up on the window seat that wraps around the tower in this quiet spot.

- Laundry Room: A tub makes this large room practical for crafts as well as laundry.

- Master Suite: A vaulted ceiling gives grace to the sitting area, and the garden bath with a walk-in closet and whirlpool tub adds luxury.

Rear Elevation

Main Level Floor Plan

Basement Level Floor Plan

Copyright by designer/architect.

Plan #101030

Dimensions: 63' W x 63' D
Levels: 1
Square Footage: 2,071
Bedrooms: 3
Bathrooms: 2½
Foundation: Crawl space or basement
Materials List Available: No
Price Category: D

This lovely three-bedroom brick home with an optional bonus room above the three-car garage is just what you've been looking for.

Features:

• Family Room: This large room, with its high ceiling and cozy fireplace, is great for entertaining.

• Kitchen: This kitchen boasts a built-in pantry and a peninsula opening into the breakfast nook.

• Master Suite: This suite, with its 14-ft.-high ceiling and private sitting area, is a perfect place to relax after a long day. The bath has a double vanity, large walk-in closet, and soaking tub.

• Bedrooms: Two additional bedrooms feature walk-in closets and share a private bathroom.

Images provided by designer/architect.

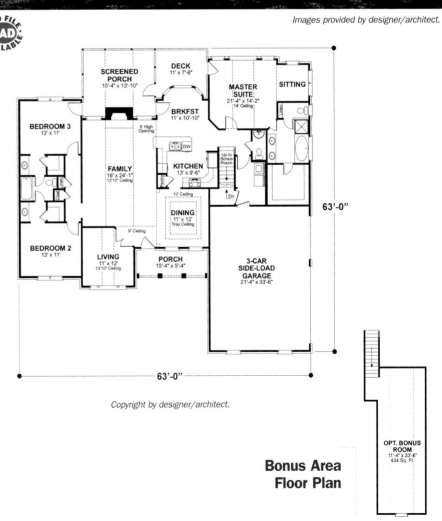

Copyright by designer/architect.

Bonus Area Floor Plan

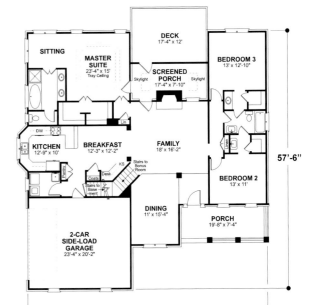

Copyright by designer/architect.

DECK

BEDROOM 3
14X11

BRKFST
11X9
11' CEILING

MASTER
BEDROOM
16X15

MORNING
PORCH

14' CEILING

KITCHEN
13X12
11' CEILING

FAMILY ROOM
17X19

LINEN

PLANT
SHELF

UP

PANTRY

SHLVS

BEDROOM 2
14X11

LIVING
11X12

FOYER

DINING
13X11
11' CEILING

DN

LNDRY
TUB

WSHR
DRYER

STORAGE

◀ 53 ▶

BONUS ROOM ABOVE

GARAGE
23X20

◀ 68 ▶

Plan #101008

Dimensions: 68' W x 53' D

Levels: 1

Square Footage: 2,088

Bedrooms: 3

Bathrooms: 2½

Foundation: Basement

Materials List Available: Yes

Price Category: D

Images provided by designer/architect.

CAD FILE AVAILABLE CAD

SMARTtip

Accentuating Your Bathroom with Details

No matter how big or small the room, details will pull the style together. Some of the best details that you can include are the smallest—drawer pulls from an antique store or shells in a glass jar or just left on the countertop. Add period flavor with crown molding, or dress up contemporary fixtures with polished stone fittings.

Copyright by designer/architect.

DECK
17'-4" x 12'

SITTING

MASTER
SUITE
23'-4" x 15'
Tray Ceiling

SCREENED
PORCH
17'-4" x 7'-10"

Skylight

Skylight

BEDROOM 3
13' x 12'-10"

KITCHEN
12'-9" x 10'

DW

BREAKFAST
12'-3" x 12'-2"

FAMILY
18' x 16'-2"

Lin

BEDROOM 2
13' x 11'

57'-6"

Pantry

KS

Desk

Stairs to
Bonus
Room

Stairs to
Base-
ment

Coats

2-CAR
SIDE-LOAD
GARAGE
23'-4" x 20'-2"

DINING
11' x 15'-4"

PORCH
19'-8" x 7'-4"

57'-8"

Plan #101028

Dimensions: 57'8" W x 57'6" D

Levels: 1

Square Footage: 1,963

Bedrooms: 3

Bathrooms: 2

Foundation: Basement

Materials List Available: No

Price Category: D

Images provided by designer/architect.

CAD FILE AVAILABLE CAD

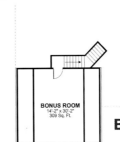

BONUS ROOM
14'-2" x 30'-2"
309 Sq. Ft.

Bonus Area Floor Plan

Plan #271017

Dimensions: 50' W x 37'2" D
Levels: 2
Square Footage: 1,835
Main Level Sq. Ft.: 928
Upper Level Sq. Ft.: 907
Bedrooms: 3
Bathrooms: 2½
Foundation: Basement
Materials List Available: Yes
Price Category: D

Images provided by designer/architect.

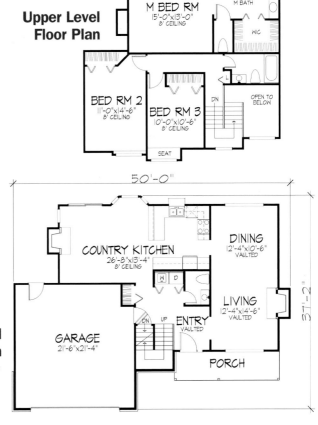

Upper Level Floor Plan

Main Level Floor Plan

Copyright by designer/architect.

Plan #311004

Dimensions: 68'2" W x 57'4" D
Levels: 1
Square Footage: 2,046
Bedrooms: 3
Bathrooms: 2½
Foundation: Crawl space, slab, or basement
Materials List Available: Yes
Price Category: D

Images provided by designer/architect.

Copyright by designer/architect.

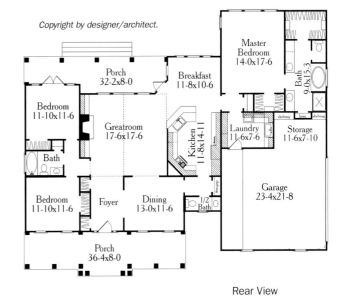

Rear View

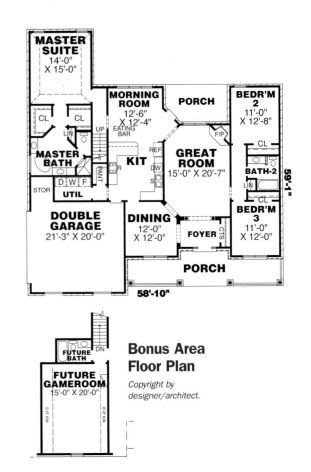

Plan #241007

Dimensions: 58'10" W x 59'1" D

Levels: 1

Square Footage: 2,036

Bedrooms: 3

Bathrooms: 2

Foundation: Crawl space, slab

Materials List Available: No

Price Category: D

Images provided by designer/architect.

Bonus Area Floor Plan

Copyright by designer/architect.

Plan #161111

Dimensions: 45' W x 42'2" D

Levels: 2

Square Footage: 1,921

Main Level Sq. Ft.: 968

Upper Level Sq. Ft.: 953

Bedrooms: 4

Bathrooms: 2½

Foundation: Basement

Materials List Available: Yes

Price Category: D

Images provided by designer/architect.

Upper Level Floor Plan

Copyright by designer/architect.

Main Level Floor Plan

Rear Elevation

Plan #141011

Dimensions: 54' W x 60'6" D

Levels: 1

Square Footage: 1,869

Bedrooms: 3

Bathrooms: 2

Foundation: Crawl space, slab, or basement

Materials List Available: Yes

Price Category: D

The blending of brick and stone on this plan gives the home an old-world appeal.

Features:

- Ceiling Height: 8 ft. unless otherwise noted.

- Tall Ceilings: The main living areas feature dramatic 12-ft. ceilings.

- Open Plan: This home's open floor plan maximizes the use of space and makes it flexible. This main living area has plenty of room for large gatherings.

- Kitchen: The kitchen is integrated into the main living area. It features a breakfast room that is ideal for informal family meals.

- Master Suite: You'll enjoy unwinding at the end of the day in this luxurious space. It's located away from the rest of the house for maximum privacy.

- Secondary Bedrooms: You have the option of adding extra style to the secondary bedrooms by including volume ceilings.

Copyright by designer/architect.

Plan #181094

Dimensions: 50' W x 39' D
Levels: 2
Square Footage: 2,099
Main Level Sq. Ft.: 1,060
Upper Level Sq. Ft.: 1,039
Bedrooms: 4
Bathrooms: 2½
Foundation: Basement
Materials List Available: Yes
Price Category: D

Images provided by designer/architect.

The curved covered porch makes this is a great place to come home to.

Features:

• Entry: This air-lock entry area with closet will help keep energy costs down.

• Family Room: This gathering area features a fireplace and is open to the kitchen and the dining area.

• Kitchen: U-shaped and boasting an island and a walk-in pantry, this kitchen is open to the dining area.

• Master Suite: This large retreat features a fireplace and a walk-in closet. The master bath has dual vanities, a separate shower, and a large tub.

• Bedrooms: Located upstairs with the master suite are three additional bedrooms. They share a common bathroom, and each has a large closet.

Rear View

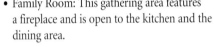

Main Level Floor Plan

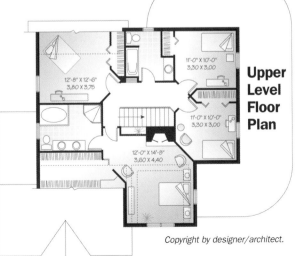

Upper Level Floor Plan

Copyright by designer/architect.

Plan #351069

Dimensions: 78' W x 49'6" D
Levels: 1
Square Footage: 2,008
Bedrooms: 3
Bathrooms: 2½
Foundation: Crawl space or slab
Materials List Available: No
Price Category: F

Images provided by designer/architect.

This is a great house with a functional split-floor-plan layout.

Features:

- **Entertaining Areas:** A large dining area for those family get-togethers and an expansive great room with a gas log fireplace and vaulted ceiling will make entertaining easy.

- **Master Suite:** This expansive suite has a large sitting area, his and her walk-in closets, a jetted tub, and a walk-in shower.

- **Storage Areas:** The home features plenty of storage space; a large utility room will help stow away your odds and ends.

- **Expansion:** Flex space can be used as a home office/study, playroom, and/or entertainment center. There is even a bonus room above the garage.

Main Level Floor Plan

Upper Level Floor Plan

Copyright by designer/architect.

Plan #161008

Dimensions: 64'2" W x 46'6" D
Levels: 1
Square Footage: 1,860
Bedrooms: 3
Bathrooms: 2
Foundation: Slab
Materials List Available: No
Price Category: D

Images provided by designer/architect.

If you enjoy casual living and formal entertaining, this delightful floor plan will attract your eye.

Features:

- **Great Room:** A sloped ceiling and corner fireplace combine to provide this great room with an open and cozy atmosphere, perfect for relaxing evenings.

- **Kitchen:** This kitchen offers ample counter and cabinet space. A convenient snack bar provides a view to the breakfast area and great room

- **Master Suite:** Enjoy the elegance and style of this master suite, with its deluxe bath, large walk-in closet, and secluded alcove.

- **Laundry Room:** You will appreciate the ample counter space in this large laundry room with utility closet.

- **Porch:** From the breakfast area, enjoy a relaxed meal on this rear covered porch in warm weather.

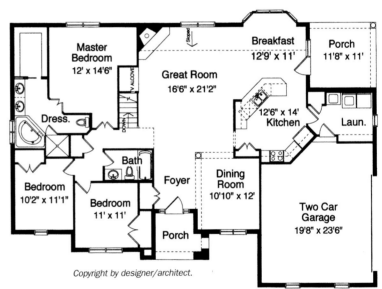

Copyright by designer/architect.

SMARTtip

Espaliered Fruit Trees

Try a technique used by the royal gardeners at Versailles—espalier. They trained the fruit trees to grow flat against the walls, creating patterns. It's not difficult, especially if you go to a reputable nursery and purchase an apple or pear tree that has already been espaliered. Plant it against a flat surface that's in a sunny spot.

Copyright by designer/architect.

Images provided by designer/architect.

Plan #221020

Dimensions: 69'8" W x 43' D

Levels: 1

Square Footage: 1,859

Bedrooms: 3

Bathrooms: 2½

Foundation: Basement

Materials List Available: No

Price Category: D

CAD FILE AVAILABLE

Rear Elevation

Copyright by designer/architect.

Rear View

Plan #311009

Dimensions: 68' W x 56'6" D

Levels: 1

Square Footage: 1,894

Bedrooms: 3

Bathrooms: 2½

Foundation: Crawl space, slab, or basement

Materials List Available: Yes

Price Category: D

Images provided by designer/architect.

Basement Stair Option

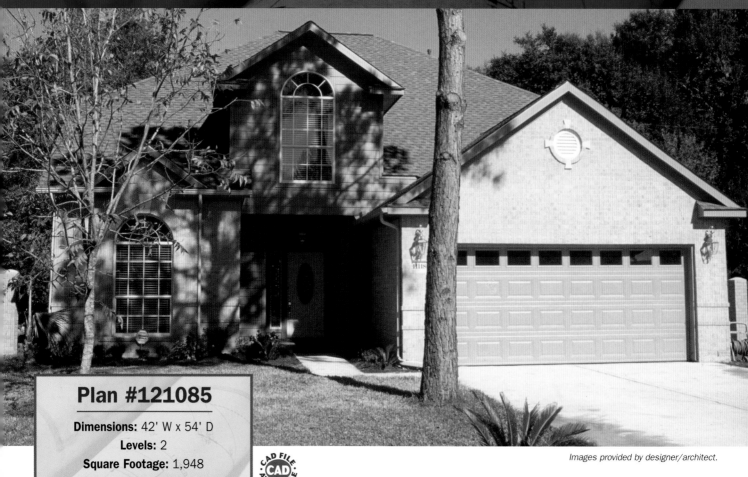

Plan #121085

Dimensions: 42' W x 54' D
Levels: 2
Square Footage: 1,948
Main Level Sq. Ft.: 1,517
Upper Level Sq. Ft.: 431
Bedrooms: 4
Bathrooms: 3
Foundation: Basement
Materials List Available: Yes
Price Category: D

Images provided by designer/architect.

You'll love the spacious feeling in this home, with its generous rooms and excellent design.

Features:

- Great Room: This room is lofty and open, thanks in part to the transom-topped windows that flank the fireplace. However, you can furnish to create a cozy nook for reading or a private spot to watch TV or enjoy some quiet music.

- Kitchen: Wrapping counters add an unusual touch to this kitchen, and a pantry gives extra storage area. A snack bar links the kitchen with a separate breakfast area.

- Master Suite: A tiered ceiling adds elegance to this area, and a walk-in closet adds practicality. The private bath features a sunlit whirlpool tub, separate shower, and double vanity.

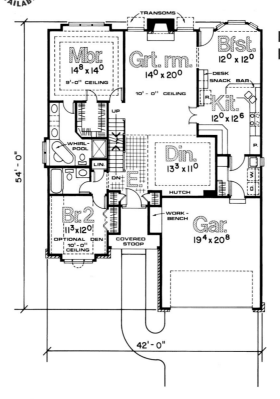

Main Level Floor Plan

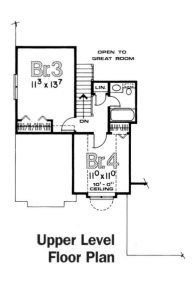

Upper Level Floor Plan

Copyright by designer/architect.

- Upper-Level Bedrooms: The upper-level placement is just right for these bedrooms, which share an amenity-filled full bathroom.

Plan #311001

Dimensions: 65'11" W x 67'9" D

Levels: 1

Square Footage: 2,085

Bedrooms: 3

Bathrooms: 2½

Foundation: Crawl space, slab, or basement

Materials List Available: No

Price Category: D

Images provided by designer/architect.

Copyright by designer/architect.

Rear View

Optional Bonus Area

Plan #191032

Dimensions: 80'4" W x 52' D

Levels: 1

Square Footage: 2,091

Bedrooms: 3

Bathrooms: 2

Foundation: Slab

Materials List Available: No

Price Category: D

Images provided by designer/architect.

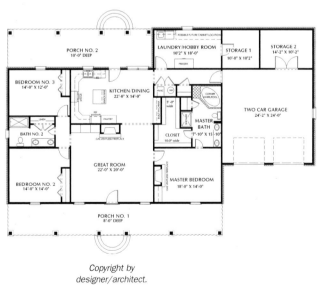

Copyright by designer/architect.

Plan #151004

Dimensions: 64'8" W x 62'1" D

Levels: 1

Square Footage: 2,107

Bedrooms: 4

Bathrooms: 2½

Foundation: Crawl space, slab, or basement

CompleteCost List Available: Yes

Price Category: D

Images provided by designer/architect.

Copyright by designer/architect.

Plan #211006

Dimensions: 61' W x 77' D

Levels: 1

Square Footage: 2,177

Bedrooms: 3

Bathrooms: 2

Foundation: Crawl space or slab

Materials List Available: Yes

Price Category: D

Images provided by designer/architect.

SMARTtip

DECK Furniture Style

Mix-and-match tabletops, frames, and legs are stylish. Combine materials such as glass, metal, wood, and mosaic tiles.

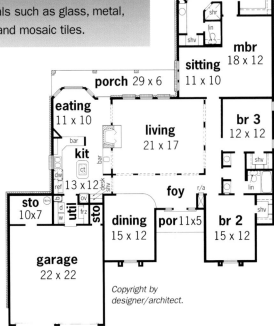

Copyright by designer/architect.

Plan #241002

Dimensions: 65' W x 59'8" D

Levels: 1

Square Footage: 2,154

Bedrooms: 4

Bathrooms: 2½

Foundation: Slab

Materials List Available: No

Price Category: D

Images provided by designer/architect.

Copyright by designer/architect.

Optional Basement Level Floor Plan

Plan #271079

Dimensions: 104' W x 55' D

Levels: 1

Square Footage: 2,228

Bedrooms: 1-3

Bathrooms: 1½

Foundation: Daylight basement

Materials List Available: No

Price Category: E

Images provided by designer/architect.

CAD FILE AVAILABLE

Copyright by designer/architect.

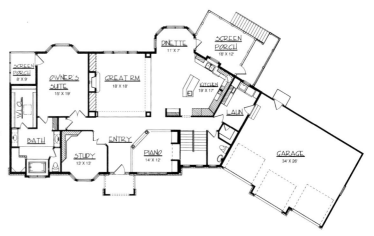

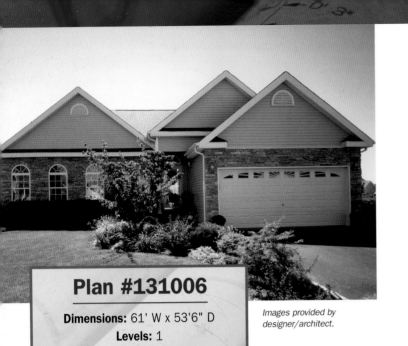

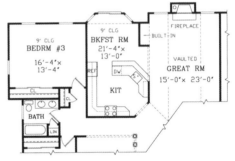

Copyright by designer/architect.

Plan #131006

Dimensions: 61' W x 53'6" D

Levels: 1

Square Footage: 2,193

Bedrooms: 3

Bathrooms: 2

Foundation: Crawl space, slab, or basement

Materials List Available: Yes

Price Category: E

Images provided by designer/architect.

Alternate Floor Plan

Plan #101087

Dimensions: 64'4" W x 42' D

Levels: 1

Square Footage: 2,197

Bedrooms: 3

Bathrooms: 2½

Foundation: Basement

Material List Available: Yes

Price Category: D

Images provided by designer/architect.

Copyright by designer/architect.

Plan #161016

Dimensions: 59'4" W x 58'8" D

Levels: 2

Square Footage: 2,101

Main Level Sq. Ft.: 1,626

Upper Level Sq. Ft.: 475

Bedrooms: 3

Bathrooms: 2½

Foundation: Basement, optional crawl space available for extra fee

Materials List Available: Yes

Price Category: D

Note: Home in photo reflects a modified garage entrance.

Images provided by designer/architect.

Features:

- **Great Room:** Made for relaxing and entertaining, the great room is sunken to set it off from the rest of the house. A balcony from the second floor looks down into this spacious area, making it easy to keep track of the kids while they are playing.

- **Kitchen:** Convenience marks this well laid-out kitchen where you'll love to cook for guests and for family.

- **Master Bedroom:** A vaulted ceiling complements the unusual octagonal shape

of the master bedroom. Located on the first floor, this room allows some privacy from the second floor bedrooms. It is also ideal for anyone who no longer wishes to climb stairs to reach a bedroom.

Rear Elevation

You'll love the exciting roofline that sets this elegant home apart from its neighbors as well as the embellished, solid look that declares how well-designed it is—from the inside to the exterior.

CAD FILE AVAILABLE

Main Level Floor Plan

Deck

Breakfast 9-2 x 16

Sunken Great Room 16-10 x 21

Kitchen 8 x 13-4

Bath

Walk-in closet

Dining Room 16 x 11-8

Foyer

Master Bedroom 14 x 17-4

Slope ceiling   Slope ceiling

Bath

Hall

Laundry

58'-8"

Two-car Garage 21 x 20-8

Copyright by designer/architect.

59'-4"

Upper Level Floor Plan

Bedroom 15 x 10-8

Great Room Below

Bath

Bedroom 14 x 10-6

Foyer Below

Plan #101010

Dimensions: 70' W x 47' D

Levels: 1

Square Footage: 2,187

Bedrooms: 4

Bathrooms: 2½

Foundation: Crawl space, slab, or basement

Materials List Available: Yes

Price Category: D

Images provided by designer/architect.

This stately ranch features a brick-and-stucco exterior, layered trim, and copper roofing returns.

Features:

- Ceiling Height: 11 ft. unless otherwise noted.

- Special Ceilings: Vaulted and raised ceilings adorn the living room, family room, dining room, foyer, kitchen, breakfast room, and master suite.

- Kitchen: This roomy kitchen is brightened by an abundance of windows.

- Breakfast Room: Located off the kitchen, this breakfast room is the perfect spot for informal family meals.

- Master Suite: This truly exceptional master suite features a bath, and a spacious walk in closet.

- Morning Porch: Step out of the master bedroom, and greet the day on this lovely porch.

- Additional Bedrooms: The three additional bedrooms each measure approximately 11 ft. x 12 ft. Two of them have walk-in closets.

Copyright by designer/architect.

SMARTtip
Using Slipcovers in Your Dining Area

Change the look of your dining room by slipcovering chairs. Short-skirted slipcovers give a more informal appearance; fabrics in graphic patterns, such as checks or floral prints, complement this style of slipcover best. Long-skirted covers are elegant additions to a formal dining room, particularly in solid color or tone-on-tone fabrics. Ties, buttons, or trim can add personality.

Plan #151534

Dimensions: 37'8" W x 71'6" D
Levels: 2
Square Footage: 2,237
Main Level Sq. Ft.: 1,708
Upper Level Sq. Ft.: 529
Bedrooms: 3
Bathrooms: 2½
Foundation: Crawl space or slab
CompleteCost List Available: Yes
Price Category: E

Images provided by designer/architect.

This home has dormers with copper roofing and a covered porch for lovely street appeal.

Features:

- **Foyer:** As you enter through this foyer you'll find a study/home office or extra bedroom, if needed, across from the formal dining room, with its column-lined entry.

- **Great Room:** This large room, with its built-in wet bar and large fireplace, is centrally located for a family-oriented atmosphere.

- **Breakfast Room:** This large room provides access to the covered grilling porch, which is perfect for entertaining.

- **Master Suite:** After a long day, retire to this suite, which provides French-door entry to the elegant master bath, complete with a whirlpool tub, separate shower, and large walk-in closet.

Main Level Floor Plan

Copyright by designer/architect.

- **Upper Level:** The upstairs has a built-in computer desk for study time, two bedrooms, a full bathroom, and a large optional game/bonus room.

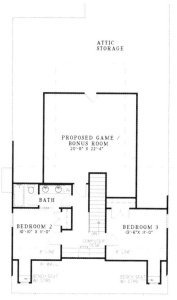

Upper Level Floor Plan

Front View

Plan #101017

Dimensions: 57' W x 51' D
Levels: 2
Square Footage: 2,253
Main Level Sq. Ft.: 1,719
Upper Level Sq. Ft.: 534
Opt. Upper Level Bonus Sq. Ft.: 247
Bedrooms: 4
Bathrooms: 3
Foundation: Basement
Materials List Available: No
Price Category: E

Images provided by designer/architect.

This alluring two-story "master-down" design blends a spectacular floor plan with a lovely facade to create a home that's simply irresistible.

Features:

• Entry: You're welcomed by an inviting front porch and greeted by a beautiful leaded glass door leading to this two-story entry.

• Family Room: A corner fireplace and a window wall with arched transoms accent this dramatic room.

• Master Suite: This sumptuous suite includes a double tray ceiling, sitting area, and his and her walk-in closets. The master bathroom features dual vanities, a corner tub, and a shower.

• Bedrooms: Located upstairs, these two additional bedrooms share a Jack-and-Jill bathroom.

Main Level Floor Plan

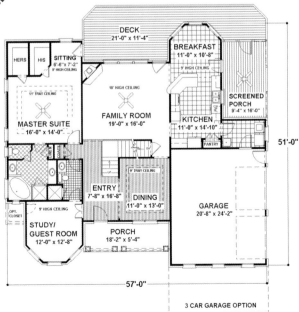

Upper Level Floor Plan

Copyright by designer/architect.

Plan #101011

Dimensions: 71'2" W x 58'1" D
Levels: 1
Square Footage: 2,184
Bedrooms: 3
Bathrooms: 3
Foundation: Crawl space, slab, basement, walkout
Materials List Available: Yes
Price Category: D

A classic design and spacious interior add up to a flexible design suitable to any modern lifestyle.

Features:

- Ceiling Height: 9 ft. unless otherwise noted.

- Formal Dining Room: A decorative square column and a tray ceiling adorn this elegant dining room.

Kitchen

- Screened Porch: Enjoy summer breezes in style by stepping out of the French doors into this vaulted screened porch.

- Kitchen: Does everyone want to hang out in the kitchen while you are cooking? No problem. True to the home's country style, this huge 14-ft.-3-in. x 22-ft.-6-in. has plenty of room for helpers.

- The kitchen is open to the vaulted family room.

- Patio or Deck: This pleasant outdoor area is accessible from both the screened porch and the master bedroom.

- Master Suite: This luxurious suite includes a double tray ceiling, a sitting area, two walk-in closets, and an exquisite bath.

Images provided by designer/architect.

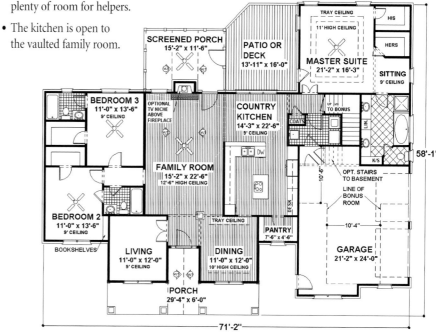

Copyright by designer/architect.

Plan #271076

Dimensions: 69' W x 57' D

Levels: 1

Square Footage: 2,188

Bedrooms: 2-4

Bathrooms: 1½-2½

Foundation: Daylight basement

Materials List Available: No

Price Category: D

Images provided by designer/architect.

CAD FILE AVAILABLE

Optional Basement Level Floor Plan

Copyright by designer/architect.

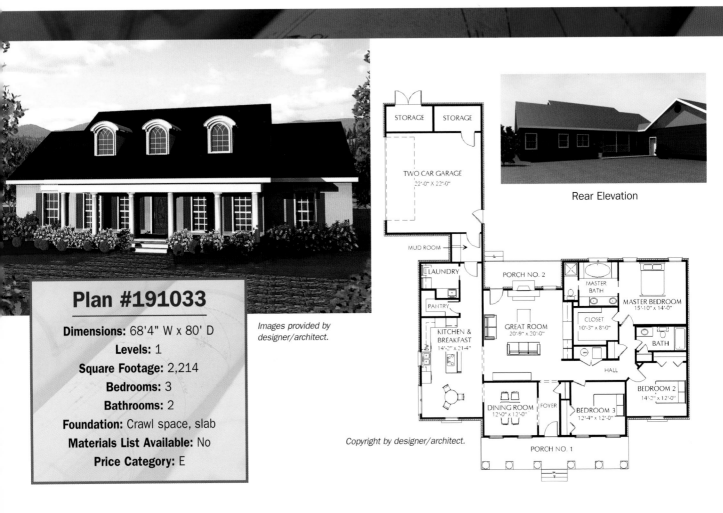

Plan #191033

Dimensions: 68'4" W x 80' D

Levels: 1

Square Footage: 2,214

Bedrooms: 3

Bathrooms: 2

Foundation: Crawl space, slab

Materials List Available: No

Price Category: E

Images provided by designer/architect.

Rear Elevation

Copyright by designer/architect.

Plan #351007

Dimensions: 73'8"W x 53'2" D

Levels: 1

Square Footage: 2,251

Bedrooms: 3

Bathrooms: 2½

Foundation: Crawl space, slab, or basement

Materials List Available: Yes

Price Category: E

Images provided by designer/architect.

This three-bedroom brick home with arched window offers traditional styling that features an open floor plan.

Features:

- **Great Room:** This room has a 12-ft.-high ceiling and a corner fireplace.

- **Kitchen:** This kitchen boasts a built-in pantry and a raised bar open to the breakfast area.

- **Dining Room:** This area features a vaulted ceiling and a view of the front yard.

- **Master Bedroom:** This private room has an office and access to the rear porch.

- **Master Bath:** This bathroom has a double vanity, large walk-in closet, and soaking tub.

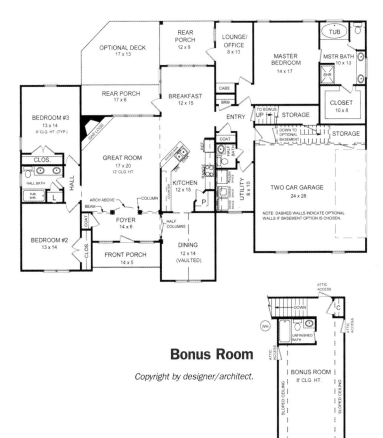

Bonus Room

Copyright by designer/architect.

Plan #151484

Dimensions: 53'6" W x 76'10" D
Levels: 1.5
Square Footage: 2,211
Bedrooms: 3
Bathrooms: 2
Foundation: Crawl space or slab
CompleteCost List Available: Yes
Price Category: E

This traditional design, perfect for narrow lot, incorporates 10-ft.-tall boxed ceilings and 8-in. round columns.

 CAD FILE AVAILABLE

Images provided by designer/architect.

Features:

- Dining Room: This room is centrally located and looks through to the great room, which allows access to the rear grilling porch.

- Master Suite: The split-bedroom plan gives the ultimate in privacy to this suite, complete with a large walk-in closet and a bath with amenities galore.

- Kitchen: At the other end of the house from the master suite is this kitchen and breakfast room combo with island seating, a built-in bench seat, and a walk-in pantry.

- Den: Down the hall from the kitchen is this den or extra bedroom. Private access to the full bathroom makes it great for guests.

Front View

Bonus Area Floor Plan
Copyright by designer/architect.

Copyright by designer/architect.

Plan #221017

Dimensions: 65' W x 56' D

Levels: 1

Square Footage: 2,229

Bedrooms: 3

Bathrooms: 2

Foundation: Basement

Materials List Available: No

Price Category: E

Images provided by designer/architect.

Rear Elevation

Plan #321009

Dimensions: 55'8" W x 46'4" D

Levels: 1

Square Footage: 2,295

Bedrooms: 3

Bathrooms: 2

Foundation: Basement

Materials List Available: Yes

Price Category: E

Images provided by designer/architect.

Rear View

Optional Basement Level Floor Plan

Copyright by designer/architect.

Plan #161098

Dimensions: 72' W x 55'10" D

Levels: 1

Square Footage: 2,283

Bedrooms: 3

Bathrooms: 2

Foundation: Basement

Material List Available: No

Price Category: E

This home, as shown in the photograph, may differ from the actual blueprints. For more detailed information, please check the floor plans carefully.

Images provided by designer/architect.

This spacious single-level home with 9-ft.-high ceiling heights is designed with formal and informal spaces.

Features:

• Dining Room: This open room and the great room are defined by columns and dropped ceilings.

• Great Room: This gathering area features a fireplace and a triple sliding glass door to the rear yard.

• Kitchen: This spacious kitchen with large pantry and angled counter serves the informal dining area and solarium, creating a comfortably relaxed gathering place.

• Master Suite: Designed for luxury, this suite, with its high-style tray ceiling, offers a whirlpool tub, double-bowl vanity, and large walk-in closet.

Rear Elevation

Kitchen

Copyright by designer/architect.

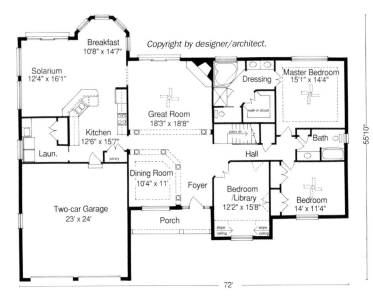

Plan #441043

Dimensions: 48' W x 56' D
Levels: 2
Square Footage: 2,277
Main Level Sq. Ft.: 1,563
Upper Level Sq. Ft.: 714
Bedrooms: 3
Bathrooms: 2½
Foundation: Crawl space; slab or basement available for fee
Material List Available: No
Price Category: E

Images provided by designer/architect.

With a nod to the details of the Arts and Crafts movement, this appealing bungalow has an eye-catching covered front porch, cedar-shingle accents, and light-catching windows.

Features:

- Foyer: This main foyer separates a cozy den on the left from the formal dining room on the right.

- Kitchen: A butler's pantry connects the dining room and this convenient kitchen; an angled peninsula containing the cooktop joins the area to a casual nook.

- Master Suite: This suite includes the master bath, which has a spa tub, separate shower, walk-in closet, compartmented toilet, and dual lavatories.

- Upper Level: On this upper level you'll find a bathroom with dual vanities to serve the two family bedrooms.

Main Level Floor Plan

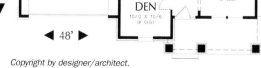

Copyright by designer/architect.

Upper Level Floor Plan

Rear Elevation

Images provided by designer/architect.

Plan #151447

Dimensions: 65'2" W x 63'8" D
Levels: 1
Square Footage: 2,147
Bedrooms: 4
Bathrooms: 2½
Foundation: Crawl space and slab
CompleteCost List Available: Yes
Price Category: D

The exquisite exterior of this split-bedroom offering hints at the stylish features waiting to be found inside.

Features:

- **Great Room:** Meticulous living spaces, including this living space, branch off from the foyer, and all share 10-ft.-high ceilings. Enjoy an appetizer by the fireplace here, or step outside and lounge on the festive patio until mealtime.

- **Kitchen:** This island work space has everything the chef in the family would want. The breakfast room merges with this area, allowing conversation during cleanup.

- **Master Suite:** This suite is accented by a stepped, boxed ceiling and his and her walk-in closets. The master bath has a marvelous step-up whirlpool tub, dual vanities, and a compartmentalized lavatory.

- **Bedrooms:** The three family bedrooms, located on the opposite side of the home from the master suite, share a hall bathroom.

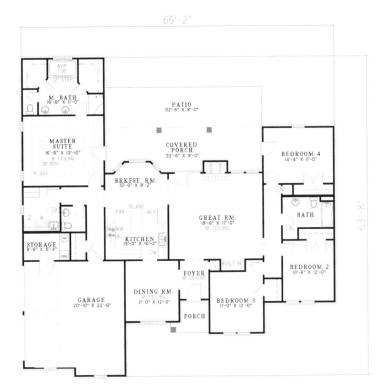

Copyright by designer/architect.

Plan #351055

Dimensions: 73'8" W x 58'4" D
Levels: 1
Square Footage: 2,251
Bedrooms: 3
Bathrooms: 2½
Foundation: Crawl space, slab, or basement
Materials List Available: Yes
Price Category: E

This beautiful and versatile plan features three bedrooms, two baths, and a three-car garage.

Features:

- **Great Room:** Featuring a 12-ft.-high raised ceiling and a gas fireplace, this large gathering area is open to the kitchen.

- **Kitchen:** This peninsula kitchen has a walk-in pantry and a raised bar, which is open into the great room.

- **Master Suite:** An office/lounge, jetted tub, large walk-in shower, large walk-in closet, and privacy porch set this suite apart.

- **Bedrooms:** The two secondary bedrooms have large closets and share a common bathroom.

Images provided by designer/architect.

Main Level Floor Plan

Bonus Area Floor Plan

Copyright by designer/architect.

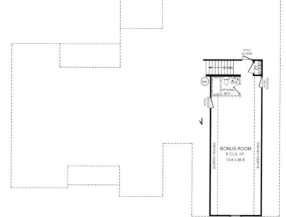

Plan #271075

Dimensions: 80' W x 52' D

Levels: 1

Square Footage: 2,233

Bedrooms: 2-4

Bathrooms: 1½-3½

Foundation: Basement

Materials List Available: No

Price Category: E

Images provided by designer/architect.

CAD FILE AVAILABLE · CAD

Optional Basement Level Floor Plan

Copyright by designer/architect.

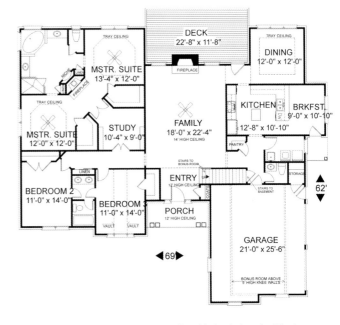

Plan #101098

Dimensions: 69' W x 62' D

Levels: 1

Square Footage: 2,398

Bedrooms: 3

Bathrooms: 2½

Foundation: Slab or basement

Materials List Available: Yes

Price Category: E

Images provided by designer/architect.

CAD FILE AVAILABLE · CAD

Copyright by designer/architect.

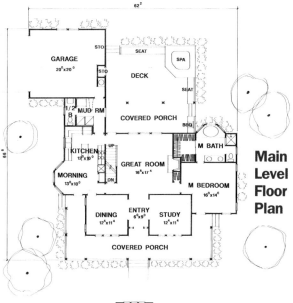

Main Level Floor Plan

GARAGE 20'0" x 20'0"
STO
SEAT
SPA
DECK
SEAT
1/2 B
MUD RM
COVERED PORCH
BBQ
KITCHEN 12'4" x 10'0"
UP
GREAT ROOM 16'5" x 17'4"
M BATH
MORNING 13'0" x 10'0"
DN
M BEDROOM 16'8" x 14'0"
DINING 12'4" x 11'4"
ENTRY 6'5" x 9'0"
STUDY 12'4" x 11'4"
COVERED PORCH

Upper Level Floor Plan
Copyright by designer/architect.

STO
BEDRM 2 11'8" x 14'4"
BATH 2
DN
BEDRM 3 10'10" x 16'10"
STORAGE
AC
STO
PLAYROOM 16'8" x 9'4"

Plan #331002

Dimensions: 62'2" W x 66'8" D
Levels: 2
Square Footage: 2,299
Main Level Sq. Ft.: 1,517
Upper Level Sq. Ft.: 782
Bedrooms: 3
Bathrooms: 2½
Foundation: Crawl space, slab, or basement
Materials List Available: No
Price Category: E

Images provided by designer/architect.

Upper Level Floor Plan

LOFT 17'4" x 14'4"
OPEN BELOW

Main Level Floor Plan

3- CAR GARAGE 21'5" x 29'0"
KITCHEN
GUEST SUITE 11' x 10'8"
WIC
BATH
DINING 9' x 13'
MASTER SUITE 15' x 15'
GREAT ROOM 24'4" x 18'4"

Basement Level Floor Plan
Copyright by designer/architect.

SHOP AREA
SHOP AREA
BDRM. #3 16'8" x 12'10"
REC ROOM 24'4" x 16'0"
BDRM. #4 13'4" x 12'10"

Plan #451114

Dimensions: 80'8" W x 50'8" D
Levels: 2
Square Footage: 3,892
Main Level Sq. Ft.: 1,781
Upper Level Sq. Ft.: 330
Basement Level Sq. Ft.: 1,781
Bedrooms: 4
Bathrooms: 3
Foundation: Slab
Material List Available: No
Price Category: H

Images provided by designer/architect.

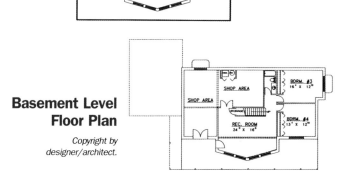

Plan #321037

Dimensions: 78'8" W x 50'6" D

Levels: 1

Square Footage: 2,397

Bedrooms: 3

Bathrooms: 2

Foundation: Basement or walkout

Materials List Available: Yes

Price Category: E

Come home to this three-bedroom stucco home with arched windows.

Features:

- Dining Room: Just off the entry is this formal room, with its vaulted ceiling.

- Great Room: This large room has a vaulted ceiling and a fireplace.

- Kitchen: A large pantry and an abundance of counter space make this kitchen a functional work space.

- Master Suite: This suite has a large walk-in closet and a private bath.

- Bedrooms: The two additional bedrooms share a common bathroom.

Images provided by designer/architect.

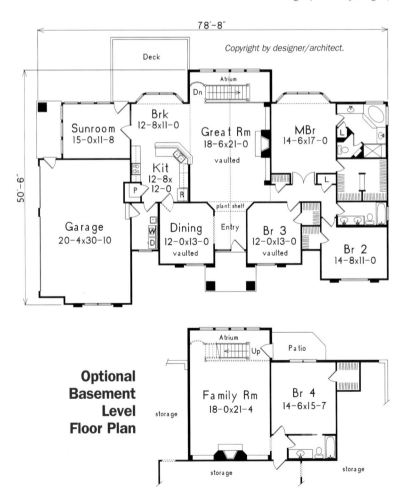

Optional Basement Level Floor Plan

Plan #441007

Dimensions: 70' W x 64' D
Levels: 1
Square Footage: 2,197
Bedrooms: 4
Bathrooms: 2½
Foundation: Crawl space
Materials List Available: No
Price Category: D

Images provided by designer/architect.

Welcome to this roomy ranch, embellished with a brick facade, intriguing roof peaks, and decorative quoins on all the front corners.

Features:

- Great Room: There's a direct sightline from the front door through the trio of windows in this room. The rooms are defined by columns and changes in ceiling height rather than by walls, so light bounces from dining room to breakfast nook to kitchen.

- Kitchen: The primary workstation in this kitchen is a peninsula, which faces the fireplace. The peninsula is equipped with a sink, dishwasher, downdraft cooktop, and snack counter.

- Den/Home Office: Conveniently located off the foyer, this room would work well as a home office.

- Master Suite: The double doors provide an air of seclusion for this suite. The vaulted bedroom features sliding patio doors to the backyard and an arch-top window. The adjoining bath is equipped with a whirlpool tub, shower, double vanity, and walk-in closet.

- Secondary Bedrooms: The two additional bedrooms, each with direct access to the shared bathroom, occupy the left wing of the ranch.

Rear Elevation

Copyright by designer/architect.

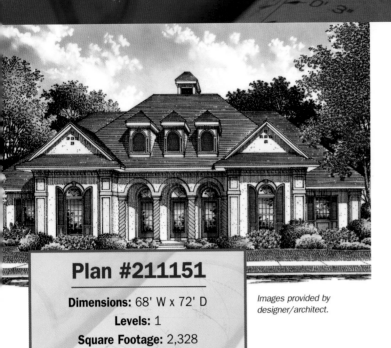

Plan #211151

Dimensions: 68' W x 72' D

Levels: 1

Square Footage: 2,328

Bedrooms: 3

Bathrooms: 2

Foundation: Slab

Material List Available: No

Price Category: E

Images provided by designer/architect.

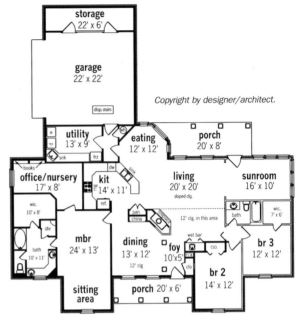

Copyright by designer/architect.

Plan #121057

Dimensions: 64' W x 57'2" D

Levels: 1

Square Footage: 2,311

Bedrooms: 3

Bathrooms: 2½

Foundation: Basement

Materials List Available: Yes

Price Category: E

Images provided by designer/architect.

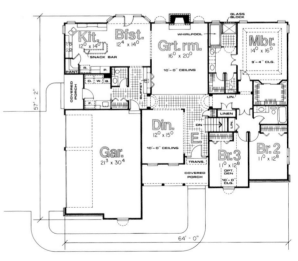

Copyright by designer/architect.

SMARTtip

Installing Crown Molding

Test for the direction and location of ceiling joists with a stud sensor, by tapping with a hammer to hear the sound of hollow or solid areas or by tapping in test finishing nails.

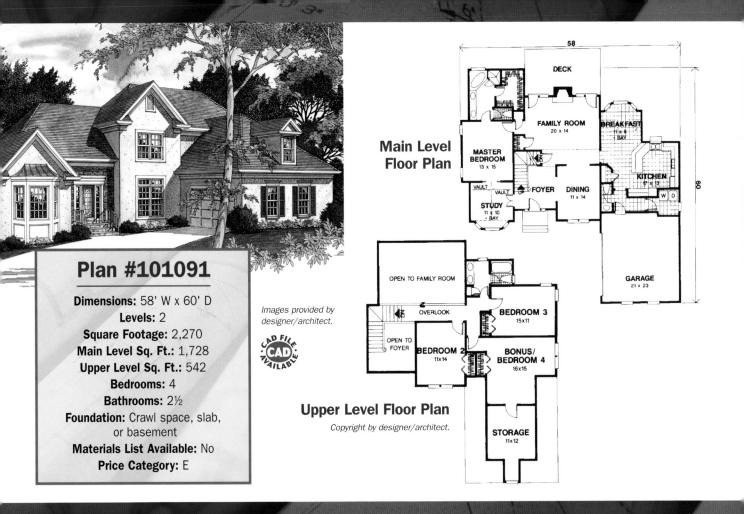

Plan #101091

Dimensions: 58' W x 60' D
Levels: 2
Square Footage: 2,270
Main Level Sq. Ft.: 1,728
Upper Level Sq. Ft.: 542
Bedrooms: 4
Bathrooms: 2½
Foundation: Crawl space, slab, or basement
Materials List Available: No
Price Category: E

Images provided by designer/architect.

CAD FILE AVAILABLE

Main Level Floor Plan

Upper Level Floor Plan

Copyright by designer/architect.

Plan #151028

Dimensions: 36' W X 69' D
Levels: 2
Square Footage: 2,252
Main Level Sq. Ft.: 1,694
Upper Level Sq. Ft.: 558
Bedrooms: 3
Bathrooms: 3
Foundation: Crawl space, slab; optional basement plan available for extra fee
CompleteCost List Available: Yes
Price Category: E

Images provided by designer/architect.

CAD FILE AVAILABLE

Main Level Floor Plan

Upper Level Floor Plan

Copyright by designer/architect.

Plan #131045

Dimensions: 81'4" W x 68'3" D
Levels: 1
Square Footage: 2,347
Bedrooms: 4
Bathrooms: 2½
Foundation: Crawl space, slab, or basement
Materials List Available: Yes
Price Category: E

Images provided by designer/architect.

You'll love the character and flexibility in siting that the angled design gives to this contemporary ranch-style home.

Features:

- **Porch:** A wraparound rear porch adds distinction to this lovely home.

- **Great Room:** Facing the rear of the house, this great room has a high, stepped ceiling, fireplace, and ample space for built-ins.

- **Kitchen:** This large room sits at an angle to the great room and is adjacent to both a laundry room and extra powder room.

- **Office:** Use the 4th bedroom as a home office, study, or living room, depending on your needs.

- **Master Suite:** This area is separated from the other bedrooms in the house to give it privacy. The beautiful bay window at the rear, two large walk-in closets, and luxurious bath make it an ideal retreat after a hectic day.

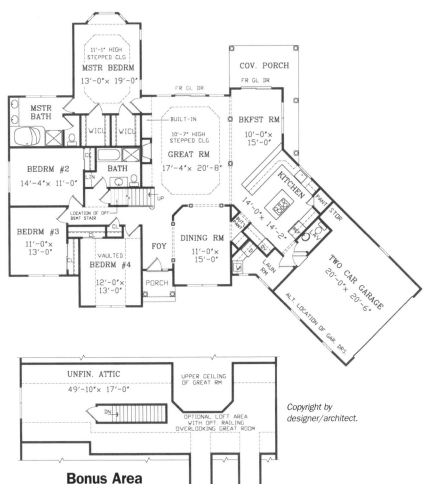

Copyright by designer/architect.

Plan #101033

Dimensions: 62' W x 69'2" D
Levels: 1
Square Footage: 2,260
Bedrooms: 3
Bathrooms: 3
Foundation: Basement
Material List Available: No
Price Category: E

CAD FILE AVAILABLE — CAD

The standing-seam roof over the entry porch makes this home stand out.

Features:

- Family Room: This gathering area features an over-13-ft.-tall ceiling, a built-in entertainment center, and a fireplace.

- Kitchen: This large kitchen has a built-in pantry and is open to the breakfast nook.

- Master Suite: This suite provides a dramatic extended bow-window wall with a clear view to the pool. It also offers his and her walk-in closets, a sitting area, and direct access to the covered rear porch.

- Bedrooms: The two additional bedrooms share a Jack-and-Jill bathroom Bedroom 2 has a walk-in closet.

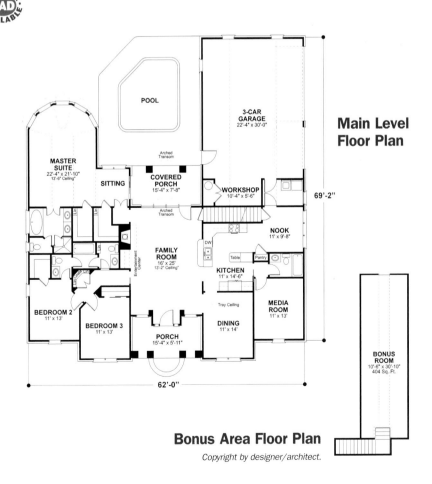

Main Level Floor Plan

Bonus Area Floor Plan

Plan #321041

Dimensions: 64' W x 34' D

Levels: 2

Square Footage: 2,286

Main Level Sq. Ft.: 1,283

Upper Level Sq. Ft.: 1,003

Bedrooms: 4

Bathrooms: 2½

Foundation: Crawl space, slab, or basement

Materials List Available: No

Price Category: E

If you love the way these gorgeous windows look from the outside, you'll be thrilled with the equally gracious interior of this home.

Features:

- Entryway: This two-story entryway shows off the fine woodworking on the railing and balustrades.

- Living Room: The large front windows form a glamorous background in this spacious room.

- Family Room: A handsome fireplace and a sliding glass door to the backyard enhance the open design of this room.

- Breakfast Room: Large enough for a crowd, this room makes a perfect dining area.

- Kitchen: The angled bar and separate pantry are highlights in this step-saving design.

- Master Suite: Enjoy this suite's huge walk-in closet, vaulted ceiling, and private bath, which features a double vanity, tub, and shower stall.

Images provided by designer/architect.

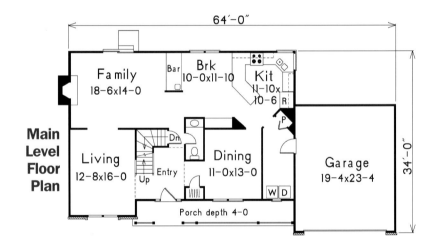

Main Level Floor Plan

Upper Level Floor Plan

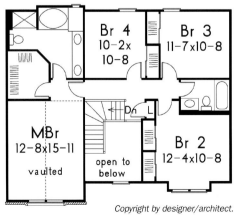

Front View

Copyright by designer/architect.

Plan #101034

Dimensions: 57' W x 62' D
Levels: 2
Square Footage: 2,470
Main Level Sq. Ft.: 1,916
Upper Level Sq. Ft.: 554
Bedrooms: 4
Bathrooms: 4
Foundation: Basement
Material List Available: No
Price Category: E

Images provided by designer/architect.

This spectacular two-story "master-down" design blends a luxurious and flexible floor plan with an unforgettable façade to create a simply exquisite home design.

CAD FILE AVAILABLE

Features:

- Entry: An inviting front porch welcomes you to this dramatic two-story entry, which is adorned by a lovely radius glass window above.

- Family Room: Beyond the stairs is this dramatic room, with its sloped ceiling, fireplace, and built-in cabinets.

- Master Suite: This magnificent suite includes a tray ceiling, a bowed rear window-wall, his

and her closets, a fitness area, and a bath with a 6-ft.-round spa and sit-down shower.

- Upper Level: Upstairs, there are two spacious bedrooms, each with direct access to the full bathroom. The bonus room provides additional flexible space to suit the needs of your family. All upper-level rooms have 8-ft.-high ceilings.

- Rear Porch: This large screened-in porch is the perfect place to relax after a long day at the office.

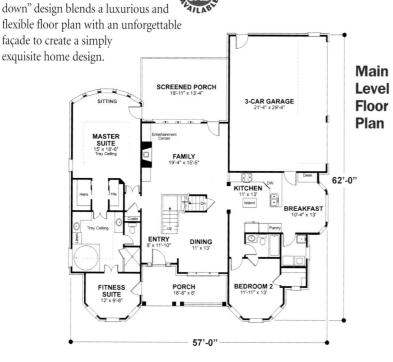

Main Level Floor Plan

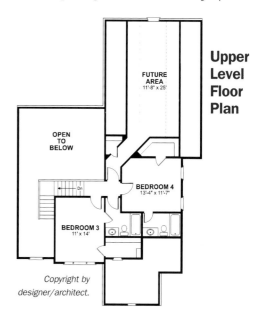

Upper Level Floor Plan

Copyright by designer/architect.

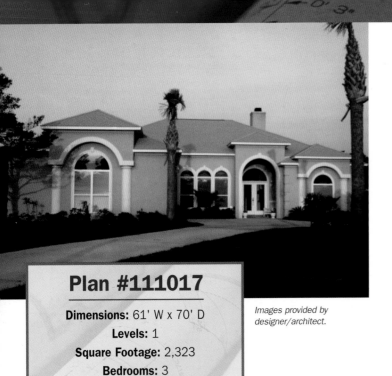

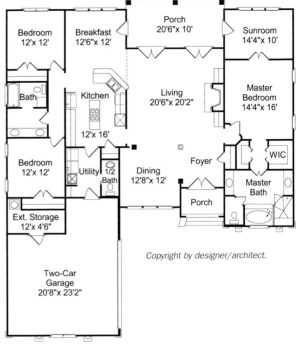

Images provided by designer/architect.

Copyright by designer/architect.

Plan #111017

Dimensions: 61' W x 70' D

Levels: 1

Square Footage: 2,323

Bedrooms: 3

Bathrooms: 2½

Foundation: Monolithic slab

Materials List Available: No

Price Category: E

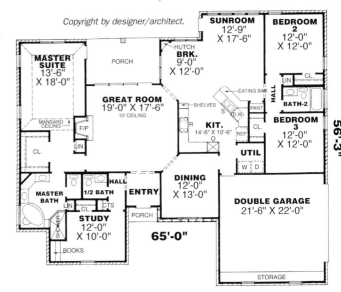

Images provided by designer/architect.

Copyright by designer/architect.

Plan #241001

Dimensions: 65' W x 56'3" D

Levels: 1

Square Footage: 2,350

Bedrooms: 3

Bathrooms: 2½

Foundation: Slab

Materials List Available: No

Price Category: E

SMARTtip

Kitchen Counters

Make use of counter inserts to help with the cooking chores. For example, ceramic tiles inlaid in a laminate counter create a heat-proof landing zone near the range. A marble or granite insert is tailor-made for pastry chefs. And a butcher-block inlay is a great addition to the food prep area.

Plan #121017

Dimensions: 54' W x 50' D
Levels: 2
Square Footage: 2,353
Main Level Sq. Ft.: 1,653
Upper Level Sq. Ft.: 700
Bedrooms: 4
Bathrooms: 2½
Foundation: Basement
Materials List Available: Yes
Price Category: E

Images provided by designer/architect.

The dramatic two-story entry with bent staircase is the first sign that this is a gracious home.

Features:

- Ceiling Height: 8 ft. except as noted.

- Great Room: A row of transom-topped windows and a tall, beamed ceiling add a sense of spaciousness to this family gathering area.

- Formal Dining Room: The bayed window helps make this an inviting place to entertain.

- See-through Fireplace: This feature spreads warmth and coziness throughout the informal areas of the home.

- Breakfast Area: This sunny area shares a see-through fireplace with the great room. It's the perfect place to start the day.

- Master Suite: Here are all the features you expect to find in large luxury homes. Wake up to tall, sloped ceilings, and enjoy the corner whirlpool, separate shower, and vanity. A large walk-in closet provides plenty of wardrobe storage.

Main Level Floor Plan

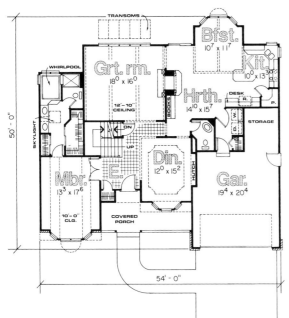

Upper Level Floor Plan

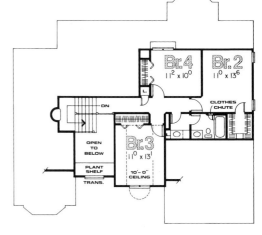

Copyright by designer/architect.

Plan #441044

Dimensions: 54' W x 47' D

Levels: 2

Square Footage: 2,277

Main Level Sq. Ft.: 1,563

Upper Level Sq. Ft.: 714

Bedrooms: 5

Bathrooms: 2½

Foundation: Crawl space; slab or basement available for fee

Materials List Available: No

Price Category: E

Images provided by designer/architect.

This handsome design takes its initial cues from the American farmhouse style, but it blends in a wonderful mixture of exterior materials to enliven the look. Cedar battens, lap siding, and stone accents work together for an out-of-the-ordinary facade.

Features:

• **Open Living:** The floor plan is thoughtfully created and holds just the right amount of space for exceptional livability. An open living area, comprising a vaulted great room, dining room, and large kitchen, lies to the rear of the main level and can take advantage of backyard views and a patio.

• **Den:** This room, which is located at the front of the main level, may also become an additional bedroom if you need the space.

• **Master Suite:** This suite is located on the main level. It features a salon with a vaulted ceiling and a bath with a spa tub, separate shower, and compartmented toilet.

• **Bonus Space:** This space on the upper level complements two family bedrooms and a shared full bathroom.

Main Level Floor Plan

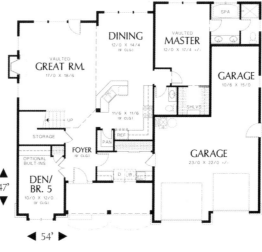

Upper Level Floor Plan

Copyright by designer/architect.

Rear Elevation

Plan #141029

Dimensions: 55' W x 42' D
Levels: 2
Square Footage: 2,289
Main Level Sq. Ft.: 1,382
Upper Level Sq. Ft.: 907
Bedrooms: 4
Bathrooms: 2½
Foundation: Basement
Materials List Available: Yes
Price Category: E

Images provided by designer/architect.

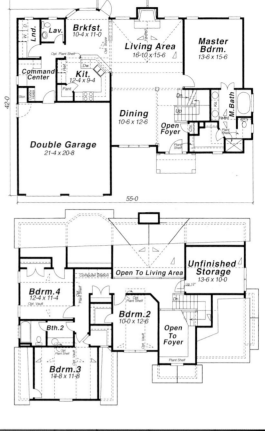

Main Level Floor Plan

Upper Level Floor Plan

Copyright by designer/architect.

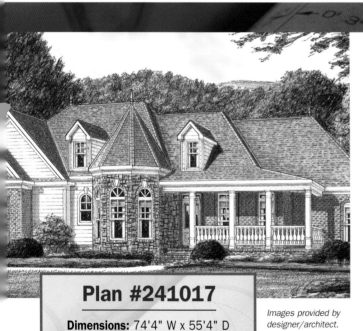

Plan #241017

Dimensions: 74'4" W x 55'4" D
Levels: 1
Square Footage: 2,431
Bedrooms: 4
Bathrooms: 2½
Foundation: Slab
Materials List Available: No
Price Category: E

Images provided by designer/architect.

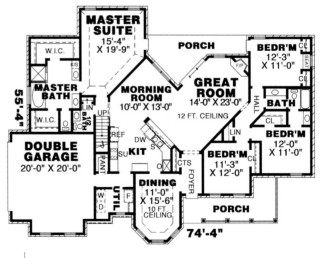

Bonus Area

Copyright by designer/architect.

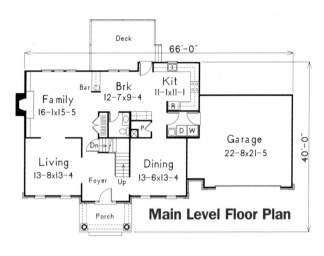

Main Level Floor Plan

Deck

66'-0"

Family
16-1x15-5

Bar

Brk
12-7x9-4

Kit
11-1x11-1

R

Garage
22-8x21-5

40'-0"

Living
13-8x13-4

Dn

Up

Foyer

Dining
13-6x13-4

P

D W

Porch

Plan #321046

Dimensions: 66' W x 40' D

Levels: 2

Square Footage: 2,411

Main Level Sq. Ft.: 1,293

Upper Level Sq. Ft.: 1,118

Bedrooms: 3

Bathrooms: 2½

Foundation: Basement

Materials List Available: Yes

Price Category: E

Images provided by designer/architect.

Upper Level Floor Plan

Study
11-5x11-8

Br 3
11-11x10-0

L

MBr
13-8x15-4

open to below

Dn

Br 2
13-8x11-0

vaulted

Copyright by designer/architect.

Main Level Floor Plan

COVERED DECK/SCREENED PORCH
31'-8" x 10'-6"
Vaulted Ceiling

DINING
11'-5" x 16'
Vaulted Ceiling

HEARTH ROOM
15' x 15'-11"
Vaulted Ceiling

SITTING
11'-4" x 9'-2"
Vaulted Ceiling

MASTER SUITE
16' x 15'
Raised Tray Ceiling

FAMILY
18' x 19'
Vaulted Ceiling

KITCHEN
15' x 17'
Raised Ceiling

NOOK
9'-11" x 9'-4"

BEDROOM 2
11'-0" x 16'-4"

BEDROOM 3
11' x 14'
Vaulted Ceiling

COVERED PORCH
11' x 5'

3-CAR GARAGE
21' x 33'

74'-8"

71'-4"

Plan #101035

Dimensions: 71'4" W x 74'8" D

Levels: 1

Square Footage: 2,461

Bedrooms: 3

Bathrooms: 3½

Foundation: Basement

Material List Available: No

Price Category: E

Images provided by designer/architect.

CAD FILE AVAILABLE

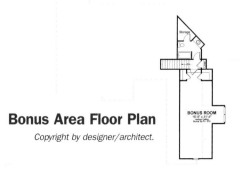

Storage

BONUS ROOM
16'-8" x 31'-4"
Vaulted Ceiling

Bonus Area Floor Plan

Copyright by designer/architect.

Plan #151530

Dimensions: 38'10" W x 70'4" D
Levels: 2
Square Footage: 2,146
Main Level Sq. Ft.: 1,654
Upper Level Sq. Ft.: 492
Bedrooms: 3
Bathrooms: 2½
Foundation: Crawl space or slab
CompleteCost List Available: Yes
Price Category: D

Images provided by designer/architect.

Gables, columns, and architectural detailing give this home a warm feeling reminiscent of your grandmother's house.

CAD FILE AVAILABLE

Features:

- **Foyer:** The cozy porch gently welcomes you into this column-lined foyer, which separates the formal dining room from the large great room with fireplace.

- **Kitchen:** This kitchen with breakfast room is centrally located and looks out at the lovely courtyard patio, which is perfect for entertaining.

- **Master Suite:** Your perfect hideaway awaits you in this spacious suite, with its large walk-in closet and master bath packed with amenities.

- **Upper Level:** The upstairs has two bedrooms, each with private access to the full bathroom, as well as future bonus space when desired.

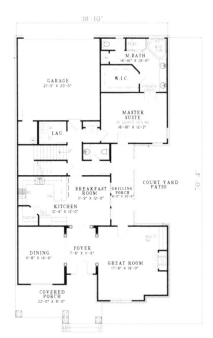

Main Level Floor Plan
Copyright by designer/architect.

Upper Level Floor Plan

Front View

Plan #441035

Dimensions: 50' W x 56' D

Levels: 2

Square Footage: 2,196

Main Level Sq. Ft.: 1,658

Upper Level Sq. Ft.: 538

Bedrooms: 4

Bathrooms: 2½

Foundation: Crawl space; slab or basement available for fee

Materials List Available: No

Price Category: D

Images provided by designer/architect.

This home's stone-and-cedar-shingle facade is delightfully complemented by French Country detailing, dormer windows, and shutters at the large arched window and its second-story sister.

Features:

- Great Room: Containing a fireplace and double doors to the rear yard, this large room is further enhanced by a vaulted ceiling.

- Kitchen: This cooking center has an attached nook with corner windows overlooking the backyard.

- Master Suite: This suite is well designed with a vaulted ceiling and Palladian window. Its bath sports a spa tub.

- Bonus Space: This huge space, located on the second level, provides for a future bedroom, game room, or home office. Two dormer windows grace it.

- Garage: A service hall, with laundry alcove, opens to this garage. There is space enough here for three cars or two and a workshop.

Main Level Floor Plan

Copyright by designer/architect.

Upper Level Floor Plan

Rear Elevation

Plan #221034

Dimensions: 63'8" W x 56'4" D

Levels: 2

Square Footage: 2,415

Main Level Sq. Ft.: 1,691

Upper Level Sq. Ft.: 724

Bedrooms: 4

Bathrooms: 2½

Foundation: Basement

Materials List Available: No

Price Category: E

Images provided by designer/architect.

This spacious two-story brick home features tons of amenities that you would normally expect in a much larger home.

CAD FILE AVAILABLE

Features:

- Kitchen: The breakfast bar in this kitchen overlooks both the nook and the great room, creating the illusion of additional space.

- Great Room: The two-story ceiling in this room is made comfortable by a wall that features a fireplace and built-ins.

- Master Suite: This suite features a spacious bath and large walk-in closet, while the bedroom itself has a stepped ceiling.

- Upper Level: Upstairs you'll love the balcony, which overlooks the great room from above, and you'll be pleasantly surprised to find three additional bedrooms and a full bathroom.

Rear Elevation

Main Level Floor Plan

Upper Level Floor Plan

Copyright by designer/architect.

Plan #101012

Dimensions: 69'4" W x 62'9" D

Levels: 1

Square Footage: 2,288

Bedrooms: 3

Bathrooms: 2½

Foundation: Crawl space, slab, basement, or walkout

Materials List Available: No

Price Category: E

Images provided by designer/architect.

This classic brick ranch boasts traditional styling and an exciting up-to-date floor plan.

Features:

- Ceiling Height: 9 ft. unless otherwise noted.

- Front Porch: Guests will be welcome by this inviting front porch, which features a 12-ft. ceiling.

- Family Room: This warm and inviting room measures 16 ft. x 19 ft. It features a 14-ft. ceiling and a rear wall of windows. French doors lead to an enormous deck.

- Kitchen: This unique angled kitchen is open to the hearth room and eating areas, all of which enjoy vaulted ceilings and are surrounded by windows. The hearth room has a TV niche.

- Master Suite: This 16-ft. x 15-ft. master suite is truly sumptuous, with its 12-ft. ceiling, sitting area, two walk-in closets, and full-featured bath.

- Bonus Room: Here is plenty of storage or room for future expansion. Just beyond the entry are stairs leading to a bonus room measuring approximately 12 ft. x 21 ft.

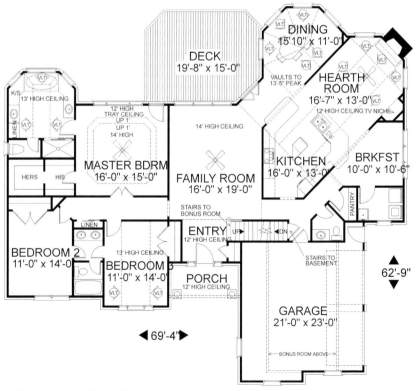

Copyright by designer/architect.

Kitchen

Dining Room

Living Room

Hearth Room

Master Bedroom

Bedroom

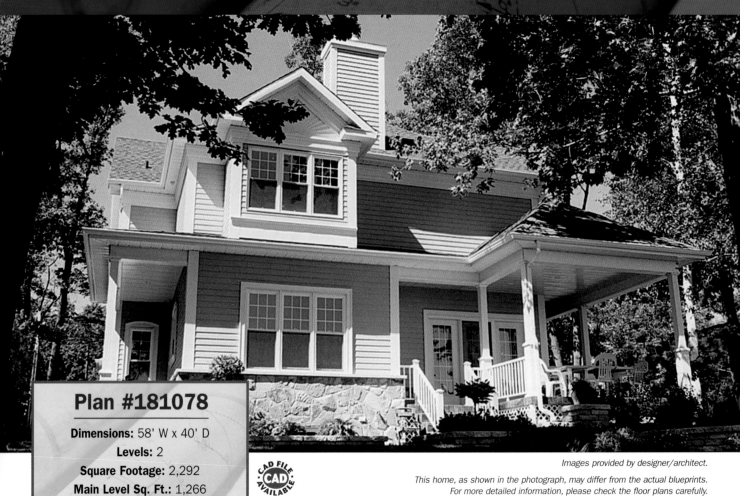

Plan #181078

Dimensions: 58' W x 40' D

Levels: 2

Square Footage: 2,292

Main Level Sq. Ft.: 1,266

Upper Level Sq. Ft.: 1,026

Bedrooms: 4

Bathrooms: 2½

Foundation: Full basement

Materials List Available: Yes

Price Category: E

Images provided by designer/architect.

This home, as shown in the photograph, may differ from the actual blueprints. For more detailed information, please check the floor plans carefully.

This two-story home will be a fine addition to any neighborhood.

Features:

- Living Room: This gathering area is open to the kitchen and will warm you with its cozy fireplace.

- Kitchen: This island kitchen has a raised bar that looks into the living room, and it provides access to the rear porch.

- Master Suite: This private area has a cozy fireplace in the sleeping area. The master bath features dual vanities, a walk-in closet, and a large tub.

- Bedrooms: The two additional bedrooms are located upstairs with the master suite and share the Jack-and-Jill bathroom.

Main Level Floor Plan

Upper Level Floor Plan

Copyright by designer/architect.

Plan #441048

Dimensions: 48' W x 40' D
Levels: 2
Square Footage: 2,453
Main Level Sq. Ft.: 1,118
Upper Level Sq. Ft.: 1,335
Bedrooms: 4
Bathrooms: 2½
Foundation: Crawl space
Materials List Available: No
Price Category: E

Images provided by designer/architect.

The perfect-size plan and a pretty facade add up to a great home for your family. The combination of wood siding and stone complements a carriage-style garage door and cedar-shingle detailing on the outside of this home.

CAD FILE AVAILABLE

Features:

- **Entry:** The interior opens though this angled front entry, with the den on the left and a half-bathroom on the right. The den has a comfortable window seat for dreaming and gazing.

- **Kitchen:** The dining area adjoins this island kitchen, which has a roomy pantry and built-in desk.

- **Master Suite:** This vaulted suite features a spa bath, walk-in closet with window seat, and separate tub and shower.

- **Upper Level:** All bedrooms are located on this level. Bedroom 3 has a walk-in closet. The laundry area is also located here to make wash day trouble free.

Rear Elevation

Copyright by designer/architect.

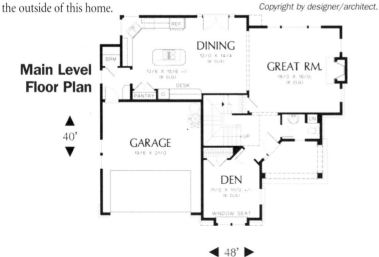

Main Level Floor Plan

Upper Level Floor Plan

Plan #121074

Dimensions: 68'8" W x 47'8" D

Levels: 2

Square Footage: 2,486

Main Level Sq. Ft.: 1,829

Upper Level Sq. Ft.: 657

Bedrooms: 4

Bathrooms: 2½

Foundation: Basement

Materials List Available: Yes

Price Category: E

Images provided by designer/architect.

Enjoy the natural light that streams through the many lovely windows in this well-designed home.

Features:

- **Living Room:** This room is sure to be your family's headquarters, thanks to the lovely 15-ft. ceiling, stacked windows, central location, and cozy fireplace.

- **Dining Room:** A boxed ceiling adds formality to this well-positioned room.

- **Kitchen:** The island cooktop in this kitchen is so large that it includes a snack bar area. A pantry gives ample storage space, and a built-in desk—where you can set up a computer station or a record-keeping area—adds efficiency.

- **Master Suite:** For the sake of privacy, this master suite is located on the opposite side of the home from the other living areas. You'll love the roomy bedroom and luxuriate in the private bath with its many amenities.

Main Level Floor Plan

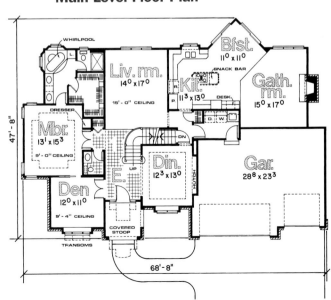

Upper Level Floor Plan

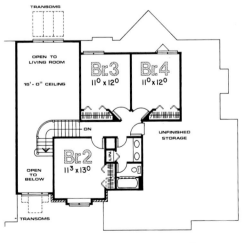

Copyright by designer/architect.

Plan #341060

Dimensions: 75'10" W x 56'2" D

Levels: 1.5

Square Footage: 2,349

Bonus unfinished Sq. Ft.: 706

Bedrooms: 3

Bathrooms: 2½

Foundation: Crawl space

Materials List Available: Yes

Price Category: E

Images provided by designer/architect.

Classic forms and luxurious spaces combine to create a contemporary abode that is just right for the homeowner who demands the best.

Features:

- **Family Room:** This spacious room boasts a gas log fireplace and French doors to the screened back porch.

- **Kitchen:** With an elevated bar that's ideal for informal breakfasts and snacks, this kitchen also features a cooktop and a walk-in pantry.

- **Master Suite:** Located for privacy away from the other bedrooms, this suite has a large walk-in closet and a private full bath with garden tub, separate shower, and double vanity.

- **Bedrooms:** The two additional bedrooms are located near the home office and share the hall bathroom.

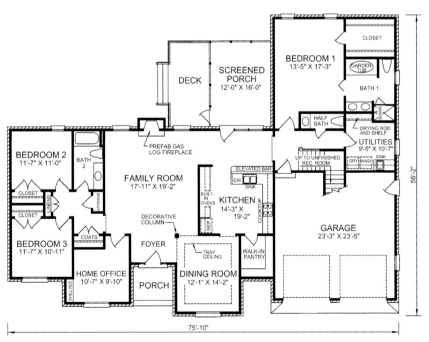

Copyright by designer/architect.

Plan #441041

Dimensions: 49' W x 45' D
Levels: 2
Square Footage: 2,164
Main Level Sq. Ft.: 1,171
Upper Level Sq. Ft.: 993
Bedrooms: 3
Bathrooms: 2½
Foundation: Crawl space; slab or basement available for fee
Material List Available: No
Price Category: D

The use of decorative brick or stone as the accent on the façade of this home adds a rich texture to an already inviting design.

Images provided by designer/architect.

Features:

- Great Room: With large windows, which give a view of the backyard and allow natural light to flood the room, a vaulted ceiling, and a fireplace, this area is perfect for large gatherings.

- Kitchen: This kitchen has an abundance of cabinets and counter space as well as a pantry cabinet. The raised bar is open to the dining room.

- Dining Room: You can serve formal or informal meals here while you enjoy the view of the backyard. Step through the door, and you are on the rear porch.

- Bedrooms: All three bedrooms reside on the upper level. The master bedroom is vaulted and has a walk-in closet, and the master bath boasts a spa tub and double sinks. The family bedrooms share the full bathroom in the hallway.

- Garage: This large front-loading garage has room for tree cars or two cars and a shop area.

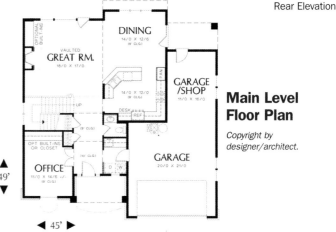

Rear Elevation

Upper Level Floor Plan

Main Level Floor Plan

Copyright by designer/architect.

Plan #311003

Dimensions: 70'10" W x 65'4" D

Levels: 2

Square Footage: 2,428

Main Level Sq. Ft.: 2,348

Upper Level Sq. Ft.: 80

Bedrooms: 3

Bathrooms: 2½

Foundation: Crawl space, slab

Materials List Available: Y

Price Category: E

Images provided by designer/architect.

If you admire the gracious colonnaded porch, curved brick steps, and stunning front windows, you'll fall in love with the interior of this home.

Features:

- **Great Room:** Enjoy the vaulted ceiling, balcony from the upper level, and fireplace with flanking windows that let you look out to the patio.

- **Dining Room:** Columns define this formal room, which is adjacent to the breakfast room.

- **Kitchen:** A bayed sink area and extensive curved bar provide visual interest in this well-designed kitchen, which every cook will love.

- **Breakfast Room:** Huge windows let the sun shine into this room, which is open to the kitchen.

- **Master Suite:** The sitting area is open to the rear porch for a special touch in this gorgeous suite. Two walk-in closets and a vaulted ceiling and double vanity in the bath will make you feel completely pampered.

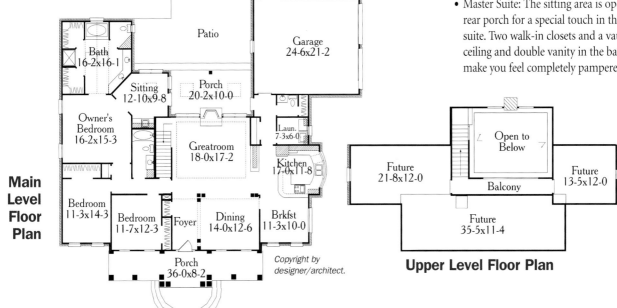

Main Level Floor Plan

Bath 16-2x16-1

Patio

Garage 24-6x21-2

Sitting 12-10x9-8

Porch 20-2x10-0

Owner's Bedroom 16-2x15-3

Greatroom 18-0x17-2

Laun. 7-3x6-0

Kitchen 17-0x11-8

Bedroom 11-3x14-3

Bedroom 11-7x12-3

Foyer

Dining 14-0x12-6

Brkfst 11-3x10-0

Porch 36-0x8-2

Copyright by designer/architect.

Upper Level Floor Plan

Open to Below

Future 21-8x12-0

Future 13-5x12-0

Balcony

Future 35-5x11-4

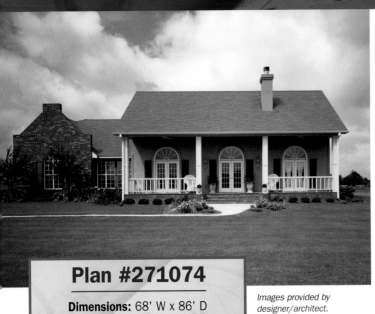

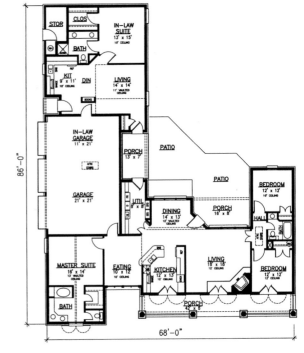

Plan #271074

Dimensions: 68' W x 86' D

Levels: 1

Square Footage: 2,400

Bedrooms: 4

Bathrooms: 3

Foundation: Crawl space or slab

Materials List Available: No

Price Category: E

Images provided by designer/architect.

Copyright by designer/architect.

Main Level Floor Plan

Plan #101100

Dimensions: 48' W x 50' D

Levels: 2

Square Footage: 2,479

Main Level Sq. Ft.: 1,720

Upper Level Sq. Ft.: 759

Bedrooms: 3

Bathrooms: 2½

Foundation: Crawl space or basement

Materials List Available: Yes

Price Category: E

Images provided by designer/architect.

Upper Level Floor Plan

Copyright by designer/architect.

Plan #351011

Dimensions: 73'8" W x 53'2" D

Levels: 1

Square Footage: 2,251

Bedrooms: 3

Bathrooms: 2½

Foundation: Crawl space, slab, or basement

Materials List Available: Yes

Price Category: E

Images provided by designer/architect.

CAD FILE AVAILABLE

Bonus Room Floor Plan

Copyright by designer/architect.

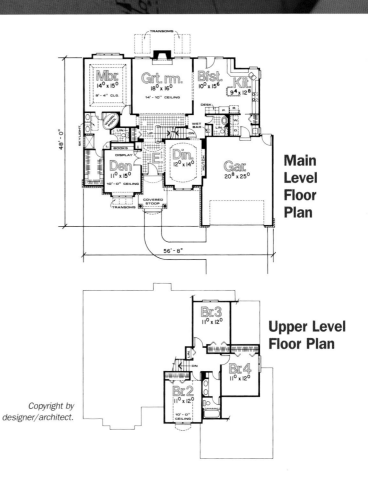

Plan #121088

Dimensions: 56'8" W x 48' D

Levels: 2

Square Footage: 2,340

Main Level Sq. Ft.: 1,701

Upper Level Sq. Ft.: 639

Bedrooms: 4

Bathrooms: 2½

Foundation: Basement

Materials List Available: Yes

Price Category: E

Images provided by designer/architect.

CAD FILE AVAILABLE

Main Level Floor Plan

Upper Level Floor Plan

Copyright by designer/architect.

Plan #121068

Dimensions: 54' W x 49'10" D

Levels: 2

Square Footage: 2,391

Main Level Sq. Ft.: 1,697

Upper Level Sq. Ft.: 694

Bedrooms: 4

Bathrooms: 2½

Foundation: Basement

Materials List Available: Yes

Price Category: E

This home, as shown in the photograph, may differ from the actual blueprints. Images provided by designer/architect. For more detailed information, please check the floor plans carefully.

This home allows you a great deal of latitude in the way you choose to finish it, so you can truly make it "your own."

Features:

• Living Room: Located just off the entryway, this living room is easy to convert to a stylish den. Add French doors for privacy, and relish the style that the 12-ft. angled ceiling and picturesque arched window provide.

• Great Room: The highlight of this room is the two-sided fireplace that easily adds as much design interest as warmth to this area. The three transom-topped windows here fill the room with light.

• Kitchen: A center island, walk-in pantry, and built-in desk combine to create this wonderful kitchen, and the attached gazebo breakfast area adds the finishing touch.

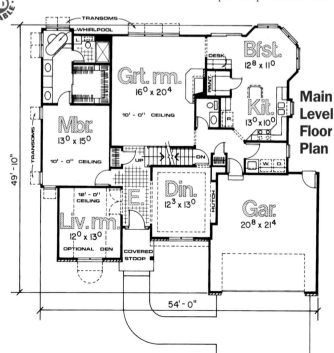

Main Level Floor Plan

Upper Level Floor Plan

Copyright by designer/architect.

Plan #321005

Dimensions: 69' W x 53'8" D
Levels: 1
Square Footage: 2,483
Bedrooms: 3
Bathrooms: 2
Foundation: Basement
Materials List Available: Yes
Price Category: E

You'll love the grand feeling of this home, which combines with the very practical features that make living in it a pleasure.

Features:

- Porch: The open brick arches and Palladian door set the tone for this magnificent home.

- Great Room: An alcove for the entertainment center and vaulted ceiling show the care that went into designing this room.

- Dining Room: A tray ceiling sets off the formality of this large room.

- Kitchen: The layout in this room is designed to make your work patterns more efficient and to save you steps and time.

- Study: This quiet room can be a wonderful refuge, or you can use it for a fourth bedroom if you wish.

- Master Suite: Made for relaxing at the end of the day, this suite will pamper you with luxuries.

Images provided by designer/architect.

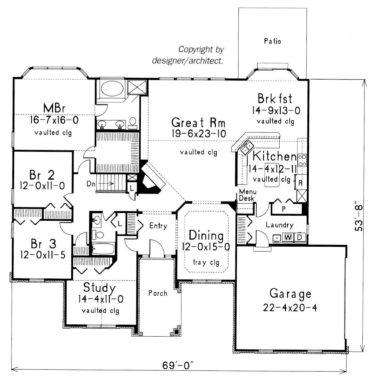

Copyright by designer/architect.

SMARTtip

Art in Pools

The tiled walls and floor of a pool make great canvases for art, so incorporate a serious or whimsical design. Also, make the stairs wide and shallow to form a wading area for kids.

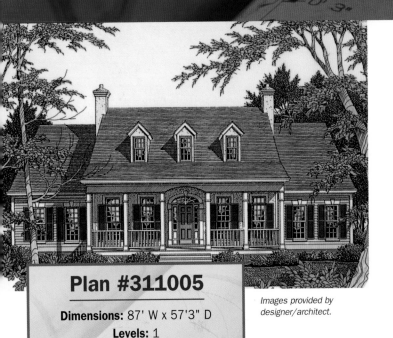

Copyright by designer/architect.

Storage 4-11x12-6

Garage 21-7x21-5

Porch 9-0x21-6

Bath

Desk

Laun. 5-5x6-0

Master Bedroom 14-3x15-11

Greatroom 18-7x15-11

Breakfast 12-7x10-1

Bedroom 13-3x11-0

Optional Stair Dn | Up

Kitchen 12-7x11-3

Bath

M.Bath

Study/Guest 12-7x12-7

Foyer

Dining 12-7x11-2

Bedroom 13-3x10-2

Porch 32-8x6-0

Images provided by designer/architect.

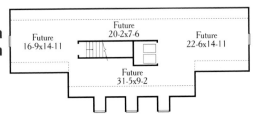

Bonus Area Floor Plan

Future 16-9x14-11 | Future 20-2x7-6 | Future 22-6x14-11

Future 31-5x9-2

Plan #311005

Dimensions: 87' W x 57'3" D

Levels: 1

Square Footage: 2,497

Bedrooms: 3

Bathrooms: 2½

Foundation: Crawl space, slab, or basement

Materials List Available: Yes

Price Category: E

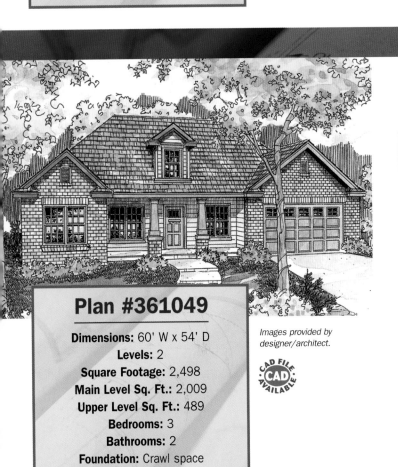

Images provided by designer/architect.

CAD FILE AVAILABLE

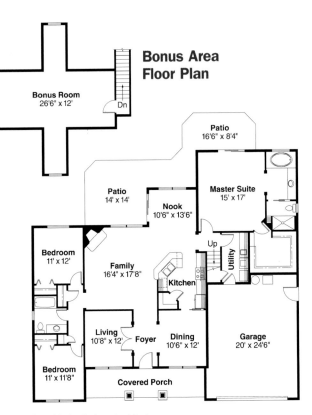

Bonus Area Floor Plan

Bonus Room 26'6" x 12'

Dn

Patio 16'6" x 8'4"

Patio 14' x 14'

Nook 10'6" x 13'6"

Master Suite 15' x 17'

Bedroom 11' x 12'

Family 16'4" x 17'8"

Kitchen

Up

Utility

Living 10'8" x 12'

Foyer

Dining 10'6" x 12'

Garage 20' x 24'6"

Bedroom 11' x 11'8"

Covered Porch

Copyright by designer/architect.

Plan #361049

Dimensions: 60' W x 54' D

Levels: 2

Square Footage: 2,498

Main Level Sq. Ft.: 2,009

Upper Level Sq. Ft.: 489

Bedrooms: 3

Bathrooms: 2

Foundation: Crawl space

Material List Available: No

Price Category: E

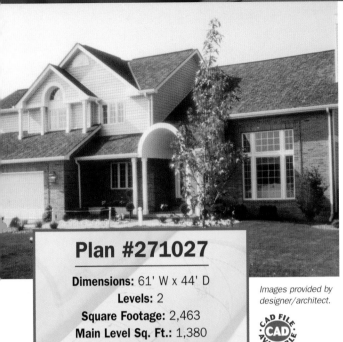

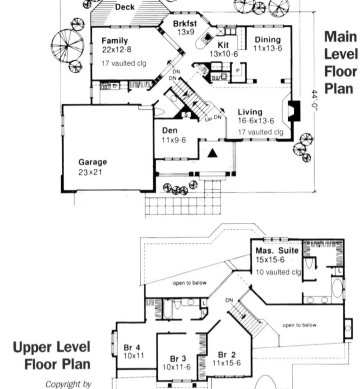

Main Level Floor Plan

Deck

Brkfst
13x9

Family
22x12-8
17 vaulted clg

Kit
13x10-6

Dining
11x13-6

Living
16-6x13-6
17 vaulted clg

Den
11x9-6

Garage
23 x21

60'-4"

44'-0"

Images provided by designer/architect.

CAD FILE AVAILABLE

Plan #271027

Dimensions: 61' W x 44' D

Levels: 2

Square Footage: 2,463

Main Level Sq. Ft.: 1,380

Upper Level Sq. Ft.: 1,083

Bedrooms: 4

Bathrooms: 2½

Foundation: Basement

Materials List Available: Yes

Price Category: D

Upper Level Floor Plan

Mas. Suite
15x15-6
10 vaulted clg

open to below

open to below

Br 4
10x11

Br 3
10x11-6

Br 2
11x15-6

Copyright by designer/architect.

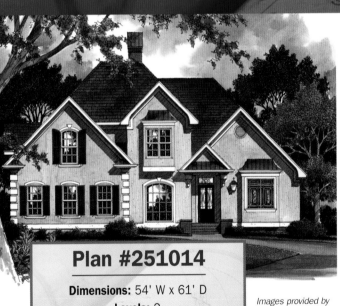

Main Level Floor Plan

Deck

Sun Room
11x14'-4'

Kitchen
11x13

Breakfast
10x13

Master
15x15
Vaulted Clg.

Vaulted Clg.

See Thru Fireplace

Family Room
16x18

Dining
11x13

Foyer

Bath

Storage

Laundry

Stoop

Garage
22x23

Drive

54'

61'

Images provided by designer/architect.

CAD FILE AVAILABLE

Plan #251014

Dimensions: 54' W x 61' D

Levels: 2

Square Footage: 2,210

Main Level Sq. Ft.: 1,670

Upper Level Sq. Ft.: 540

Bedrooms: 3

Bathrooms: 2½

Foundation: Crawl space, basement

Materials List Available: Yes

Price Category: E

Upper Level Floor Plan

Br.#2
14x12

Bath

Br.#3
11x13

Opt. Bonus Area
15x28

Copyright by designer/architect.

Plan #361059

Dimensions: 77' W x 63' D

Levels: 1

Square Footage: 2,470

Bedrooms: 3

Bathrooms: 2½

Foundation: Crawl space

Material List Available: No

Price Category: E

Images provided by designer/architect.

CAD FILE AVAILABLE

Patio
18' x 14'

Vaulted Covered Patio
12' x 12'

Nook
11' x 11'

Master Suite
15' x 16'2"

Family
15' x 17'10"

Bedroom
11'2" x 11'

Kitchen

Utility

Bedroom
10'6" x 11'8"

Garage
29'8" x 24'10"

Dining
11'6" x 12'10"

Entry

Living
13' x 17'6"

Den
14'2" x 11'

Covered Porch

Copyright by designer/architect.

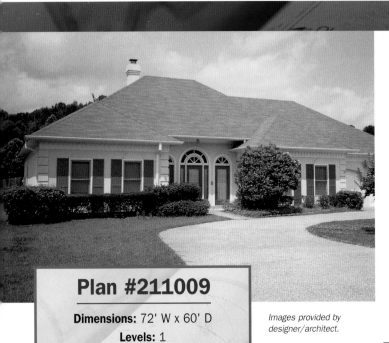

Plan #211009

Dimensions: 72' W x 60' D

Levels: 1

Square Footage: 2,396

Bedrooms: 4

Bathrooms: 2

Foundation: Slab

Materials List Available: Yes

Price Category: E

Images provided by designer/architect.

Copyright by designer/architect.

mbr
16 x 15

wic

patio

sky light

br 2
16 x 11

porch
18 x 8

bkfst
10 x 10

bath

sto
12 x 9

util

br 3
12 x 12

living
20 x 20

garage
22 x 22

kit 14 x 10

br 4
14 x 12

foy
16x5

porch 16 x 4

dining
17 x 14

SMARTtip

Ornaments in a Garden

Placement is everything with ornaments in a garden. Some elements are best sitting by themselves. Others are better when they are part of a cohesive whole, perhaps placed in the greenery at a corner or flanking a structure.

Plan #121097

Dimensions: 58' W x 42'8" D

Levels: 2

Square Footage: 2,417

Main Level Sq. Ft.: 1,162

Upper Level Sq. Ft.: 1,255

Bedrooms: 4

Bathrooms: 2½

Foundation: Basement

Materials List Available: Yes

Price Category: E

This design is ideal if you're looking for a home that will be easy to expand through the years.

Features:

- **Entry:** A balcony from the upper level overlooks this two-story entryway.

- **Study:** Add French doors to make this bayed room an expansion of the family room.

- **Family Room:** This room is positioned so that friends and family will congregate here.

- **Dining Room:** A built-in serving cabinet from the kitchen makes serving meals a pleasure.

- **Kitchen:** A roll-away butcher-block island, full pantry, and snack bar add convenience.

- **Breakfast Area:** Patio doors in this bayed area lead to a private porch where you'll love to dine.

- **Unfinished area:** Use this area for storage or future expansion.

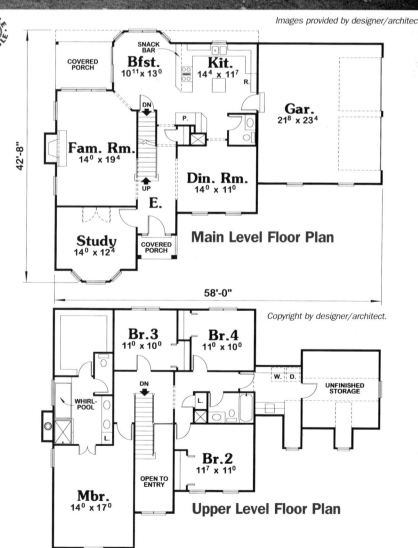

Images provided by designer/architect.

Main Level Floor Plan

Copyright by designer/architect.

Upper Level Floor Plan

Plan #121080

Dimensions: 56' W x 49' D

Levels: 2

Square Footage: 2,384

Main Level Sq. Ft.: 1,616

Upper Level Sq. Ft.: 768

Bedrooms: 4

Bathrooms: 2½

Foundation: Slab

Materials List Available: Yes

Price Category: E

This home, as shown in the photograph, may differ from the actual blueprints. Images provided by designer/architect. For more detailed information, please check the floor plans carefully.

This design is ideal if you want a generously sized home now and room to expand later.

Features:

• Living Room: Your eyes will be drawn towards the ceiling as soon as you enter this lovely room. The ceiling is vaulted, giving a sense of grandeur, and a graceful balcony from the second floor adds extra interest to this room.

• Kitchen: Designed with lots of counter space to make your work convenient, this kitchen also shares an eating bar with the breakfast nook.

• Breakfast Nook: Eat here or go out to the adjoining private porch where you can enjoy your meal in the morning sunshine.

• Master Suite: The bayed area in the bedroom makes a picturesque sitting area. French doors in the bedroom open to a private bath that's fitted with a whirlpool tub, separate shower, two vanities, and a walk-in closet.

Main Level Floor Plan

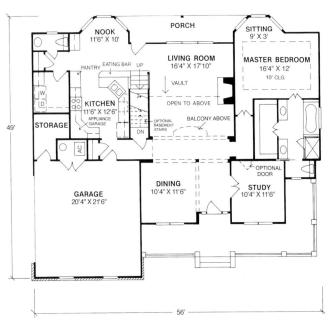

Upper Level Floor Plan

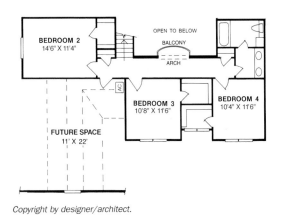

Copyright by designer/architect.

Plan #321050

Dimensions: 49' W x 42' D

Levels: 2

Square Footage: 2,336

Main Level Sq. Ft.: 1,291

Upper Level Sq. Ft.: 1,045

Bedrooms: 4

Bathrooms: 2½

Foundation: Basement

Materials List Available: Yes

Price Category: E

Images provided by designer/architect.

This traditional-looking home has an interior filled with up-to-date design elements and amenities.

Features:

- **Family Room:** The spacious family room is lit by a wall of windows punctuated by a handsome fireplace.

- **Living Room:** The vaulted ceiling emphasizes the sunken floor in this spacious room.

- **Dining Room:** Convenient to the kitchen, this room is also isolated enough for formal parties.

- **Kitchen:** The L-shaped work area and center island make this room an efficient work space.

- **Breakfast Room:** You'll find a doorway to the backyard in the bayed area of this friendly, comfortable room.

- **Master Suite:** The bedroom has a vaulted ceiling and two walk-in closets, and the bath has a tub, two vanities, and a separate shower.

Main Level Floor Plan

Upper Level Floor Plan

Copyright by designer/architect.

Plan #111006

Dimensions: 56' W x 67' D
Levels: 1
Square Footage: 2,241
Bedrooms: 4
Bathrooms: 2½
Foundation: Slab
Materials List Available: No
Price Category: E

Images provided by designer/architect.

You'll love this plan if you're looking for a home with fantastic curb appeal on the outside and comfortable amenities on the inside.

Features:

- **Foyer:** This lovely foyer opens to both the living and dining rooms.

- **Dining Room:** Three columns in this room accentuate both its large dimensions and its slightly formal air.

- **Living Room:** This room gives an airy feeling, and the fireplace here makes it especially inviting when the weather's cool.

- **Kitchen:** This G-shaped kitchen is designed to save steps while you're working, and the ample counter area adds even more to its convenience. The breakfast bar is a great gathering area.

- **Master Suite:** Two walk-in closets provide storage space, and the bath includes separate vanities, a standing shower, and a deluxe corner bathtub.

Front Elevation

Copyright by designer/architect.

Two-Car Garage 21'3"x 23'9"

Porch

Master Bath

WIC   WIC

Utility

1/2 Bath

Master Bedroom 19'1"x 14'1"

Living 22'6"x 16'6"

Bath

Breakfast 12'3"x 10'9"

Bedroom 11'1"x 11'1"

Kitchen 12'3"x 11'11"

Dining 12'5"x 13'7"

Foyer

Porch

Bedroom 11'3"x 11'1"

Bedroom 11'1"x 12'1"

Plan #161108

Dimensions: 57'6" W x 50'6" D
Levels: 2
Square Footage: 2,500
Main Level Sq. Ft.: 1,787
Upper Level Sq. Ft.: 713
Bedrooms: 4
Bathrooms: 2½
Foundation: Crawl space, slab, or basement; walkout for fee
Material List Available: *Yes*
Price Category: E

The brick and stone add a unique contrast to this house.

CAD FILE AVAILABLE · CAD

Images provided by designer/architect.

Features:

- Great Room: This gathering area has a tray ceiling at over 12 ft. tall and a cozy fireplace. It is open to the breakfast room, allowing for casual entertaining.

- Dining Room: This formal room is just off the foyer and features a 9-ft.-high ceiling.

- Master Suite: Located on the main level for privacy, this private retreat has a tray ceiling in the sleeping area. The master bath boasts a large tub, dual vanities, and a walk-in closet.

- Upper Level: This level is where you'll find the three secondary bedrooms. Each has ample space, and they share the full bathroom.

Rear Elevation

Main Level Floor Plan

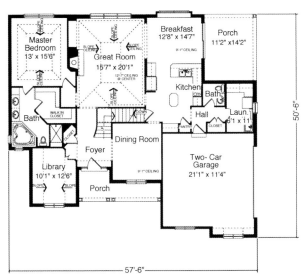

Upper Level Floor Plan

Copyright by designer/architect.

Plan #201061

Dimensions: 64'10" W x 54'10" D

Levels: 1

Square Footage: 2,387

Bedrooms: 4

Bathrooms: 2½

Foundation: Crawl space, slab

Materials List Available: Yes

Price Category: E

Images provided by designer/architect.

The classic good looks of the exterior hint at the clean lines you'll find on the interior of this home.

Features:

- **Den:** You're sure to love the decorative ceiling, fireplace flanked by cabinets and shelves, and windowed wall with doors that open to the porch.

- **Porch:** Running the length of the den, the rear porch is an ideal place for summer entertaining.

- **Dining Room:** Arched windows let light pour into this room, with its boxed column entryway.

- **Eating Nook:** You'll love the large windows, which let light pour into this sizable family eating nook.

- **Kitchen:** A long, U-shaped counter helps to make this kitchen layout an efficient place to work. Use one side of the counter as a snack bar, too.

- **Master Suite:** The large bedroom features a decorative ceiling, and the bath includes a walk-in closet, two vanities, tub, and separate shower.

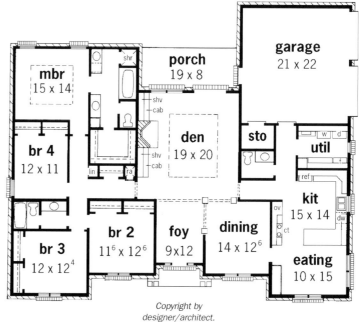

Copyright by designer/architect.

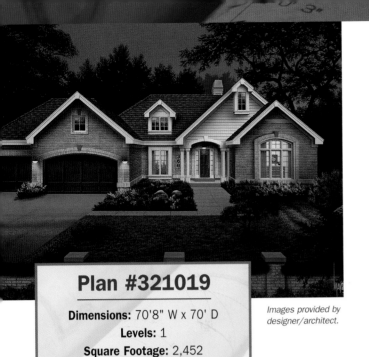

Plan #321019

Dimensions: 70'8" W x 70' D

Levels: 1

Square Footage: 2,452

Bedrooms: 4

Bathrooms: 2½

Foundation: Basement

Materials List Available: Yes

Price Category: E

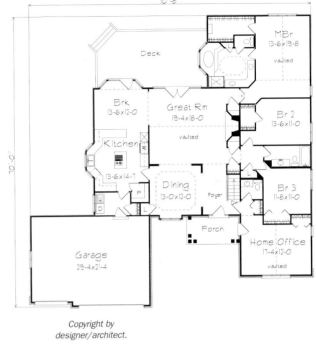

Images provided by designer/architect.

Copyright by designer/architect.

Plan #121095

Dimensions: 65'4" W x 48'8" D

Levels: 2

Square Footage: 2,282

Main Level Sq. Ft.: 1,597

Upper Level Sq. Ft.: 685

Bedrooms: 4

Bathrooms: 2½

Foundation: Basement

Materials List Available: Yes

Price Category: E

Images provided by designer/architect.

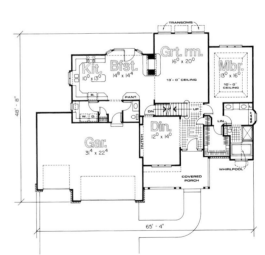

Main Level Floor Plan

Upper Level Floor Plan

Copyright by designer/architect.

Stone Materials and Patterns

Building with stone can be both the hardest and most satisfying project a homeowner can undertake. You need to be in good physical condition and lift stones carefully to protect your back. There's no hurry. After all, you are building something that will stand for a long time.

Choosing Stone

Although many types of stone are available throughout the country, only a few are suitable for building. Besides being accessible, suitable stones must satisfy certain requirements of strength, hardness, workability, and durability.

Rubble wall construction has stones that are irregular in size and shape. Fieldstone is one type of rubble, while quarried rubble comes from fragments left over after stonecutting. Random rubble walls are usually dry-laid but can also be mortared.

Coursed rubble walls have a neater appearance than random rubble walls but are more difficult to construct and require a large selection of stone. Rubble stones can also be roughly squared with a brick hammer to fit more easily. Coursed rubble walls can be used for foundations as well as garden and retaining walls.

Mosaic is a tighter version of a random rubble wall. Large and smaller stones are fitted together tightly. To ensure that all of the pieces fit without large gaps, the stones are first laid out on the ground, face down, and test-fitted in the order in which they will be installed.

Ashlar is quarry cut to produce smooth, flat bedding surfaces that stack easily. It is generally cut into small rectangles with sawed or dressed faces. Ashlar patterns are not really random, and as with brick, a variety of bond pattern are used: coursed, random, and combination.

Coursed ashlar has a formal appearance and requires precisely cut stone. Ashlar mortar joints are sometimes used as a decorative element in the overall pattern. They may be colored to complement the stone, raked concave like block joints, or filled and dressed to stand out from the face of the wall.

The following article was reprinted from *Ultimate Guide to Masonry and Concrete* (Creative Homeowner 2006).

Stone Patterns

Random Rubble

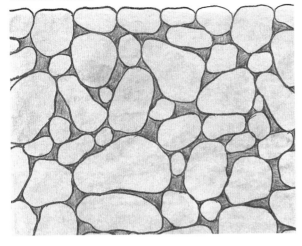

Coursed Ashlar

Coursed Rubble

Random Ashlar

Mosaic Rubble

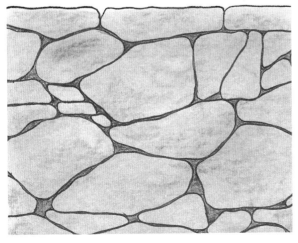

Combination Ashlar

Estimating Materials

To estimate how many cubic yards of stone you will need, multiply the length of your wall times the height times the width in feet to get cubic feet, and divide by 27 to get cubic yards. If you are using ashlar stone, add about 10 percent to your order for breakage and waste. If you are using rubble stone, add at least 25 percent. Waste depends a lot on how you plan the layout.

To estimate flagstone for a patio or walk, figure the square footage by multiplying the length times the width. The stone supplier will be able to tell you how much stone you will need based on this figure.

Special Stone Tools

For cutting and shaping stone, you'll need a small sledgehammer that is tempered to strike metal tools safely. A compact, short-handled 2-pound hammer works well. A brick hammer is helpful for chipping off small pieces of rock. A stonemason's hammer is similar to a brick hammer but heavier with a broader edge. A rubber mallet is used to seat flagstones in sand. Stone chisels, available with differently shaped heads, are used to break stones. To lay out stone walls, patios, or walks you'll need wood stakes, mason's twine, and a spade.

Planning can produce interlocked walls where stones form part of the face and the top at the same time.

order direct: 1-800-523-6789

Common Types of Building Stone

Bluestone: uniform and dense; used for caps and hearths.

Limestone: soft and workable in light grays and tans.

Rubble: irregular shapes, sizes, and colors of fieldstone.

Flagstone: quarried into paving slabs ½ to 2 in. thick.

Synthetic Stone: manufactured in regular widths.

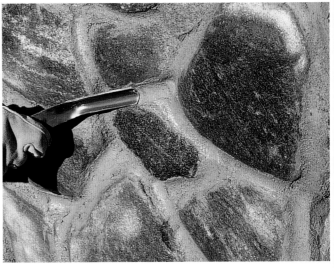

Cut Stone: real stone with one flat-cut side for facing.

Cutting and Shaping

Working with uniform sizes is one way to eliminate the toughest part of working with stone: cutting it. This is a job you want to do as little as possible because it is difficult, time consuming, and easy to get wrong with a hammer blow that breaks a stone in the wrong place.

If you use irregular shapes and sizes, some cutting and trimming will almost always be necessary. But you can minimize cutting with good planning and careful selection of compatible stones. It pays to make a complete dry layout of a flagstone walkway, for example, trying different combinations of shapes and sizes that nestle together with a minimum of trimming.

Cutting Stone

When you are laying stone in mortar, you often can hide slightly irregular shapes by burying them in the mortar joints. When you are dry-laying stones without mortar, the fit of the stones usually must be more precise both for aesthetics and stability. For both types of stonework though, you will often have to cut and shape individual stones to make them fit better. Whenever you are cutting stone, be sure to wear heavy leather gloves and safety goggles.

While granite is difficult to cut, limestone, sandstone, and slate are relatively easy to work with once you get the knack. First, position the stone on solid ground for firm, even support. Do not lay the stone on concrete because the hard concrete surface may cause the stone to break in the wrong place. The job will be easier (and safer) if you build a small sand box, as shown below. Even a shallow bed of sand can support irregular shapes while you score cut lines and break stones to fit your layout.

You can mark the cutting line with chalk, a pencil, or a scratch awl. Then use a hardened stone chisel to score the cut by positioning the blade of the chisel along the intended line and tapping lightly with a hammer.

You need to move the chisel along the scored line as you strike with a heavy hammer or mallet. In most cases, you'll need to cover the same ground again, setting the chisel in the groove and gradually making the score line deeper.

Sometimes a stone will break along the line before you have scored it all the way. This is a tricky part of the process. For some stones light hammer blows will score a line; for others, you'll need heavier blows.

Once the score line is complete, strike one sharp blow to break the stone. It helps to position the stone with the score line over a pipe or narrow strip of wood that serves as a fulcrum. Remove any small bumps or protrusions with a point chisel, placing the point at the base of the bump and tapping with the hammer.

Cutting Flagstone

1 **If you have many stones to trim,** build a small sand box in which you can nestle irregular stones.

2 **Score the stone** along your mark with a stone chisel, tapping firmly with a 2-lb. hammer.

Planning can produce interlocked walls where stones form part of the face and the top at the same time.

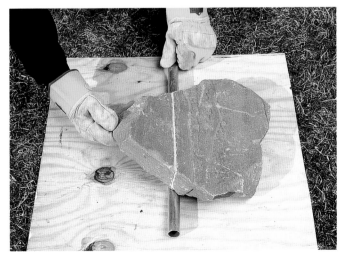

3 **After scoring the line several times,** insert a pipe or narrow board under the score line.

4 **The pipe provides a fulcrum** that helps the stone break cleanly when you strike it.

Maintenance and Repair

Properly laid on a solid footing, stone structures should last in definitely. They don't, due to the weak link—the mortar joints. Various stresses can cause small cracks and slight crumbling that are the skin-deep indicators of deeper problems to come, unless you repoint—the term for cleaning out and replacing deteriorated mortar joints.

Once mortar joints are cracked, water can seep in, which erodes the wall even more. In winter, of course, the water freezes up and causes much more damage.

You can check joints by eye and with a screwdriver to find sections that are loose or spongy. Don't worry about every hairline crack. The key is to have a sound foundation for new mortar—no matter how deep you have to dig to find it. In some areas you may need to pry out loose chunks that extend well under the stone.

To give new mortar a good bite in the wall, old joints should be excavated at least as deep as the joint is wide—preferably twice as deep. Once the joint is clean, simply pack in fresh mortar and smooth out its surface (a process called tooling), normally with a slight concave shape to match surrounding joints. During this process you may

Common Problems in Stone Walls

Stacked seams in several courses of stone create weak spots that often need repointing.

The lack of tie stones bridging the seam between a wall and a pillar creates a weak link and open seams.

Cracked concrete caps designed to shed water off a wall expose the joints underneath to erosion.

Mortar erosion in large joints causes heavy stones to settle, which can undermine a wall.

want to insert a small piece of stone to support any major stone that has settled due to the mortar erosion. You can also use small wooden wedges cut to just the right shape. Once the mortar sets up, simply remove them and fill in the small holes.

Different Cleaning Procedures

There are four basic ways to clean large expanses of stone: by sandblasting and by using chemicals, steam, or water.

All are big projects, generally for contractors.

■ **Sandblasting.** An abrasive sandblast treatment is the equivalent of sanding a wood floor. It takes away surface and embedded dirt—and often some of the masonry, too. You need to test the pressure and abrasion on any soft stone.

■ **Chemical cleaning.** Contractors can tailor a mix of chemicals according to job conditions— for example, to remove algae, oil, or other staining.

The structure may do better this way, but, in some cases, surrounding vegetation may not. Some mixes can require a lot of set up time to mask and protect plants, soil, and wood trim on buildings.

■ **Steam cleaning.** Steam can remove embedded dirt without the risks posed by sandblasting (because it's not abrasive) and chemical cleaning (because it's not caustic—merely burning hot).

■ **Water cleaning.** Combined with a cleaner, such as a mild solution of muri-

---

Repointing Cracked Stone Walls

TOOLS

■ **Hammer**

■ **Stone chisel**

■ **Trowel**

■ **Striking tool**

■ **Whiskbroom or brush**
   to clean joints

■ **Safety glasses and work gloves**

MATERIALS

■ **Mortar mix**

1 **Chip out loose mortar** using a 2-lb. hammer and stone chisel. Then brush the joints free of debris.

2 **Push fresh mortar** fully into the joints using a small pointed trowel, and compress the seams.

3 **Use a striking tool** (or the handle of any implement that fits) to firm and smooth the seams.

atic acid, washing and rinsing can clear surface dirt. You can also use a pressure-washer, testing first to be sure the spray does not erode the mortar joints.

Dealing with Stains

Stains from iron and steel hardware, such as shutter hinges, can be scrubbed away using oxalic acid and water.

(Always observe the label cautions of powerful cleaners.)

To deal with mold and mildew, use undiluted household bleach, which you can wash away with a scrub brush. Cutting the bleach with an equal amount of warm water should be strong enough to cure mild deposits over a larger area.

On older homes with roofs that have needed repairs, tar may have dripped through old leaks or gutter seams and lodged on the masonry below. Tar will clean up with a solvent such as benzene. But instead of using a solvent that may spread the stain, use a razor knife to cut away almost all of the deposit before cleaning. If an embedded stain remains, which is likely, make a soupy mix of benzene and a binder such as sawdust and pat it in place at least overnight. This mixture will draw out more of the stain.

Planning can produce interlocked walls where stones form part of the face and the top at the same time.

Cleaning Stone

Washing with water and a mild, over-the-counter solution of muriatic acid is effective on surface dirt and embedded mortar dust. You should always check the results ahead of time by cleaning a small section. Washing with very hard water may leave traces of mineral deposits. Masonry often has enough variation to camouflage minor discolorations.

Wash the wall, and let it dry before applying a clear sealer.

Four Keys to Building Strong Stone Walls

Maximum Number of staggered seams

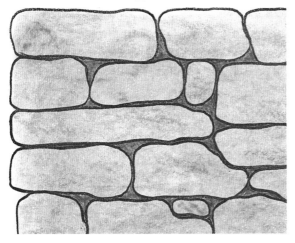

Interlocked corners in every course

Full mortar bed under cap stone

Deadman extension stones in retaining walls

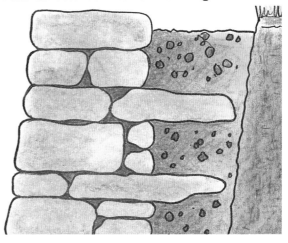

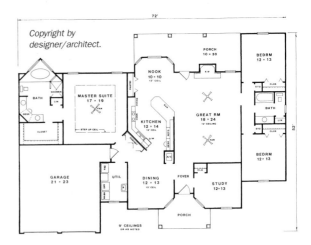

Copyright by
designer/architect.

Plan #171004

Dimensions: 72' W x 52' D

Levels: 1

Square Footage: 2,256

Bedrooms: 3

Bathrooms: 2

Foundation: Crawl space, slab

Materials List Available: Yes

Price Category: E

SMARTtip

Windows – Privacy

You can easily stencil a work of art onto a windowpane, perhaps only as a border around the edge. Choose or create a design that gives you as little or as much privacy and light control as you need. Use a ready-made stencil or a piece of openwork fabric such as lace, or mask a design onto the glass using tape and a razor knife. Then apply glass paint or frosted glass spray, referring to the instructions and guidelines that come with the product.

Plan #141031

Dimensions: 58'4" W x 30' D

Levels: 2

Square Footage: 2,367

Main Level Sq. Ft.: 1,025

Upper Level Sq. Ft.: 1,342

Bedrooms: 4

Bathrooms: 2½

Foundation: Basement

Materials List Available: No

Price Category: E

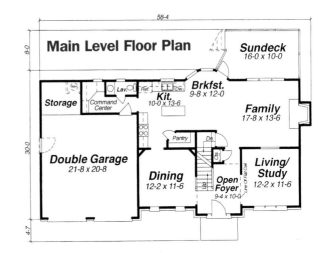

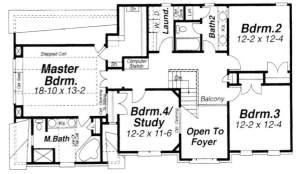

Copyright by
designer/architect.

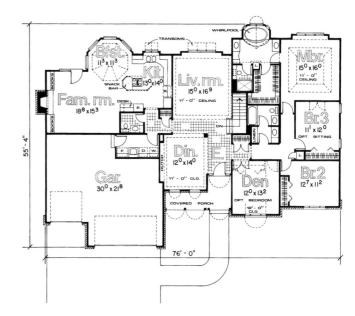

Plan #121003

Dimensions: 76' W x 55'4" D

Levels: 1

Square Footage: 2,498

Bedrooms: 4

Bathrooms: 2½

Foundation: Basement

Materials List Available: Yes

Price Category: E

Images provided by designer/architect.

CAD FILE AVAILABLE

Copyright by designer/architect.

Main Level Floor Plan

Plan #161039

Dimensions: 61' W x 41'8" D

Levels: 2

Square Footage: 2,320

Main Level Sq. Ft.: 1,595

Upper Level Sq. Ft.: 725

Bedrooms: 4

Bathrooms: 2½

Foundation: Basement

Materials List Available: Yes

Price Category: E

Images provided by designer/architect.

Upper Level Floor Plan

Copyright by designer/architect.

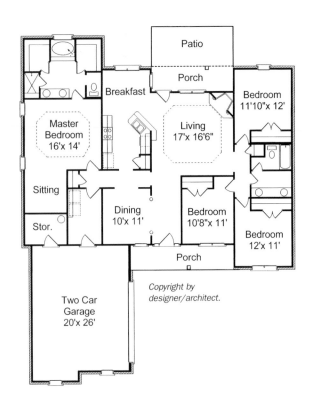

Images provided by designer/architect.

Copyright by designer/architect.

Plan #111015

Dimensions: 64' W x 58' D

Levels: 1

Square Footage: 2,208

Bedrooms: 4

Bathrooms: 2

Foundation: Slab

Materials List Available: No

Price Category: E

Images provided by designer/architect.

Rear View

Copyright by designer/architect.

Plan #111016

Dimensions: 72' W x 76' D

Levels: 1

Square Footage: 2,240

Bedrooms: 3

Bathrooms: 2½

Foundation: Basement

Materials List Available: No

Price Category: E

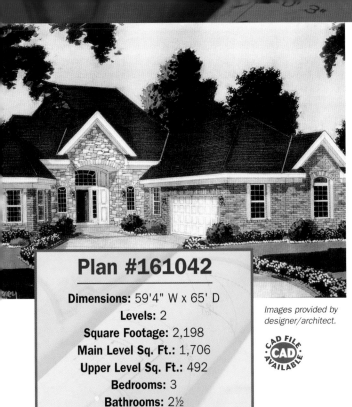

Plan #161042

Dimensions: 59'4" W x 65' D
Levels: 2
Square Footage: 2,198
Main Level Sq. Ft.: 1,706
Upper Level Sq. Ft.: 492
Bedrooms: 3
Bathrooms: 2½
Foundation: Basement
Materials List Available: Yes
Price Category: D

Images provided by designer/architect.

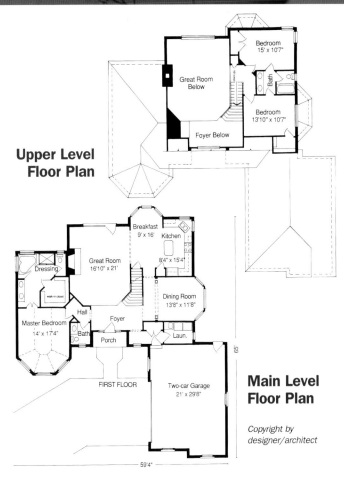

Upper Level Floor Plan

Main Level Floor Plan

Copyright by designer/architect

Plan #211010

Dimensions: 81' W x 84' D
Levels: 1
Square Footage: 2,503
Bedrooms: 3
Bathrooms: 2½
Foundation: Slab
Materials List Available: Yes
Price Category: E

Images provided by designer/architect.

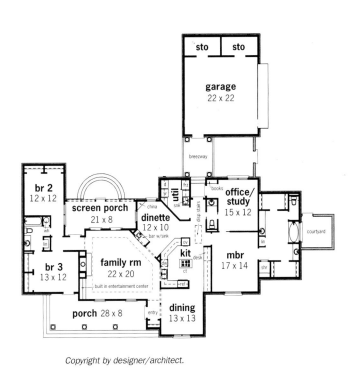

Copyright by designer/architect.

WOOD DECK
22-3 x 22-8

DINETTE
VAULTED CLG
14-6 x 10-2

WALL ABOVE

GREAT RM
20-6 x 15-4
VAULTED CLG

DW

KITCHEN
13-6 x 11-0

OV

WORK ISLAND

3 CAR GARAGE
23-6 x 33-4

WALL ABV

Main Level Floor Plan

PANTRY

SHWR

BATH 3

BENCH ENTRY

REFR

FRZR

CLOS

LANDING

UP
DN

BUILT IN SHLVS

WINDOW SEAT

FOYER

OFFICE
11-0 x 13-6
BUILT IN SHLVS

PORCH

BEDRM 4
11-4 x 11-0

Images provided by designer/architect.

GREAT ROOM BELOW
VAULTED CLG

M BEDRM
TRAY CLG
17-0 x 15-4

M BATH

Upper Level Floor Plan

Copyright by designer/architect.

HALL

DN

BALC

BATH 2

LIN

W.I.C.

LND

W.I.C.

STORAGE

BEDRM 2
11-0 x 13-6

BEDRM 3
10-9 x 12-0

Plan #261008

Dimensions: 68' W x 64'6" D

Levels: 2

Square Footage: 2,226

Main Level Sq. Ft.: 1,689

Upper Level Sq. Ft.: 537

Bedrooms: 4

Bathrooms: 3

Foundation: Basement

Materials List Available: No

Price Category: E

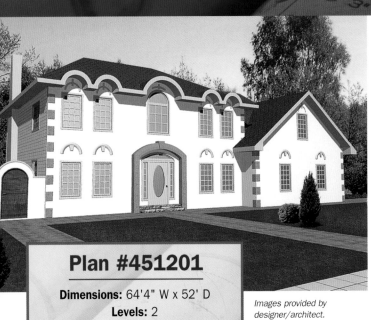

OPEN DECK
33-4 x 12-0

NOOK
11-2 x 11-10

KITCHEN
16-10 x 15-2

LIVING ROOM
20-2 x 20-4

OVEN PROBE

BARREL VAULT

3-CAR GARAGE
23-2 x 31-2

DEN
11-0 x 14-0

DINING
13-10 x 13-6

FOYER
10-6 x 14-0

Main Level Floor Plan

Images provided by designer/architect.

CAD FILE AVAILABLE CAD

Copyright by designer/architect.

COVERED PORCH

M. BATH
4-10 x 13-2

SITTING
10-10 x 15-0

MASTER SUITE
13-8 x 20-0

DOWN

OPEN TO BELOW

W-I-C
11-0 x 14

W-I-C
9 x 13

BDRM. #2
12-0 x 14-0

Upper Level Floor Plan

Plan #451201

Dimensions: 64'4" W x 52' D

Levels: 2

Square Footage: 2,800

Main Level Sq. Ft.: 1,466

Upper Level Sq. Ft.: 1,334

Bedrooms: 2

Bathrooms: 2 full, 2 half

Foundation: Crawl space

Material List Available: No

Price Category: F

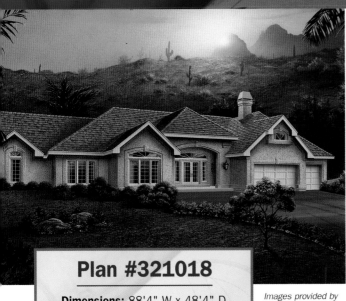

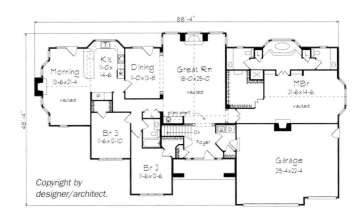

Copyright by designer/architect.

Plan #321018

Dimensions: 88'4" W x 48'4" D
Levels: 1
Square Footage: 2,523
Bedrooms: 3
Bathrooms: 2
Foundation: Basement
Materials List Available: Yes
Price Category: E

Images provided by designer/architect.

Main Level Floor Plan

Plan #161017

Dimensions: 61' W x 37'6" D
Levels: 2
Square Footage: 2,653
Main Level Sq. Ft.: 1,365
Upper Level Sq. Ft.: 1,288
Bedrooms: 4
Bathrooms: 2½
Foundation: Basement
Materials List Available: Yes
Price Category: F

Images provided by designer/architect.

CAD FILE AVAILABLE

Upper Level Floor Plan

Copyright by designer/architect.

Plan #151384

Dimensions: 76'8" W x 77'7" D
Levels: 1.5
Square Footage: 2,742
Bedrooms: 3
Bathrooms: 2½
Foundation: Crawl space or slab
CompleteCost List Available: Yes
Price Category: F

With its fine detailing, this is a home created for the ages.

Features:

- **Great Room:** A fireplace nicely settled between built-ins punctuates this enormous room.

- **Hobby Room:** This oversized room offers space galore for those do-it-yourself home projects.

- **Master Suite:** This elaborate suite presents an entire wall of built-ins, along with an angled private entrance to the porch.

- **Bedrooms:** The two secondary bedrooms are located on the opposite side of the home from the master suite and share the full bathroom adjacent to Bedroom 2.

Bonus Area Floor Plan

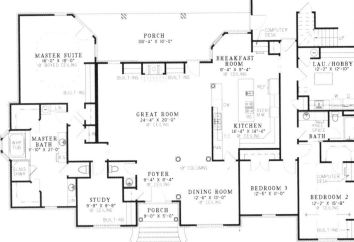

Front View

Images provided by designer/architect.

Plan #441036

Dimensions: 60' W x 50' D
Levels: 2
Square Footage: 2,902
Main Level Sq. Ft.: 1,617
Upper Level Sq. Ft.: 1,285
Bedrooms: 3
Bathrooms: 2½
Foundation: Crawl space
Materials List Available: No
Price Category: F

Features:

- Great Room: Come in and relax in this room, with its media center and fireplace. Look onto the backyard through the large windows.

- Kitchen: This kitchen is wonderfully appointed, containing an island cooktop, walk-in pantry, built-in desk, and corner sink. The laundry room is nearby.

- Master Suite: This suite is especially noteworthy, opening from double doors and boasting a walk-in closet and a bath with a spa tub, separate shower, double vanities, and compartmented toilet.

- Bedrooms: Two additional bedrooms share the upper level with the master suite. Both bedrooms have large closets and share a Jack-and-Jill bathroom.

It's a natural: a two-story traditional with board-and-batten siding, cedar shingles, stone detail at the foundation and Craftsman-inspired porch columns.

CAD FILE AVAILABLE CAD

Main Level Floor Plan

Upper Level Floor Plan

Copyright by designer/architect.

Plan #321051

Dimensions: 69'8" W x 46' D

Levels: 2

Square Footage: 2,624

Main Level Sq. Ft.: 1,774

Upper Level Sq. Ft.: 850

Bedrooms: 4

Bathrooms: 2½

Foundation: Basement

Materials List Available: Yes

Price Category: F

The dramatic exterior design allows natural light to flow into the spacious living area of this home.

Features:

- **Entry:** This two-story area opens into the dining room through a classic colonnade.

- **Dining Room:** A large bay window, stately columns, and doorway to the kitchen make this room both beautiful and convenient.

- **Great Room:** Enjoy light from the fireplace or the three Palladian windows in the 18-ft. ceiling.

- **Kitchen:** The step-saving design features a walk-in pantry as well as good counter space.

- **Breakfast Room:** You'll love the light that flows through the windows flanking the back door.

- **Master Suite:** The vaulted ceiling and bayed areas in both the bed and bath add elegance. You'll love the two walk-in closets and bath with a sunken tub, two vanities, and separate shower.

This home, as shown in the photograph, may differ from the actual blueprints. For more detailed information, please check the floor plans carefully.   *Images provided by designer/architect.*

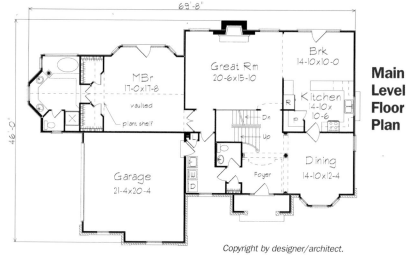

Main Level Floor Plan

Copyright by designer/architect.

Master Bath

Upper Level Floor Plan

Plan #151063

Dimensions: 64' W x 60'2" D

Levels: 1

Square Footage: 2,554

Bedrooms: 4

Bathrooms: 2½

Foundation: Crawl space or slab; basement or walkout for a fee

CompleteCost List Available: Yes

Price Category: D

This home, as shown in the photograph, may differ from the actual blueprints. For more detailed information, please check the floor plans carefully.

Images provided by designer/architect.

This home boasts a beautiful arched entry on the covered porch.

Features:

- Dining Room: Set off by columns, this room will impress your dinner guests. The triple window gives a front-yard view while allowing natural light into the space.

- Entertaining: Your family and friends will love to gather in the hearth room and the great room, which share a see-through fire place. The hearth room has access to the grilling porch for outdoor entertaining.

- Kitchen: Centrally located, this island kitchen is open to the dining room in the front and the hearth room in the rear. It features a raised bar into the hearth room.

- Master Suite: This secluded retreat resides on the opposite side of the home from the secondary bedrooms. The large master bath features a whirlpool tub, two walk-in closets, and dual vanities.

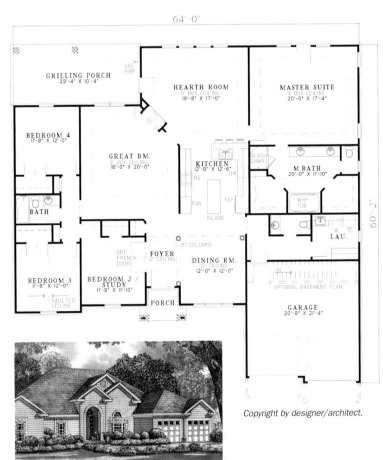

Copyright by designer/architect.

Rear View

Plan #151537

Dimensions: 70'2" W x 53'4" D

Levels: 2

Square Footage: 2,603

Main Level Sq. Ft.: 1,813

Upper Level Sq. Ft.: 790

Bedrooms: 4

Bathrooms: 2½

Foundation: Crawl space or slab

CompleteCost List Available: Yes

Price Category: F

Eye-catching covered porches and columns are used on both the front and rear of this traditional home.

Features:

- **Great Room:** A vaulted ceiling, balcony, and built-in media center enhance this great room, which is open to the kitchen and breakfast room.

- **Kitchen:** This large kitchen, with a raised bar, has an abundance of cabinets and a walk-in pantry.

- **Master Suite:** This suite and an additional bedroom or study are located on the main level for privacy and convenience.

- **Upper Level:** The upstairs has a balcony overlooking the great room. In addition, it has two bedrooms, a full bathroom, a built-in computer nook, and a large bonus room.

Main Level Floor Plan

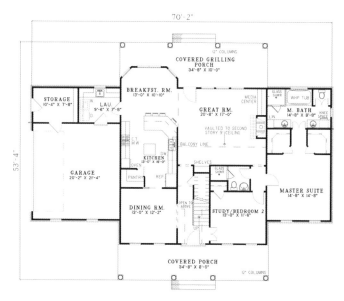

Upper Level Floor Plan

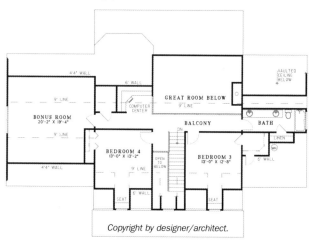

Copyright by designer/architect.

Plan #441042

Dimensions: 52' W x 45' D

Levels: 2

Square Footage: 2,538

Main Level Sq. Ft.: 1,342

Upper Level Sq. Ft.: 1,196

Bedrooms: 3

Bathrooms: 2½

Foundation: Crawl space; slab or basement available for fee

Materials List Available: No

Price Category: E

Images provided by designer/architect.

It's never too late to have a happy childhood—or the exact home you want.

CAD FILE AVAILABLE

Features:

- Foyer: This entry soars up two stories with a view to the open hallway above.

- Family Room: This large informal gathering area has large windows with a view to the backyard. It also has a two-sided fireplace, which it shares with the den.

- Kitchen: This fully equipped island kitchen has a built-in pantry and desk. The nook and family room are open to it.

- Master Suite: This private retreat includes a sitting area in the master bedroom that

provides ample space for a comfortable lounge in front of its fireplace. The master bath features a compartmentalized lavatory, spa tub, large shower, and his and her vanities.

- Bedrooms: The two additional bedrooms are located on the upper level with the master suite. Both rooms have large closets and share a common bathroom.

Rear Elevation

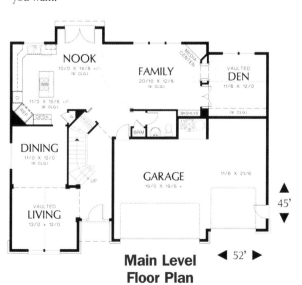

Main Level Floor Plan

◄ 52' ►

Upper Level Floor Plan

Copyright by designer/architect.

Plan #401023

Dimensions: 76' W x 63'4" D
Levels: 1
Square Footage: 2,806
Bedrooms: 3
Bathrooms: 2½
Foundation: Basement, walkout
Materials List Available: Yes
Price Category: F

Images provided by designer/architect.

The lower level of this magnificent home includes unfinished space that could have a future as a den and a family room with a fireplace. This level could also house extra bedrooms or an in-law suite.

CAD FILE AVAILABLE

Features:

- **Foyer:** On the main level, this foyer spills into a tray ceiling living room with a fireplace and an arched, floor-to-ceiling window wall.

- **Family Room:** Up from the foyer, a hall introduces this vaulted room with built-in media center and French doors that open to an expansive railed deck.

- **Kitchen:** Featured in this gourmet kitchen are a food-preparation island with a salad sink, double-door pantry, corner-window sink, and breakfast bay.

- **Master Bedroom:** The vaulted master bedroom opens to the deck, and the deluxe bath offers a raised whirlpool spa and a double-bowl vanity under a skylight.

- **Bedroom:** Two family bedrooms share a compartmented bathroom.

Foyer

Master Bathroom

Rear Elevation

Right Side Elevation

Left Side Elevation

Rear View

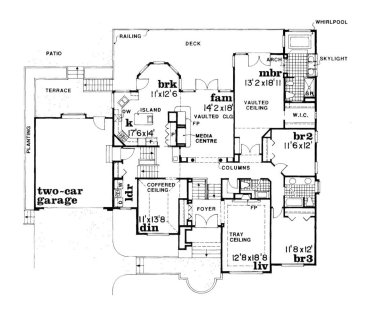

Copyright by designer/architect.

Optional Floor Plan

Front View

Master Bedroom

Kitchen

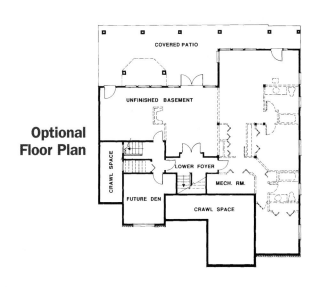

Kitchen

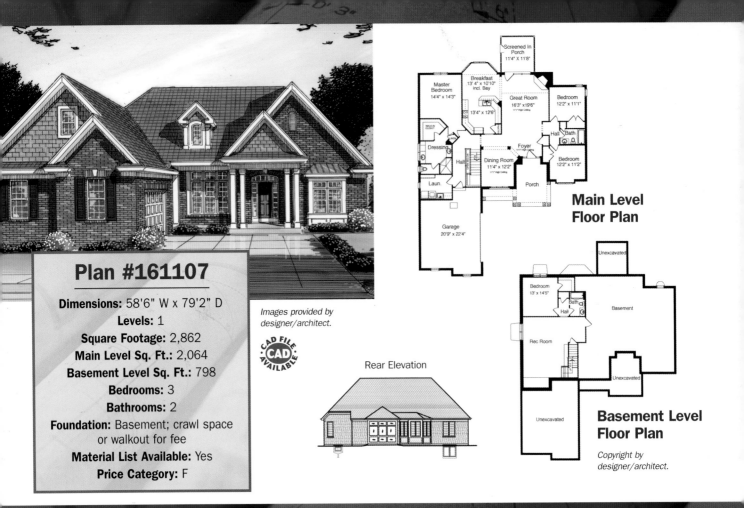

Plan #161107

Dimensions: 58'6" W x 79'2" D

Levels: 1

Square Footage: 2,862

Main Level Sq. Ft.: 2,064

Basement Level Sq. Ft.: 798

Bedrooms: 3

Bathrooms: 2

Foundation: Basement; crawl space or walkout for fee

Material List Available: Yes

Price Category: F

Images provided by designer/architect.

CAD FILE AVAILABLE

Rear Elevation

Main Level Floor Plan

Basement Level Floor Plan

Copyright by designer/architect.

Plan #181064

Dimensions: 91'4" W x 40'8" D

Levels: 2

Square Footage: 2,802

Main Level Sq. Ft.: 2,219

Upper Level Sq. Ft.: 583

Bedrooms: 4

Bathrooms: 2½

Foundation: Crawl space

Materials List Available: Yes

Price Category: F

Images provided by designer/architect.

CAD FILE AVAILABLE

Upper Level Floor Plan

Copyright by designer/architect.

Main Level Floor Plan

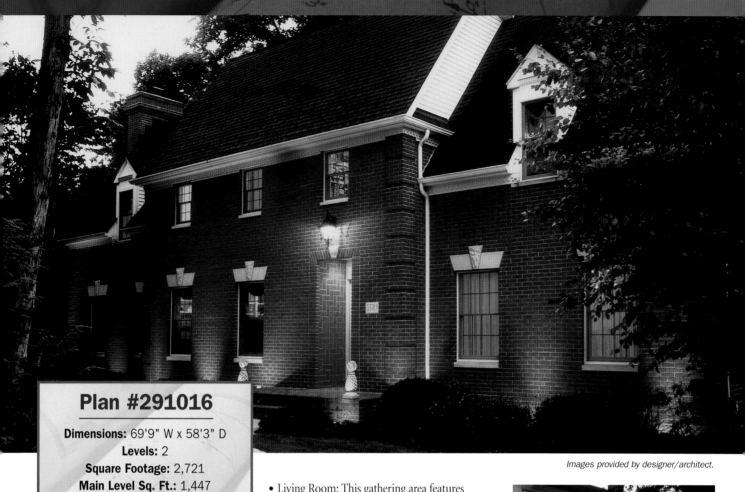

Plan #291016

Dimensions: 69'9" W x 58'3" D
Levels: 2
Square Footage: 2,721
Main Level Sq. Ft.: 1,447
Upper Level Sq. Ft.: 1,274
Bedrooms: 3
Bathrooms: 2½
Foundation: Basement
Materials List Available: No
Price Category: F

Images provided by designer/architect.

This fine example of Greek revival architecture begs to be visited!

Features:

- Entry: This area is the central hub of the home, with access to the kitchen, dining room, office, and upper level. There are two coat closets here.

- Living Room: This gathering area features a cozy fireplace and has access to the rear sunroom.

- Kitchen: Generous in size, this family-oriented kitchen has an informal dining area and a morning room that has access to the rear deck.

- Upper Level: Located upstairs are two secondary bedrooms that share the hall bathroom. The master suite, also on this level, features a private bath and a large walk-in closet.

Rear View

Upper Level Floor Plan

Main Level Floor Plan

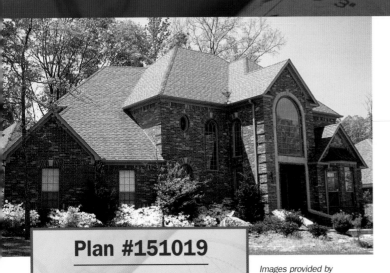

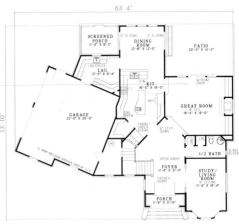

Main Level Floor Plan

Plan #151019

Dimensions: 63'4" W x 53'10" D

Levels: 2

Square Footage: 2,947

Main Level Sq. Ft.: 1,407

Upper Level Sq. Ft.: 1,540

Bedrooms: 3

Bathrooms: 2½

Foundation: Crawl space, slab; optional full basement plan available for extra fee

CompleteCost List Available: Yes

Price Category: F

Images provided by designer/architect.

CAD FILE AVAILABLE

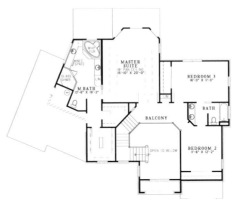

Upper Level Floor Plan

Copyright by designer/architect.

Copyright by designer/architect.

Plan #151057

Dimensions: 73'6" W x 80'6" D

Levels: 1

Square Footage: 2,951

Bedrooms: 4

Bathrooms: 3

Foundation: Crawl space, slab, or basement

CompleteCost List Available: Yes

Price Category: F

Images provided by designer/architect.

CAD FILE AVAILABLE

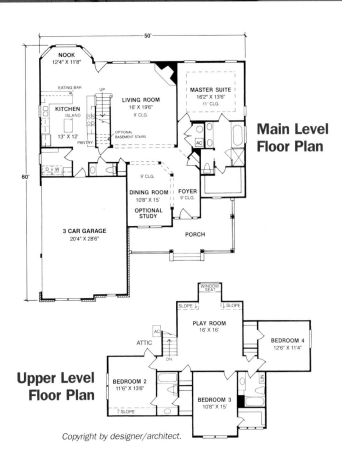

**Main Level
Floor Plan**

- NOOK 12'4" X 11'8"
- EATING BAR
- KITCHEN 13" X 12'
- UP
- PANTRY
- OPTIONAL BASEMENT STAIRS
- LIVING ROOM 16' X 19'6" 9' CLG.
- MASTER SUITE 16'2" X 13'6" 11' CLG.
- AC
- 9' CLG.
- DINING ROOM 10'8" X 15'
- FOYER 9' CLG.
- OPTIONAL STUDY
- PORCH
- 3 CAR GARAGE 20'4" X 28'6"
- D W

**Upper Level
Floor Plan**

- WINDOW SEAT
- SLOPE
- SLOPE
- PLAY ROOM 16' X 16'
- ATTIC
- AC
- DN
- BEDROOM 4 12'6" X 11'4"
- BEDROOM 2 11'6" X 13'6"
- BEDROOM 3 10'8" X 15'
- SLOPE
- LIN

Copyright by designer/architect.

Plan #121079

Dimensions: 50' W x 60' D

Levels: 2

Square Footage: 2,688

Main Level Sq. Ft.: 1,650

Upper Level Sq. Ft.: 1,038

Bedrooms: 4

Bathrooms: 3½

Foundation: Slab

Materials List Available: Yes

Price Category: F

Images provided by designer/architect.

This home, as shown in the photograph, may differ from the actual blueprints. For more detailed information, please check the floor plans carefully.

CAD FILE AVAILABLE

Plan #361061

Dimensions: 77'1" W x 80'8" D

Levels: 2

Square Footage: 2,979

Main Level Sq. Ft.: 2,375

Upper Level Sq. Ft.: 604

Bedrooms: 3

Bathrooms: 3

Foundation: Crawl space

Material List Available: No

Price Category: F

Images provided by designer/architect.

CAD FILE AVAILABLE

Main Level Floor Plan

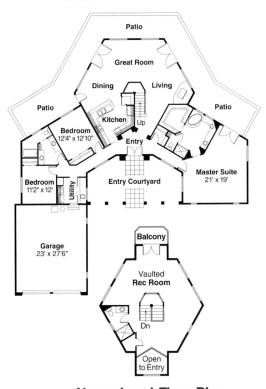

- Patio
- Great Room
- Dining
- Living
- Patio
- Patio
- Kitchen
- Up
- Bedroom 12'4" x 12'10"
- Entry
- Master Suite 21' x 19'
- Bedroom 11'2" x 12'
- Utility
- Entry Courtyard
- Garage 23' x 27'6"
- Balcony
- Vaulted Rec Room
- Dn
- Open to Entry

Upper Level Floor Plan

Copyright by designer/architect.

Plan #121067

Dimensions: 56' W x 59'4" D

Levels: 2

Square Footage: 2,708

Main Level Sq. Ft.: 1,860

Upper Level Sq. Ft.: 848

Bedrooms: 4

Bathrooms: 3½

Foundation: Basement

Materials List Available: Yes

Price Category: F

Images provided by designer/architect.

Upper Level Floor Plan

Main Level Floor Plan

Copyright by designer/architect.

Plan #321036

Dimensions: 78'4" W x 68'6" D

Levels: 1

Square Footage: 2,900

Bedrooms: 4

Bathrooms: 2½

Foundation: Basement

Materials List Available: No

Price Category: F

Images provided by designer/architect.

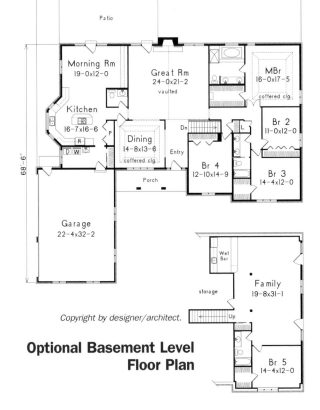

Copyright by designer/architect.

Optional Basement Level Floor Plan

Plan #161041

Dimensions: 63'4" W x 48' D
Levels: 2
Square Footage: 2,738
Main Level Sq. Ft.: 1,915
Upper Level Sq. Ft.: 823
Bedrooms: 4
Bathrooms: 3½
Foundation: Basement
Materials List Available: Yes
Price Category: F

Images provided by designer/architect.

This two-level European country home is perfect for a large family, and makes entertaining a pleasure.

Features:

• Great Room: From the foyer, view the dramatic great room with its high windows and fireplace. Open stairs with rich wood trim lead to the second floor. The balcony on the second floor draws the eye up to the vaulted ceiling and also gives an exciting bird's eye view for those looking down. You can enter the formal dining room from either the great room or the kitchen.

• Breakfast Room/Hearth Room: Appreciate these rooms as two cozy nooks or as one large space for entertaining.

• Master Bedroom: The master bedroom encourages pampering in its private sitting room with an 11-ft. ceiling and garden bath.

• Additional bedrooms: You'll find a bedroom with a private bath, and two others that share a bath on the second floor.

• Basement and Garage: A full basement and two-car garage add extra storage capabilities to this family-friendly home.

Rear Elevation

Upper Level Floor Plan

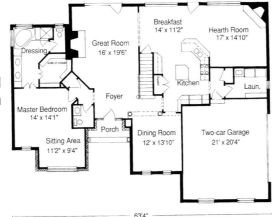

Main Level Floor Plan

Copyright by designer/architect.

Images provided by designer/architect.

Plan #151383

Dimensions: 70'4" W x 57'2" D
Levels: 1
Square Footage: 2,534
Bedrooms: 3
Bathrooms: 2
Foundation: Crawl space or slab
CompleteCost List Available: Yes
Price Category: E

The arched entry of the covered porch welcomes you to this magnificent home.

Features:

- Foyer: Welcome your guests in this warm foyer before leading them into the impressive dining room with magnificent columns framing the entry.

- Great Room: After dinner, your guests will enjoy conversation in this spacious room, complete with fireplace and built-ins.

- Study: Beautiful French doors open into this quiet space, where you'll be able to concentrate on that work away from the office.

- Rear Porch: This relaxing spot may be reached from the breakfast room or your secluded master suite.

Copyright by designer/architect.

Front View

Plan #451092

Dimensions: 100' W x 68'5" D

Levels: 1

Square Footage: 2,521

Bedrooms: 2

Bathrooms: 2½

Foundation: Walkout basement

Material List Available: No

Price Category: E

Images provided by designer/architect.

Main Level Floor Plan

Rear Elevation

Optional Basement Level Floor Plan

Copyright by designer/architect.

Plan #271080

Dimensions: 71' W x 83' D

Levels: 1

Square Footage: 2,581

Bedrooms: 3

Bathrooms: 3

Foundation: Basement

Materials List Available: Yes

Price Category: E

Images provided by designer/architect.

Copyright by designer/architect.

Main Level Floor Plan

BRK 11'-0" X 13'-6"

SUNROOM 20'-7" X 12'-4"

UTIL

GREAT ROOM 19'-1" X 16'-1"

MASTER BATH

CL.

LIN

EATING BAR

REAR ENTRY

1/2 BATH

KIT.

REF

DINING 10'-8" X 13'-0"

DOUBLE GARAGE 20'-1" X 21'-0"

MASTER SUITE 15'-1" X 16'-0"

HALL

CL.

LANDING

UP

STUDY 7'-8" X 9'-1"

FOYER

DROP CEILING

46'-0"

PORCH

68'-0"

Images provided by designer/architect.

BEDROOM 2 11'-2" X 16'-6"

BEDROOM 3 12'-9" X 12'-0"

BATH-3

LANDING DN

PLAYROOM 14'-0" X 15'-1"

SEAT

Upper Level Floor Plan

BATH 2

CL.

BALCONY

LANDING DN

CL.

BEDROOM 4 11'-0" X 11'-3"

CL.

SHOWER

SEAT

LIN

FOYER BELOW

LANDING

Copyright by designer/architect.

BALCONY

Plan #241013

Dimensions: 68' W x 46' D

Levels: 2

Square Footage: 2,779

Main Level Sq. Ft.: 1,918

Upper Level Sq. Ft.: 861

Bedrooms: 4

Bathrooms: 3½

Foundation: Crawl space, slab, basement or walkout

Materials List Available: No

Price Category: G

Images provided by designer/architect.

Rear Elevation

Patio

Porch

Bedroom 15'9" x 13'1"

Breakfast 13'5" x 11'7"

Master Bedroom 14'5" x 18'7"

Bath

Kitchen 13'9" x14'

Living 20' x 19'3"

WIC

Bedroom 12'1" x 13'1"

WIC

Dress

Utility

Dining 12'7" x 16'1"

Foyer

Master Bath

Storage 12'1" x 6'3"

Porch

Bedroom 14'7" x 13'1"

Copyright by designer/architect.

Two-Car Garage 21'3" x 22'3"

Plan #111018

Dimensions: 67' W x 79' D

Levels: 1

Square Footage: 2,745

Bedrooms: 4

Bathrooms: 3½

Foundation: Basement

Materials List Available: No

Price Category: F

Plan #171013

Dimensions: 74' W x 72' D

Levels: 1

Square Footage: 3,084

Bedrooms: 4

Bathrooms: 3½

Foundation: Crawl space or slab

Materials List Available: Yes

Price Category: G

Images provided by designer/architect.

Bonus Room

Copyright by designer/architect.

Future Rm

Copyright by designer/architect.

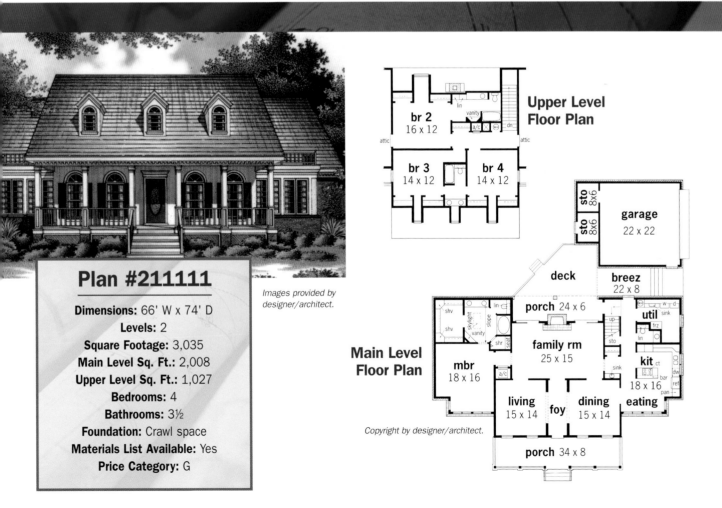

Plan #211111

Dimensions: 66' W x 74' D

Levels: 2

Square Footage: 3,035

Main Level Sq. Ft.: 2,008

Upper Level Sq. Ft.: 1,027

Bedrooms: 4

Bathrooms: 3½

Foundation: Crawl space

Materials List Available: Yes

Price Category: G

Images provided by designer/architect.

Copyright by designer/architect.

Plan #131050

Dimensions: 72'8" W x 47' D
Levels: 2
Square Footage: 2,874
Main Level Sq. Ft.: 2,146
Upper Level Sq. Ft.: 728
Bedrooms: 4
Bathrooms: 3
Foundation: Crawl space, slab, or basement
Materials List Available: Yes
Price Category: G

A gazebo and long covered porch at the entry let you know that this is a spectacular design.

Images provided by designer/architect.

Features:

- Foyer: This vaulted foyer divides the formal living room and dining room, setting the stage for guests to feel welcome in your home.
- Great Room: This large room is defined by several columns; a corner fireplace and vaulted ceiling add to its drama.
- Kitchen: An island work space separates this area from the bayed breakfast nook.
- Master Suite: You'll have privacy in this main-floor suite, which features two walk-in closets and a compartmented bath with a dual-sink vanity.
- Upper Level: The two large bedrooms share a bath and a dramatic balcony.
- Bonus Room: Walk down a few steps into this large bonus room over the 3-car garage.

Rear View

Main Level Floor Plan

Copyright by designer/architect.

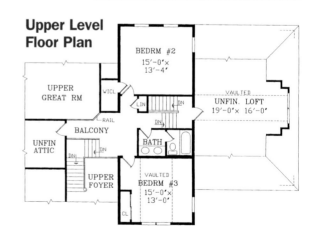

Upper Level Floor Plan

Plan #351072

Dimensions: 84' W x 54'6" D

Levels: 1

Square Footage: 2,601

Bedrooms: 4

Bathrooms: 3½

Foundation: Crawl space or slab

Material List Available: No

Price Category: F

Images provided by designer/architect.

This traditional Country home includes an open floor plan with a split-bedroom layout and other unique features.

Features:

• Porches: Large front and rear covered porches complement the livability of this home.

• Great Room: This expansive room features a vaulted ceiling and a gas log fireplace. There is access to the rear porch from this area.

• Kitchen: Fully equipped with a wraparound raised bar and walk-in pantry, this kitchen is made even more functional by the large adjoining laundry.

• Master Suite: This suite includes a raised ceiling in the master bedroom and two large walk-in closets. The master bath boasts a jetted tub and an oversized shower.

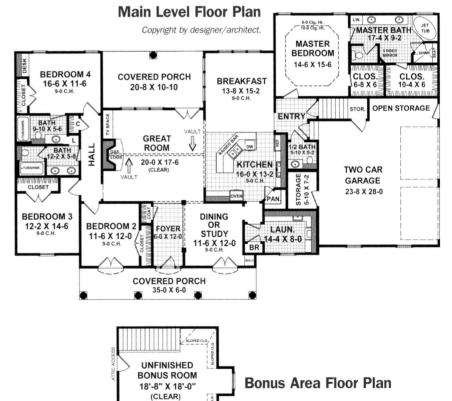

Main Level Floor Plan

Copyright by designer/architect.

Bonus Area Floor Plan

Plan #151015

Dimensions: 72'4" W x 48'4" D
Levels: 2
Square Footage: 2,789
Main Level Sq. Ft.: 1,977
Upper Level Sq. Ft.: 812
Bedrooms: 4
Bathrooms: 3
Foundation: Crawl space, slab, or basement
CompleteCost List Available: Yes
Price Category: F

Images provided by designer/architect.

The spacious kitchen that opens to the breakfast room and the hearth room make this family home ideal for entertaining.

Features:

- Great Room: The fireplace will make a cozy winter focal point in this versatile space.
- Hearth Room: Enjoy the built-in entertainment center, built-in shelving, and fireplace here.
- Dining Room: A swing door leading to the kitchen is as attractive as it is practical.
- Study: A private bath and walk-in closet make this room an ideal spot for guests when needed.
- Kitchen: An island work area, a computer desk, and an eat-in bar add convenience and utility.
- Master Bath: Two vanities, two walk-in closets, a shower with a seat, and a whirlpool tub highlight this private space.

Main Level Floor Plan

Copyright by designer/architect.

Upper Level Floor Plan

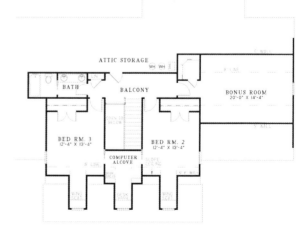

Plan #141022

Dimensions: 90' W x 93' D
Levels: 1
Square Footage: 2,911
Bedrooms: 3
Bathrooms: 2½
Foundation: Basement
Materials List Available: Yes
Price Category: F

Images provided by designer/architect.

Rear View

Second-floor dormers accent this charming country ranch, which features a gracious porch that spans its entire front. A detached garage, connected by a covered extension, creates an impressive, expansive effect.

Features:

- **Living Room:** As you enter the foyer, you are immediately drawn to this dramatic, bayed living room.

- **Study:** Flanking the foyer, this cozy study features built-in shelving and a direct-vent fireplace.

- **Kitchen:** From a massive, partially covered deck, a wall of glass floods this spacious kitchen, breakfast bay, and keeping room with light.

- **Master Suite:** Enjoy the complete privacy provided by this strategically located master suite.

- **Guest Quarters:** You can convert the bonus room, above the garage, into a guest apartment.

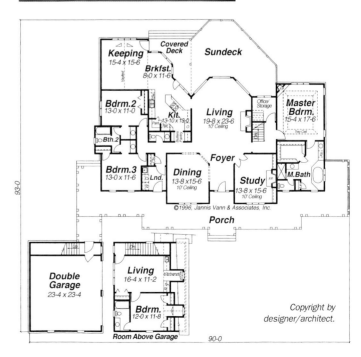

©1996, Jannis Vann & Associates, Inc.

Copyright by designer/architect.

Images provided by designer/architect.

Plan #321007

Dimensions: 76' W x 55'2" D

Levels: 1

Square Footage: 2,695

Bedrooms: 3

Bathrooms: 2½

Foundation: Basement

Materials List Available: Yes

Price Category: F

You'll love the way this spacious ranch reminds you of a French country home.

Features:

- **Foyer:** Come into this lovely home's foyer, and be greeted with a view of the gracious staircase and the great room just beyond.

- **Great Room:** Settle down by the cozy fireplace in cool weather, and reach for a book on the built-in shelves that surround it.

- **Kitchen:** Designed for efficient work patterns, this large kitchen is open to the great room.

- **Breakfast Room:** Just off the kitchen, this sunny room will be a family favorite all through the day.

- **Master Suite:** A bay window, walk-in closet, and shower built for two are highlights of this area.

- **Additional Bedrooms:** These large bedrooms both have walk-in closets and share a Jack-and-Jill bath for total convenience.

76'-0"

Copyright by designer/architect.

Patio

MBr
18-8x17-0

Br 2
14-0x14-1

Brk Rm
14-10x11-1

Great Room
18-6x23-0

Kit
15-2x11-4

MBath

Dn

Br 3
14-0x14-8

Entry

Dining
13-2x15-0

Garage
21-4x20-10

W
D

Porch

tray clg.

55'-2"

SMARTtip

Decorative Poles

Drapery poles are supported by the brackets fastened to the window frame or wall. The brackets that are provided with the poles generally coordinate and blend in with the pole finish. Brackets can be simple but also decorative. If you opt for a spectacular, attention-grabbing bracket, consider choosing less showy finials for the ends of the pole.

Images provided by designer/architect.

Plan #151593

Dimensions: 59'6" W x 64'2" D

Levels: 1.5

Square Footage: 2,542

Bonus (unfinished): 473

Bedrooms: 3

Bathrooms: 3

Foundation: Crawl space or slab

CompleteCost List Available: Yes

Price Category: E

This classic split-bedroom brick home invites guests in with vaulted ceilings in the front porch and foyer.

Features:

- Dining Room: This roomy formal room has a 12-ft.-high ceiling and a conveniently located butler's pantry.

- Great Room: In this room the fireplace warms guests while they enjoy the media center.

- Kitchen: This work space provides for all with an island and snack bar that opens to the breakfast room. Afternoon barbecues on the rear grilling porch will be a neighborhood favorite.

- Master Suite: Relax in this private suite, which has a bath with a corner whirlpool tub, split vanities, a separate shower, and a walk-in closet.

Copyright by designer/architect.

Bonus Area Floor Plan

Plan #121083

Dimensions: 72' W x 45'4" D
Levels: 2
Square Footage: 2,695
Main Level Sq. Ft.: 1,881
Upper Level Sq. Ft.: 814
Bedrooms: 4
Bathrooms: 3½
Foundation: Basement
Materials List Available: Yes
Price Category: F

Images provided by designer/architect.

You'll love this home for its soaring entryway ceiling and well-designed layout.

Features:

- Entry: A balcony from the upper level looks down into this two-story entry, which features a decorative plant shelf.
- Great Room: Comfort is guaranteed in this large room, with its built-in bookcases framing a lovely fireplace and trio of transom-topped windows along one wall.
- Living Room: Save both this formal room and the formal dining room, both of which flank the entry, for guests and special occasions.
- Kitchen: This convenient work space includes a gazebo-shaped breakfast area where friends and family will gather at any time of day.

Main Level Floor Plan

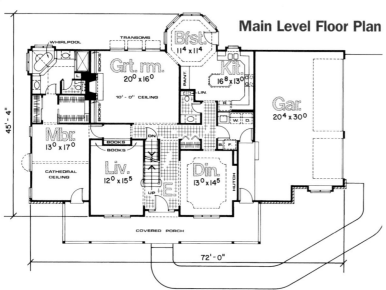

Upper Level Floor Plan

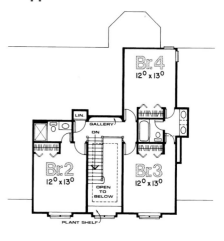

Copyright by designer/architect.

Plan #161112

Dimensions: 58'6" W x 41'6" D

Levels: 2

Square Footage: 2,896

Main Level Sq. Ft.: 1,483

Upper Level Sq. Ft.: 1,413

Bedrooms: 4

Bathrooms: 2½

Foundation: Basement

Material List Available: Yes

Price Category: D

Images provided by designer/architect.

Main Level Floor Plan

Upper Level Floor Plan

Copyright by designer/architect.

Rear Elevation

Plan #121061

Dimensions: 56' W x 52' D

Levels: 2

Square Footage: 3,025

Main Level Sq. Ft.: 1,583

Upper Level Sq. Ft.: 1,442

Bedrooms: 4

Bathrooms: 3½

Foundation: Basement

Materials List Available: Yes

Price Category: G

Images provided by designer/architect.

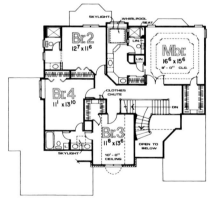

Upper Level Floor Plan

Main Level Floor Plan

Copyright by designer/architect.

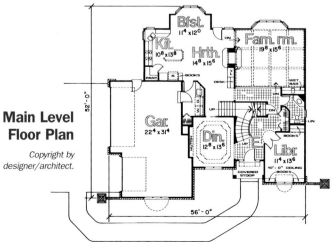

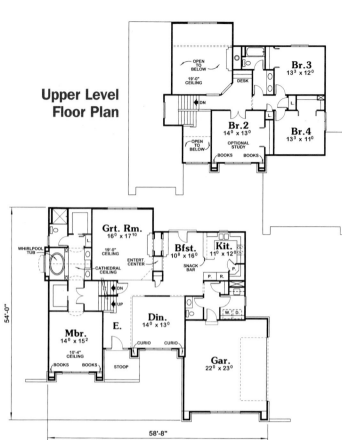

**Upper Level
Floor Plan**

**Main Level
Floor Plan**

*Copyright by
designer/architect.*

*Images provided by
designer/architect.*

Plan #121029

Dimensions: 58'8" W x 54' D

Levels: 2

Square Footage: 2,576

Main Level Sq. Ft.: 1,735

Upper Level Sq. Ft.: 841

Bedrooms: 4

Bathrooms: 2½

Foundation: Basement

Materials List Available: Yes

Price Category: E

**Main Level
Floor Plan**

*Copyright by
designer/architect.*

Upper Level Floor Plan

*Images provided by
designer/architect.*

Rear Elevation

Plan #161089

Dimensions: 64'2" W x 60'10" D

Levels: 2

Square Footage: 2,507

Main Level Sq. Ft.: 1,785

Upper Level Sq. Ft.: 722

Bedrooms: 4

Bathrooms: 2½

Foundation: Basement;
crawl space, slab or walkout for fee

Materials List Available: Yes

Price Category: E

Plan #121046

Dimensions: 65'3" W x 57'2" D
Levels: 2
Square Footage: 2,655
Main Level Sq. Ft.: 1,906
Upper Level Sq. Ft.: 749
Bedrooms: 4
Bathrooms: 2½
Foundation: Slab
Materials List Available: Yes
Price Category: F

Images provided by designer/architect.

CAD FILE AVAILABLE

Upper Level Floor Plan

Copyright by designer/architect.

Main Level Floor Plan

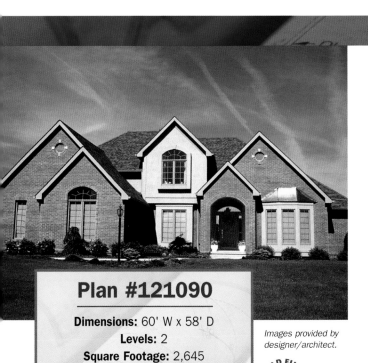

Plan #121090

Dimensions: 60' W x 58' D
Levels: 2
Square Footage: 2,645
Main Level Sq. Ft.: 1,972
Upper Level Sq. Ft.: 673
Bedrooms: 4
Bathrooms: 2½
Foundation: Basement
Materials List Available: Yes
Price Category: F

Images provided by designer/architect.

CAD FILE AVAILABLE

Main Level Floor Plan

Upper Level Floor Plan

Copyright by designer/architect.

Plan #121082

Dimensions: 68'8" W x 60' D

Levels: 2

Square Footage: 2,932

Main Level Sq. Ft.: 2,084

Upper Level Sq. Ft.: 848

Bedrooms: 4

Bathrooms: 3½

Foundation: Basement

Materials List Available: Yes

Price Category: F

Images provided by designer/architect.

Enjoy the spacious covered veranda that gives this house so much added charm.

Features:

• Great Room: A volume ceiling enhances the spacious feeling in this room, making it a natural gathering spot for friends and family. Transom-topped windows look onto the veranda, and French doors open to it.

• Den: French doors from the entry lead to this room, with its unusual ceiling detail, gracious fireplace, and transom-topped windows.

• Hearth Room: Three skylights punctuate the cathedral ceiling in this room, giving it an extra measure of light and warmth.

• Kitchen: This kitchen is a delight, thanks to its generous working and storage space.

Main Level Floor Plan

Upper Level Floor Plan

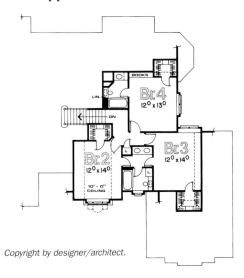

Copyright by designer/architect.

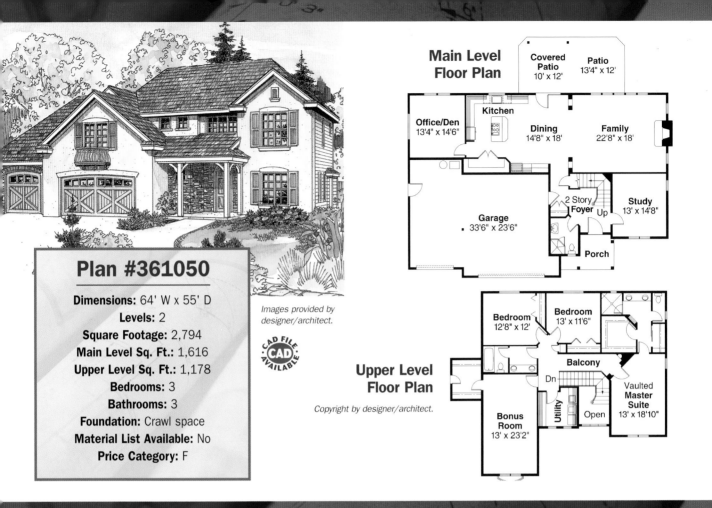

Main Level Floor Plan

Covered Patio 10' x 12'

Patio 13'4" x 12'

Office/Den 13'4" x 14'6"

Kitchen

Dining 14'8" x 18'

Family 22'8" x 18'

Garage 33'6" x 23'6"

2 Story Foyer Up

Study 13' x 14'8"

Porch

Upper Level Floor Plan

Copyright by designer/architect.

Bedroom 12'8" x 12'

Bedroom 13' x 11'6"

Balcony

Dn

Vaulted Master Suite 13' x 18'10"

Utility

Open

Bonus Room 13' x 23'2"

Images provided by designer/architect.

CAD FILE AVAILABLE

Plan #361050

Dimensions: 64' W x 55' D

Levels: 2

Square Footage: 2,794

Main Level Sq. Ft.: 1,616

Upper Level Sq. Ft.: 1,178

Bedrooms: 3

Bathrooms: 3

Foundation: Crawl space

Material List Available: No

Price Category: F

Plan #321017

Dimensions: 77' W x 36'8" D

Levels: 1

Square Footage: 2,531

Bedrooms: 1-4

Bathrooms: 1-2½

Foundation: Daylight basement

Materials List Available: Yes

Price Category: E

Images provided by designer/architect.

Main Level Floor Plan

Deck

Covered Deck

Dining 17-0x12-2 vaulted

Atrium open to below

Kit 10-6x 13-0

Great Rm 18-7x17-0 vaulted

MBr 13-0x16-8 vaulted

Garage 21-4x21-4

Porch 32-8x5-0

Br 4 12-6x11-8

Atrium Sunken

Br 2 12-6x11-8

up

Storage 16-7x12-10

Family Rm 18-6x16-2

Bar

Br 3 12-6x10-3

Optional Basement Level Floor Plan

Copyright by designer/architect.

Rear View

Main Level Floor Plan

Images provided by designer/architect.

Plan #121025

Dimensions: 60' W x 59'4" D

Levels: 2

Square Footage: 2,562

Main Level Sq. Ft.: 1,875

Upper Level Square Footage: 687

Bedrooms: 4

Bathrooms: 2½

Foundation: Basement

Materials List Available: Yes

Price Category: E

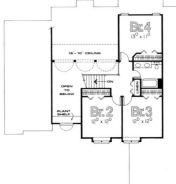

Upper Level Floor Plan

Copyright by designer/architect.

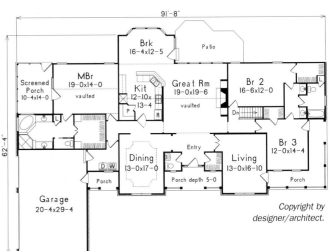

Copyright by designer/architect.

Plan #321004

Dimensions: 91'8" W x 62'4" D

Levels: 1

Square Footage: 2,808

Bedrooms: 3

Bathrooms: 2½

Foundation: Basement

Materials List Available: Yes

Price Category: F

Images provided by designer/architect.

SMARTtip

Ornaments in a Garden

Placement is everything with ornaments in a garden. Some elements are best sitting by themselves. Others are better when they are part of a cohesive whole, perhaps placed in the greenery at a corner or flanking a structure.

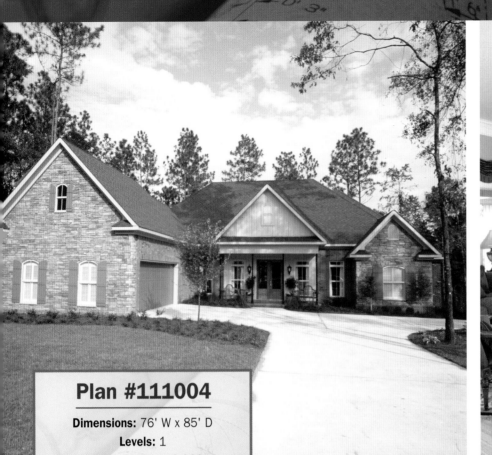

Images provided by designer/architect.   Living Room

Plan #111004

Dimensions: 76' W x 85' D

Levels: 1

Square Footage: 2,968

Bedrooms: 4

Full Bathrooms: 3½

Foundation: Slab;
crawl space available for fee

Materials List Available: No

Price Category: F

If you've been looking for a home that includes a special master suite, this one could be the answer to your dreams.

Features:

- **Living Room:** Make a sitting area around the fireplace here so that the whole family can enjoy the warmth on chilly days and winter evenings. A door from this room leads to the rear covered porch, making this room the heart of your home.

- **Kitchen:** An island with a cooktop makes cooking a pleasure in this well-designed kitchen, and the breakfast bar invites visitors at all times of day.

- **Utility Room:** A sink and a built-in ironing board make this room totally practical.

- **Master Suite:** A private fireplace in the corner sets a romantic tone for this bedroom, and the door to the covered porch allows you to sit outside on warm summer nights. The bath has two vanities, a divided walk-in closet, a standing shower, and a deluxe corner bathtub.

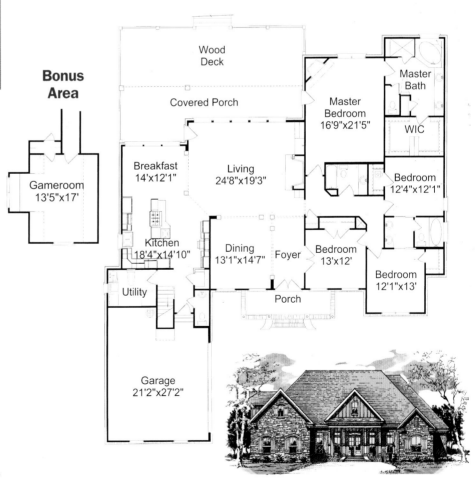

Bonus Area

Gameroom 13'5"x17'

Wood Deck

Covered Porch

Master Bedroom 16'9"x21'5"

Master Bath

WIC

Breakfast 14'x12'1"

Living 24'8"x19'3"

Bedroom 12'4"x12'1"

Kitchen 18'4"x14'10"

Dining 13'1"x14'7"

Foyer

Bedroom 13'12'

Bedroom 12'1"x13'

Utility

Porch

Garage 21'2"x27'2"

Plan #441022

Dimensions: 42' W x 53' D

Levels: 2

Square Footage: 2,820

Main Level Sq. Ft.: 1,383

Upper Level Sq. Ft.: 1,437

Bedrooms: 4

Bathrooms: 3½

Foundation: Crawl space; slab or basement available for fee

Materials List Available: No

Price Category: F

Images provided by designer/architect.

This home has all the features that are important to today's discerning homebuyer. Beautiful exterior details include multiple gables and an arched entry.

Features:

• Great Room: This spacious two-story room features a fireplace and a wall of windows to allow in an abundance of natural light.

• Kitchen: Featuring a butler's pantry and a breakfast nook, this island kitchen also has a great view of the fireplace in the great room.

• Master Suite: This suite, with its vaulted ceiling, is the perfect place for an escape after a busy day. The master bath has a walk-in closet, dual vanities, a shower, and a large tub.

• Bedrooms: A vaulted guest bedroom contains its own private bath. The two additional bedrooms and a third bath provide plenty of room for a growing family.

Rear Elevation

Main Level Floor Plan

Copyright by designer/architect.

Upper Level Floor Plan

Plan #121024

Dimensions: 60' W x 58' D

Levels: 2

Square Footage: 3,057

Main Level Sq. Ft.: 1,631

Second Level Sq. Ft.: 1,426

Bedrooms: 4

Bathrooms: 2½

Foundation: Basement

Materials List Available: Yes

Price Category: G

Images provided by designer/architect.

This distinctive home offers plenty of space and is designed for gracious and convenient living.

Features:

- Ceiling Height: 8 ft. unless otherwise noted.

- Foyer: A curved staircase in this elegant entry will greet your guests.

- Living Room: This room invites you with a volume ceiling flanked by transom-topped windows that flood the room with sunlight.

- Screened Veranda: On warm summer nights, throw open the French doors in the living room and enjoy a breeze on the huge screened veranda.

- Dining Room: This distinctive room is overlooked by the veranda.

- Family Room: At the back of the home is this comfortable family retreat with its soaring cathedral ceiling and handsome fireplace flanked by bookcases.

- Master Bedroom: This bayed bedroom features a 10-ft. vaulted ceiling.

Main Level Floor Plan

Upper Level Floor Plan

Copyright by designer/architect.

Plan #101013

Dimensions: 72' W x 66' D

Levels: 1

Square Footage: 2,564

Bedrooms: 3

Bathrooms: 2½

Foundation: Crawl space, slab, or basement

Materials List Available: Yes

Price Category: E

Images provided by designer/architect.

This exciting design combines a striking classic exterior with a highly functional floor plan.

Features:

- Ceiling Height: 9 ft. unless otherwise noted.

- Family Room: This warm and inviting room measures 18 ft. x 22 ft. It features a 14-ft. ceiling and a rear wall of windows. French doors lead to an enormous deck.

- Kitchen: This unique angled kitchen is open to the hearth room and eating areas, all of which enjoy vaulted ceilings and are surrounded by windows. The hearth room has a TV niche.

- Master Suite: This 19-ft. x 18-ft. master suite is truly sumptuous, with its 12-ft. ceiling, sitting area, two walk-in closets, and full-featured bath.

- Secondary Bedrooms: Each of the secondary bedrooms measures 11 ft. x 14 ft. and has direct access to a shared bath.

- Bonus Room: Just beyond the entry are stairs leading to this bonus room, which measures approximately 12 ft. x 21 ft.—plenty of room for storage or future expansion.

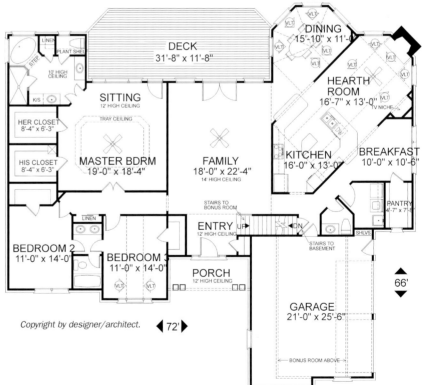

Copyright by designer/architect.

Dining Room

Hearth Room

Kitchen

Family Room

Master Bedroom

Master Bath

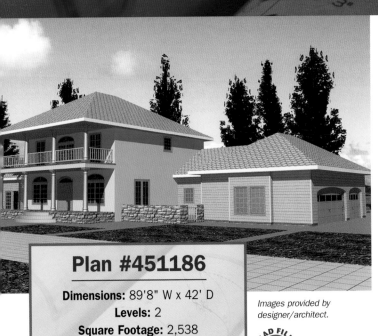

Plan #451186

Dimensions: 89'8" W x 42' D
Levels: 2
Square Footage: 2,538
Main Level Sq. Ft.: 1,795
Upper Level Sq. Ft.: 743
Bedrooms: 3
Bathrooms: 2½
Foundation: Basement
Material List Available: No
Price Category: E

Images provided by designer/architect.

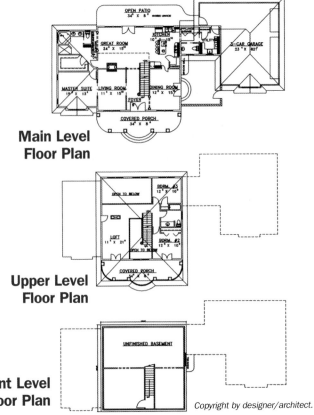

**Main Level
Floor Plan**

**Upper Level
Floor Plan**

**Basement Level
Floor Plan**

Copyright by designer/architect.

Plan #121091

Dimensions: 56' W x 50' D
Levels: 2
Square Footage: 2,689
Main Level Sq. Ft.: 1,415
Upper Level Sq. Ft.: 1,214
Bedrooms: 4
Bathrooms: 2½
Foundation: Basement
Materials List Available: Yes
Price Category: F

Images provided by designer/architect.

**Main Level
Floor Plan**

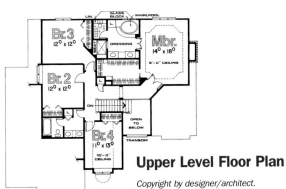

Upper Level Floor Plan

Copyright by designer/architect.

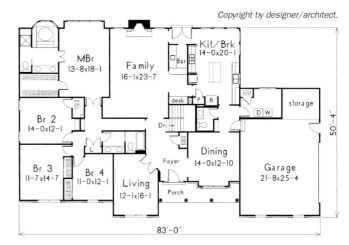

Plan #321011

Dimensions: 83' W x 50'4" D

Levels: 1

Square Footage: 2,874

Bedrooms: 4

Bathrooms: 2½

Foundation: Basement

Materials List Available: Yes

Price Category: F

Images provided by designer/architect.

SMARTtip

Drilling for Kitchen Plumbing

Drill holes for plumbing and waste lines before installing the cabinets. It is easier to work when the cabinets are out in the middle of the floor, and there is no danger of knocking them out of alignment when creating the holes if they are not screwed to the wall studs or one another yet.

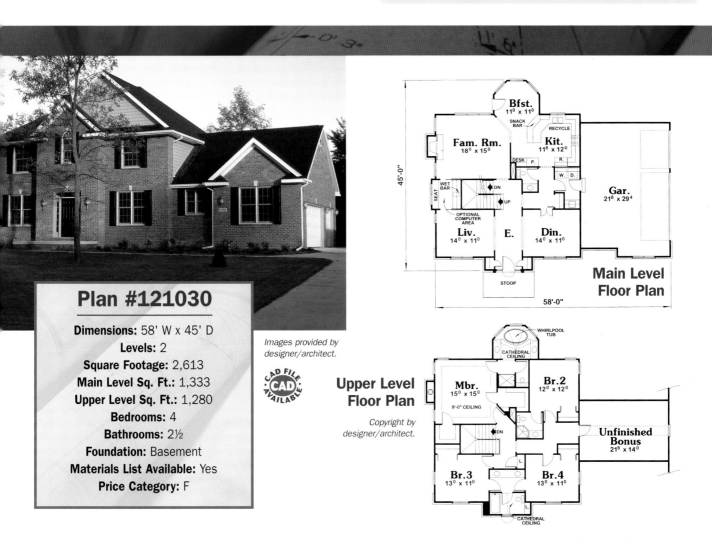

Plan #121030

Dimensions: 58' W x 45' D

Levels: 2

Square Footage: 2,613

Main Level Sq. Ft.: 1,333

Upper Level Sq. Ft.: 1,280

Bedrooms: 4

Bathrooms: 2½

Foundation: Basement

Materials List Available: Yes

Price Category: F

Images provided by designer/architect.

CAD FILE AVAILABLE

Copyright by designer/architect.

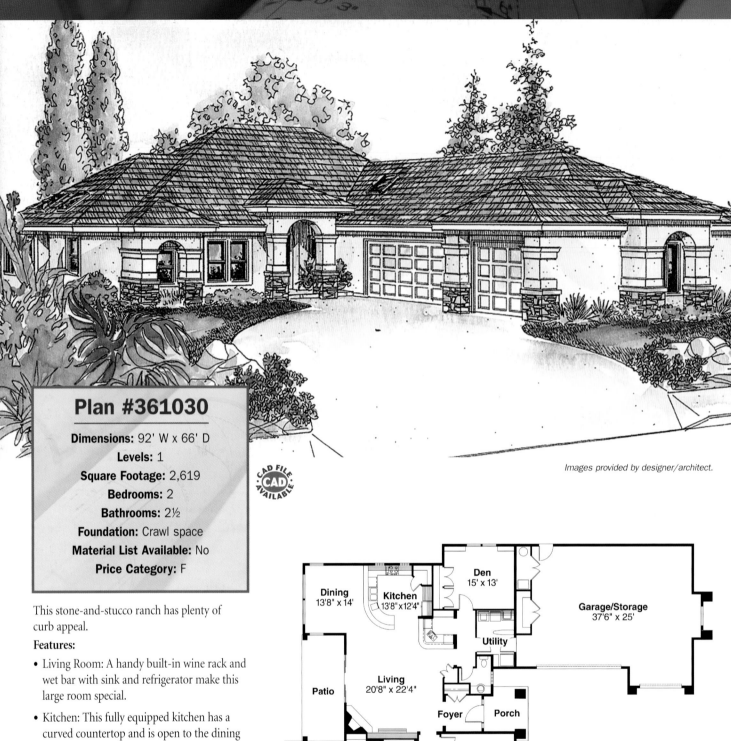

Plan #361030

Dimensions: 92' W x 66' D

Levels: 1

Square Footage: 2,619

Bedrooms: 2

Bathrooms: 2½

Foundation: Crawl space

Material List Available: No

Price Category: F

Images provided by designer/architect.

This stone-and-stucco ranch has plenty of curb appeal.

Features:

- **Living Room:** A handy built-in wine rack and wet bar with sink and refrigerator make this large room special.

- **Kitchen:** This fully equipped kitchen has a curved countertop and is open to the dining room.

- **Master Suite:** Access to the rear porch is just one amenity of this private retreat. It also boasts his and her walk-in closets and a sumptuous master bath with dual vanities, a large tub, and a separate shower.

- **Garage:** This three-car garage has room for cars, plus there is an area for storage.

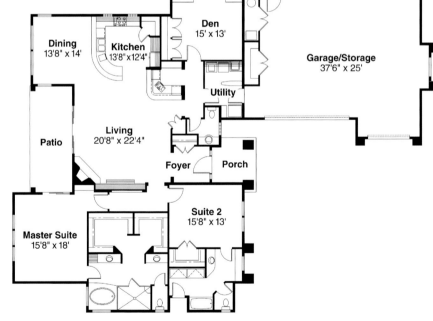

Copyright by designer/architect.

Plan #121073

Dimensions: 70' W x 52' D
Levels: 2
Square Footage: 2,579
Main Level Sq. Ft.: 1,933
Upper Level Sq. Ft.: 646
Bedrooms: 4
Bathrooms: 2½
Foundation: Basement
Materials List Available: Yes
Price Category: E

Images provided by designer/architect.

Luxury will surround you in this home with contemporary styling and up-to-date amenities at every turn.

Features:

• Great Room: This large room shares both a see-through fireplace and a wet bar with the adjacent hearth room. Transom-topped windows add both light and architectural interest to this room.

• Den: Transom-topped windows add visual interest to this private area.

• Kitchen: A center island and corner pantry add convenience to this well-planned kitchen, and a lovely ceiling treatment adds beauty to the bayed breakfast area.

• Master Suite: A built-in bookcase adds to the ambiance of this luxury-filled area, where you're sure to find a retreat at the end of the day.

Main Level Floor Plan

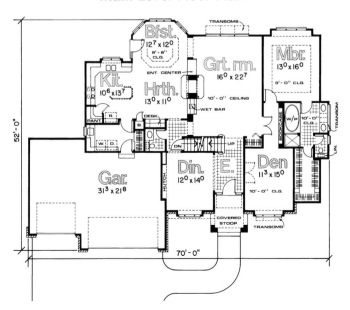

Upper Level Floor Plan

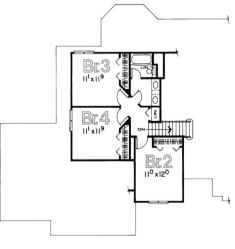

Copyright by designer/architect.

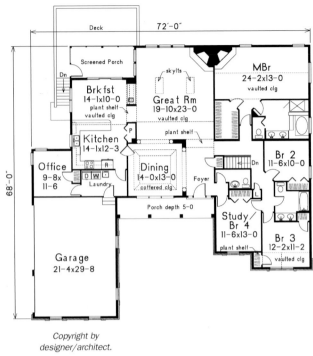

Images provided by designer/architect.

Copyright by designer/architect.

Plan #321027

Dimensions: 72' W x 68' D

Levels: 1

Square Footage: 2,758

Bedrooms: 4

Bathrooms: 2½

Foundation: Basement

Materials List Available: Yes

Price Category: F

Images provided by designer/architect.

Copyright by designer/architect.

Rear Elevation

Kitchen

Plan #221001

Dimensions: 87' W x 60' D

Levels: 1

Square Footage: 2,600

Bedrooms: 3

Bathrooms: 2½

Foundation: Basement

Materials List Available: No

Price Category: F

Plan #151018

Dimensions: 69' W x 69'10" D

Levels: 2

Square Footage: 2,755

Main Level Sq. Ft.: 2,406

Upper Level Sq. Ft.: 349

Bedrooms: 3

Bathrooms: 4½

Foundation: Crawl space, slab, or basement

CompleteCost List Available: Yes

Price Category: F

Images provided by designer/architect.

CAD FILE AVAILABLE

Main Level Floor Plan

Upper Level Floor Plan

Copyright by designer/architect.

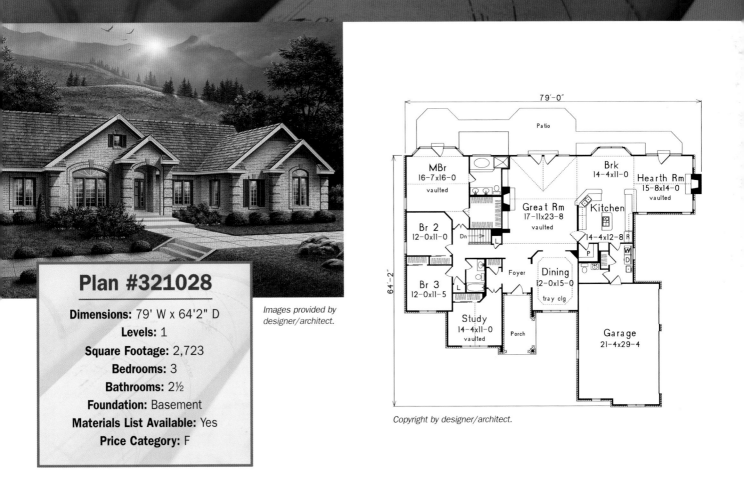

Plan #321028

Dimensions: 79' W x 64'2" D

Levels: 1

Square Footage: 2,723

Bedrooms: 3

Bathrooms: 2½

Foundation: Basement

Materials List Available: Yes

Price Category: F

Images provided by designer/architect.

Copyright by designer/architect.

Plan #361039

Dimensions: 72' W x 58'4" D

Levels: 1

Square Footage: 2,858

Bedrooms: 2

Bathrooms: 2½

Foundation: Crawl space

Material List Available: No

Price Category: F

Images provided by designer/architect.

Copyright by designer/architect.

Plan #221049

Dimensions: 62'4" W x 60' D

Levels: 2

Square Footage: 2,698

Main Level Sq. Ft.: 1,852

Upper Level Sq. Ft.: 846

Bedrooms: 4

Bathrooms: 3½

Foundation: Basement

Materials List Available: No

Price Category: F

Images provided by designer/architect.

Copyright by designer/architect.

Main Level Floor Plan

Upper Level Floor Plan

Rear Elevation

Images provided by designer/architect.

Plan #401015

Dimensions: 56' W x 50'4" D

Levels: 2

Square Footage: 2,618

Main Level Sq. Ft.: 1,464

Upper Level Sq. Ft.: 1,154

Bedrooms: 3

Bathrooms: 3

Foundation: Basement

Materials List Available: Yes

Price Category: F

High vaulted ceilings and floor-to-ceiling windows enhance the spaciousness of this home. Decorative columns separate the living room from the tray-ceiling dining room.

Features:

- Kitchen: This gourmet kitchen offers a center food-preparation island, a pantry, and a pass-through to the family room and breakfast bay.

- Family Room: This spacious room boasts a fireplace and vaulted ceiling open to the second-level hallway.

- Den: This room has a wall closet and private access to a full bath. It can be used as extra guest space if needed.

- Master Suite: Located on the second floor, this area holds a bay-windowed sitting area, a walk-in closet, and a bath with a whirlpool tub and separate shower.

- Bedrooms: Family bedrooms are at the other end of the hall upstairs and share a full bath.

CAD FILE AVAILABLE

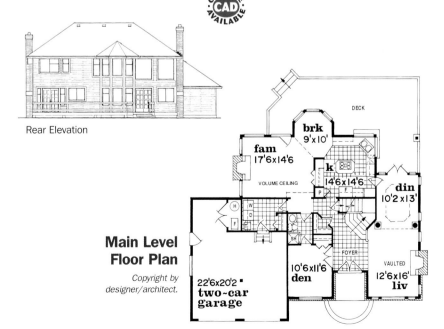

Rear Elevation

Main Level Floor Plan

Copyright by designer/architect.

Upper Level Floor Plan

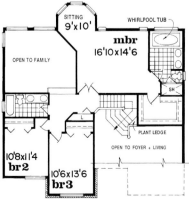

Images provided by designer/architect.

Plan #151144

Dimensions: 66'4" W x 64' D

Levels: 1

Square Footage: 2,624

Bedrooms: 4

Bathrooms: 3

Foundation: Crawl space, slab (basement option for fee)

CompleteCost List Available: Yes

Price Category: F

The traditional exterior appearance of this home gives way to a surprisingly contemporary interior design and a wealth of lovely amenities.

Features:

- Living Room: The 8-inch columns create an elegant feeling in this well-lit room.

- Dining Room: An 11-ft. ceiling makes this room ideal for hosting dinner parties or entertaining a crowd.

- Kitchen: The kitchen features a pass-through to the living room for serving convenience and a snack bar where the kids are sure to gather.

- Breakfast/Hearth Room: The fireplace is the centerpiece in winter, but you'll love the access to the grilling porch when the weather's warm.

- Master Suite: The door to the rear porch is a special feature in this private retreat, and you'll love the bath with a walk-in closet, split vanities, and a glass shower.

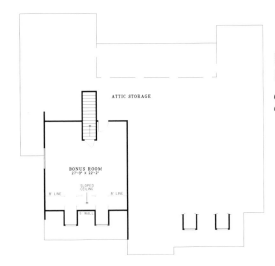

Bonus Area Floor Plan

Copyright by designer/architect.

Plan #441047

Dimensions: 50' W x 42' D
Levels: 2
Square Footage: 2,605
Main Level Sq. Ft.: 1,142
Upper Level Sq. Ft.: 1,463
Bedrooms: 3
Bathrooms: 2½
Foundation: Crawl space;
slab or basement available for fee
Material List Available: No
Price Category: F

Images provided by designer/architect.

A touch of European styling dresses the façade of this comfortable two-story home. Stone detailing on the main level and around the entryway complements board-and-batten siding above.

Features:

- **Foyer:** A side-lighted entry gains admittance to this central foyer with half-bathroom on the left. Beyond the foyer lies open living space, with the great room, dining room, and kitchen.

- **Great Room:** This room is open upward for the full two stories and is graced by the hearth and media center.

- **Dining Room:** This room has a wall of windows on one side and sliding glass doors leading to the rear yard on the other.

- **Master Suite:** On the upper level is this vaulted suite, with its vaulted bathroom. The compartmented toilet, walk-in closet, and spa tub are just a few of the coveted amenities here.

- **Bedrooms:** Bedroom 3 has a vaulted ceiling and shares the full bathroom on the other side of the stairs with Bedroom 2.

Rear Elevation

Copyright by designer/architect.

Plan #111031

Dimensions: 56' W x 53' D

Levels: 2

Square Footage: 2,869

Main Level Sq. Ft.: 2,152

Upper Level Sq. Ft.: 717

Bedrooms: 4

Bathrooms: 3

Foundation: Crawl space, slab

Materials List Available: No

Price Category: F

Images provided by designer/architect.

This home is ideal for any family, thanks to its spaciousness, beauty, and versatility.

Features:

- Ceiling Height: 9 ft.
- Front Porch: The middle of the three French doors with circle tops here opens to the foyer.
- Living Room: Archways from the foyer open to both this room and the equally large dining room.
- Family Room: Also open to the foyer, this room features a two-story sloped ceiling and a balcony from the upper level. You'll love the fireplace, with its raised brick hearth and the

two French doors with circle tops, which open to the rear porch.

- Kitchen: A center island, range with microwave, built-in desk, and dining bar that's open to the breakfast room add up to comfort and efficiency.
- Master Suite: A Palladian window and linen closet grace this suite's bedroom, and the bath has an oversized garden tub, standing shower, two walk-in closets, and double vanity.

Copyright by designer/architect.

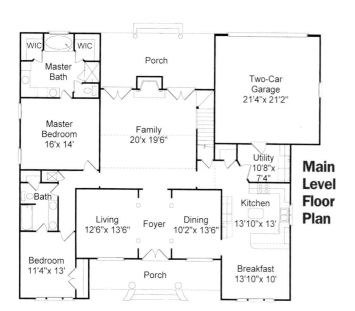

Main Level Floor Plan

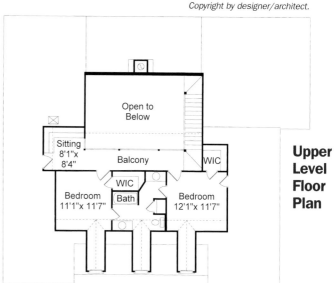

Upper Level Floor Plan

Plan #441046

Dimensions: 50' W x 42' D
Levels: 2
Square Footage: 2,606
Main Level Sq. Ft.: 1,216
Upper Level Sq. Ft.: 1,390
Bedrooms: 4
Bathrooms: 2½
Foundation: Crawl space; slab or basement for fee
Materials List Available: No
Price Category: F

Images provided by designer/architect.

Little things mean a lot, and in this design it's the little details that add up to a marvelous plan.

Features:

• **Great Room:** If you like, you might include a corner media center in this room to complement the fireplace.

• **Den:** This vaulted room lies just off the entry and opens through double doors.

• **Kitchen:** Both formal and casual dining spaces are included and flank this open kitchen, which overlooks the great room.

• **Upper Level:** Sleeping quarters are upstairs and include three family bedrooms and the master suite. Look for a spa tub, separate shower, dual sinks, and a walk-in closet in the master bath. The family bedrooms share the full bathroom, which has double sinks.

Main Level Floor Plan

Rear Elevation

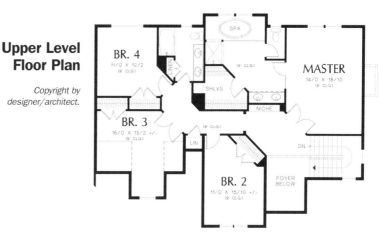

Upper Level Floor Plan

Copyright by designer/architect.

Plan #131036

Dimensions: 72' W x 69'10" D
Levels: 1
Square Footage: 2,585
Bedrooms: 4
Bathrooms: 3
Foundation: Crawl space, slab, or basement
Materials List Available: Yes
Price Category: F

Images provided by designer/architect.

This sprawling brick home features living spaces for everyone in the family and makes a lovely setting for any sort of entertaining.

Features:

- Foyer: Pass through this foyer, which leads into either the living room or dining room.
- Living Room: An elegant 11-ft. stepped ceiling here and in the dining room helps to create the formality their lines suggest.
- Great Room: This room, with its 10-ft.-7-in.-high stepped ceiling, fireplace, and many built-ins, leads to the rear covered porch.
- Kitchen: This kitchen features an island, a pantry closet, and a wraparound snack bar that serves the breakfast room and gives a panoramic view of the great room.
- Master Suite: Enjoy a bayed sitting area, walk-in closet, and private bath with garden tub.
- Office: A private entrance and access to a full bath give versatility to this room.

Copyright by designer/architect.

**Optional
Upper Level
Floor Plan**

Rear View

Great Room

Plan #151032

Dimensions: 84'4" W x 48'4" D
Levels: 2
Square Footage: 2,824
Main Level Sq. Ft.: 2,279
Upper Level Sq. Ft.: 545
Bedrooms: 4
Bathrooms: 3
Foundation: Crawl space, slab (basement option for fee)
CompleteCost List Available: Yes
Price Category: F

Images provided by designer/architect.

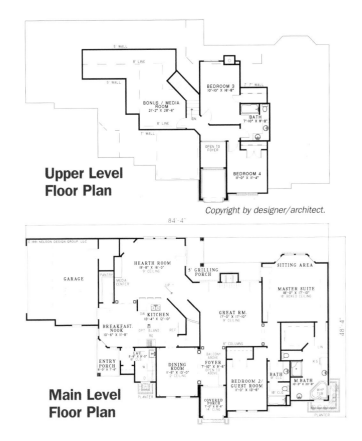

Upper Level Floor Plan

Copyright by designer/architect.

Main Level Floor Plan

Plan #121007

Dimensions: 74' W x 67'8" D
Levels: 1
Square Footage: 2,512
Bedrooms: 3
Bathrooms: 2½
Foundation: Basement
Materials List Available: Yes
Price Category: E

Images provided by designer/architect.

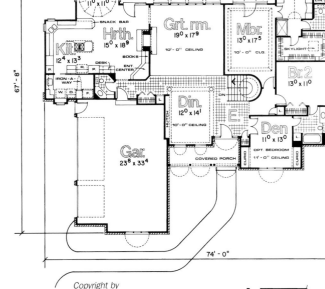

Copyright by designer/architect.

Optional Bedroom

Plan #361064

Dimensions: 130'4" W x 70'6" D

Levels: 1

Square Footage: 2,711

Bedrooms: 3

Bathrooms: 2½

Foundation: Slab

Material List Available: No

Price Category: F

Images provided by designer/architect.

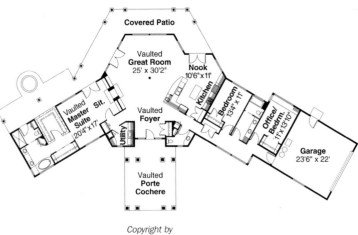

Copyright by designer/architect.

Plan #161025

Dimensions: 63'4" W x 48' D

Levels: 2

Square Footage: 2,738

Main Level Sq. Ft.: 1,915

Upper Level Sq. Ft.: 823

Bedrooms: 4

Bathrooms: 3½

Foundation: Basement

Materials List Available: No

Price Category: F

Images provided by designer/architect.

This home, as shown in the photograph, may differ from the actual blueprints. For more detailed information, please check the floor plans carefully.

Main Level Floor Plan

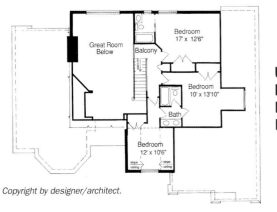

Upper Level Floor Plan

Copyright by designer/architect.

Plan #441011

Dimensions: 67' W x 46' D
Levels: 1
Square Footage: 2,898
Main Level Sq. Ft.: 1,744
Basement Level Sq. Ft.: 1,154
Bedrooms: 3
Bathrooms: 2½
Foundation: Walkout basement
Materials List Available: No
Price Category: F

Images provided by designer/architect.

Think one-story, then think again—it's a hillside home designed to make the best use of a sloping lot. Elegant in exterior appeal, this home uses high arches and a hipped room to promote a sense of style.

CAD FILE AVAILABLE

Features:

- Dining Room: Box beams and columns define this formal space, which is just off the foyer.

- Kitchen: This fully equipped kitchen has everything the chef in the family could want. Nearby is the breakfast nook with sliding glass doors to the deck, which acts as the roof for the patio below.

- Master Suite: This suite is located on the right side of the main level. The master bath is

replete with a spa tub, compartmented toilet, separate shower, and dual lavatories.

- Lower Level: The two extra bedrooms, full bathroom, and games room are on this lower floor, which adds to the great livability of the home. The wet bar in the games room is a bonus.

Rear Elevation

Main Level Floor Plan

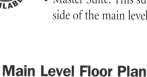

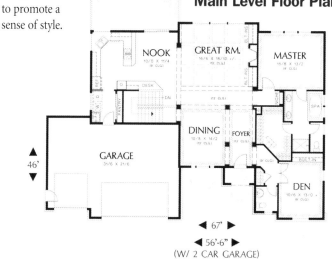

◄ 67' ►

◄ 56'-6" ►
(W/ 2 CAR GARAGE)

Basement Level Floor Plan

Copyright by designer/architect.

Images provided by designer/architect.

Plan #241008

Dimensions: 65' W x 56'8" D
Levels: 1
Square Footage: 2,526
Bedrooms: 4
Bathrooms: 3
Foundation: Slab
Materials List Available: No
Price Category: E

A covered back porch—with access from the master suite and the breakfast area—makes this traditional home ideal for siting near a golf course or with a backyard pool.

Features:

- Great Room: From the foyer, guests enter this spacious and comfortable great room, which features a handsome fireplace.

- Kitchen: This kitchen—the hub of this family-oriented home—is a joy in which to work, thanks to abundant counter space, a pantry, a convenient eating bar, and an adjoining breakfast area and sunroom.

- Master Suite: Enjoy the quiet comfort of this coffered-ceiling master suite, which features dual vanities and separate walk-in closets.

- Additional Bedrooms: Two secondary bedrooms, which share a full bath, are located at the opposite end of the house from the master suite. Bedroom 4—in front of the house—can be converted into a study.

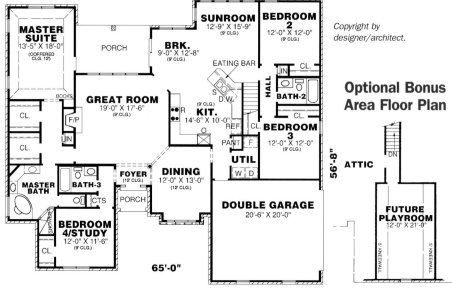

Copyright by designer/architect.

Optional Bonus Area Floor Plan

SMARTtip

Traditional-Style Kitchen Cabinetry

You can modify stock kitchen cabinetry to enjoy fine furniture-quality details. Prefabricated trims may be purchased at local lumber mills and home centers. For example, crown molding, applied to the top of stock cabinetry and stained or painted to match the door style, may be all you need. Likewise, you can replace hardware with reproduction polished-brass door and drawer knobs or pulls for a finishing touch.

Plan #121047

Dimensions: 67'8" W x 57' D
Levels: 2
Square Footage: 3,072
Main Level Sq. Ft.: 2,116
Upper Level Sq. Ft.: 956
Bedrooms: 4
Bathrooms: 3½
Foundation: Slab
Materials List Available: Yes
Price Category: G

Images provided by designer/architect.

A long porch and a trio of roof dormers give this gracious home a sophisticated country look.

Features:

- Ceiling Height: 8 ft. unless otherwise noted.

- Balcony: This balcony overlooks the entry and the staircase hall.

- Dining Room: Columns and a cased opening lend elegance, making this the perfect venue for stylish dinner parties.

- Family Room: A cathedral ceiling gives this room a light and airy feel. The handsome fireplace framed by windows is sure to become a favorite family gathering place.

- Master Bedroom: This architecturally distinctive bedroom features a bayed sitting area and a tray ceiling.

- Bedrooms: One of the bedrooms enjoys a private bath, making it a perfect guest room. Other bedrooms feature walk-in closets.

Main Level Floor Plan

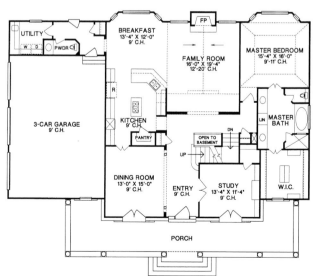

Upper Level Floor Plan

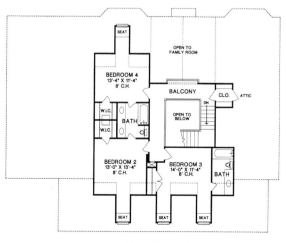

Copyright by designer/architect.

Plan #441009

Dimensions: 94' W x 53' D

Levels: 1

Square Footage: 2,650

Bedrooms: 4

Bathrooms: 2½

Foundation: Crawl space; slab or basement available for fee

Materials List Available: No

Price Category: F

You'll love to call this plan home. It's large enough for the whole family and has a façade that will make you the envy of the neighborhood.

CAD FILE AVAILABLE

Images provided by designer/architect.

Features:

- **Foyer:** The covered porch protects the entry, which has a transom and sidelights to brighten this space.

- **Great Room:** To the left of the foyer, beyond decorative columns, lies this vaulted room, with its fireplace and media center. Additional columns separate the room from the vaulted formal dining room.

- **Kitchen:** A casual nook and this island work center are just around the corner from the great room. The second covered porch can be reached via a door in the nook.

- **Master Suite:** This luxurious space boasts a vaulted salon, a private niche that could be a small study, and a view of the front yard. The master bath features a spa tub, separate shower, compartmented toilet, huge walk-in closet, and access to the laundry room.

- **Bedrooms:** The two additional bedrooms are located at the back of the plan and share the Jack-and-Jill bathroom.

Copyright by designer/architect.

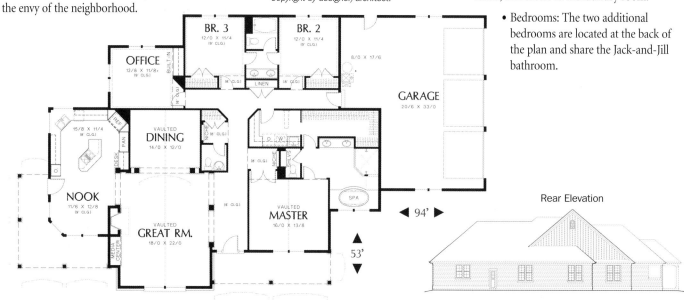

Rear Elevation

Plan #151002

Dimensions: 67' W x 66' D

Levels: 1

Square Footage: 2,444

Bedrooms: 3

Bathrooms: 2½

Foundation: Crawl space, slab, or basement

CompleteCost List Available: Yes

Price Category: E

Images provided by designer/architect.

- Kitchen: An eat-in bar is a great place to snack, and the handy computer nook allows the kids to do their homework while you cook.

- Breakfast Room: Opening from the kitchen, this area gives added space for the family to gather any time.

- Master Suite: Featuring a 10-ft. boxed ceiling, the master bedroom also has a door way that opens onto the covered rear porch. The master bathroom has a step-up whirlpool tub, separate shower, and twin vanities with a makeup area.

This gracious, traditional home is designed for practicality and convenience.

Features:

- Ceiling Height: 9 ft. except as noted below.

- Great Room: This room is ideal for entertaining, thanks to its lovely fireplace and French doors that open to the covered rear porch. Built-in cabinets give convenient storage space.

- Family Room: With access to the kitchen as well as the rear porch, this room will become your family's "headquarters."

- Study: Enjoy the quiet in this room with its 12-ft. ceiling and doorway to a private patio on the side of the house.

- Dining Room: Take advantage of the 8-in. wood columns and 12-ft. ceilings to create a formal dining area.

Copyright by designer/architect.

Plan #441014

Dimensions: 119'6" W x 87'6" D
Levels: 1
Square Footage: 3,940
Bedrooms: 3
Bathrooms: 3 full, 2 half
Foundation: Crawl space; slab or basement available for fee
Materials List Available: No
Price Category: H

Though this is but a single-story home, it satisfies and delights on many levels. The exterior has visual appeal, with varied rooflines, a mixture of materials, and graceful traditional lines.

Features:

- Great Room: This huge room boasts a sloped, vaulted ceiling, a fireplace, and built-ins. There is also a media room with double-door access.

- Kitchen: This kitchen has an island, two sink prep areas, a butler's pantry connecting it to the formal dining room, and a walk-in pantry.

- Bedrooms: Family bedrooms sit at the front of the plan and are joined by a Jack-and-Jill bathroom.

- Master Suite: This master suite is on the far right side. Its grand salon has an 11-ft.-high ceiling, a fireplace, built-ins, a walk-in closet, and a superb bathroom.

- Garage: If you need extra space, there's a bonus room on an upper level above the three-car garage.

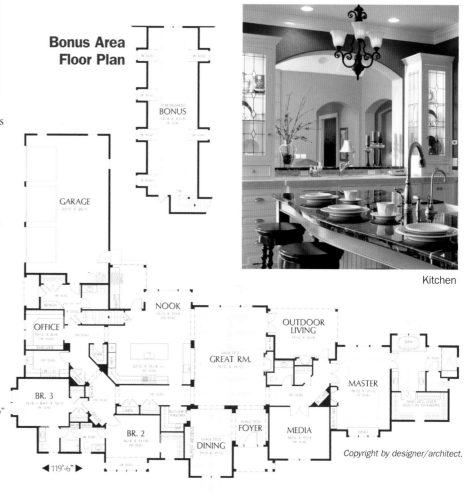

Kitchen

Plan #261001

Dimensions: 77'8" W x 49' D
Levels: 2
Square Footage: 3,746
Main Level Sq. Ft.: 1,965
Upper Level Sq. Ft.: 1,781
Bedrooms: 4
Bathrooms: 3½
Foundation: Basement
Materials List Available: No
Price Category: H

Images provided by designer/architect.

If contemporary designs appeal to you, you're sure to love this stunning home.

Features:

- Foyer: A volume ceiling here announces the spaciousness of this gracious home.

- Great Room: Also with a volume ceiling, this great room features a fireplace where you can create a cozy sitting area.

- Kitchen: Designed for the pleasure of the family cooks, this room features a large pantry, ample counter and cabinet space, and a dining bar.

- Dinette: Serve the family in style, or host casual, informal dinners for friends in this dinette with its gracious volume ceiling.

- Master Suite: A fireplace makes this suite a welcome retreat on cool nights, but even in warm weather you'll love its spaciousness and the walk-in closet. The bath features dual vanities, a whirlpool tub, and a separate shower.

Main Level Floor Plan

Copyright by designer/architect.

Upper Level Floor Plan

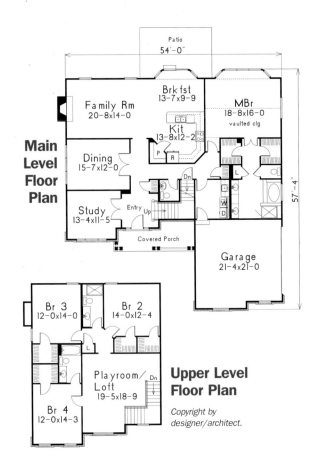

Plan #321062

Dimensions: 54' W x 57'4" D

Levels: 2

Square Footage: 3,138

Main Level Sq. Ft.: 1,958

Upper Level Sq. Ft.: 1,180

Bedrooms: 4

Bathrooms: 3½

Foundation: Basement

Materials List Available: Yes

Price Category: G

Images provided by designer/architect.

This home, as shown in the photograph, may differ from the actual blueprints. For more detailed information, please check the floor plans carefully.

Main Level Floor Plan

Upper Level Floor Plan

Copyright by designer/architect.

Plan #321016

Dimensions: 88' W x 70'8" D

Levels: 1

Square Footage: 3,814

Main Level Sq. Ft.: 3,566

Lower Level Sq. Ft.: 248

Bedrooms: 3

Bathrooms: 2½

Foundation: Daylight basement

Materials List Available: Yes

Price Category: H

Images provided by designer/architect.

Rear View

Copyright by designer/architect.

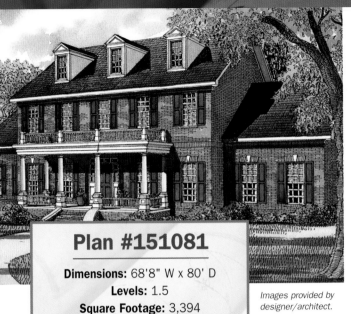

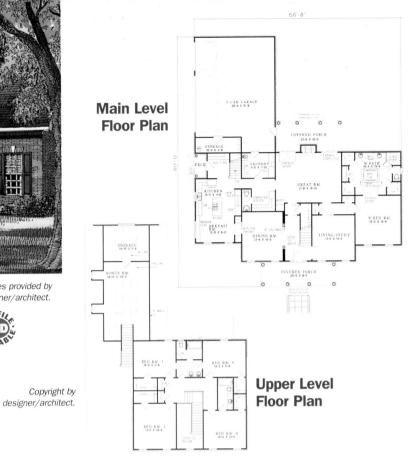

Plan #151081

Dimensions: 68'8" W x 80' D

Levels: 1.5

Square Footage: 3,394

Main Level Sq. Ft.: 2,202

Upper Level Sq. Ft.: 1,192

Bedrooms: 5

Bathrooms: 3½

Foundation: Crawl space, slab or walkout; basement for fee

CompleteCost List Available: Yes

Price Category: E

Images provided by designer/architect.

CAD FILE AVAILABLE

Copyright by designer/architect.

Main Level Floor Plan

Upper Level Floor Plan

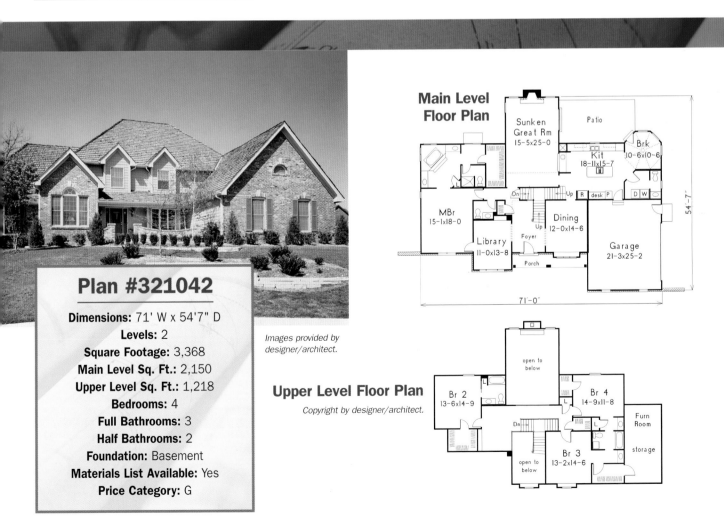

Plan #321042

Dimensions: 71' W x 54'7" D

Levels: 2

Square Footage: 3,368

Main Level Sq. Ft.: 2,150

Upper Level Sq. Ft.: 1,218

Bedrooms: 4

Full Bathrooms: 3

Half Bathrooms: 2

Foundation: Basement

Materials List Available: Yes

Price Category: G

Images provided by designer/architect.

Main Level Floor Plan

Upper Level Floor Plan

Copyright by designer/architect.

Plan #441028

Dimensions: 53'6" W x 73' D
Levels: 2
Square Footage: 3,165
Main Level Sq. Ft.: 1,268
Upper Level Sq. Ft.: 931
Lower Level Sq. Ft.: 966
Bedrooms: 4
Bathrooms: 3½
Foundation: Slab
Materials List Available: No
Price Category: G

Arts and Crafts style meets hillside design. The result is this stunning design, which fits perfectly on a sloped site.

CAD FILE AVAILABLE

Features:

- Porch: This covered porch introduces the front entry but also allows access to a mud-room and the three-car garage beyond.

- Great Room: This room is vaulted and has a fireplace, media center, and window seat in a corner window area—a cozy place to read or relax.

- Dining Room: The recess in this room is ideal for a hutch, and the double French doors open to the wide lower deck.

- Upper Level: This floor holds the two family bedrooms with walk-in closets, the shared bathroom, and the master suite. A spa tub and vaulted salon with private deck appoint the suite.

- Lower Level: This floor features another bedroom, with its full bathroom; the recreation room, which has a fireplace and wet bar; and the wine cellar.

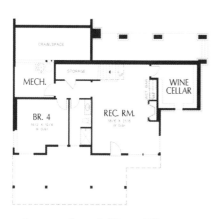

Lower Level Floor Plan
Copyright by designer/architect.

Main Level Floor Plan

Upper Level Floor Plan

Plan #151021

Dimensions: 75'2" W x 89'6" D
Levels: 2
Square Footage: 3,385
Main Level Sq. Ft.: 2,633
Upper Level Sq. Ft.: 752
Bedrooms: 4
Bathrooms: 4
Foundation: Crawl space, or slab
CompleteCost List Available: Yes
Price Category: G

Images provided by designer/architect.

From the fireplace in the master suite to the well-equipped game room, the amenities in this home will surprise and delight you.

Features:

- Great Room: A bank of windows on the far wall lets sunlight stream into this large room. The fireplace is located across the room and is flanked by the built-in media center and built-in bookshelves. Gracious brick arches create an entry into the breakfast area and kitchen.

- Breakfast Room: Move easily between this room with 10-foot ceiling either into the kitchen or onto the rear covered porch.

- Game Room: An icemaker and refrigerator make entertaining a snap in this room.

- Master Suite: A 10-ft. boxed ceiling, fireplace, and access to the rear porch give romance, while the built-ins in the closet, whirlpool tub with glass blocks, and glass shower give practicality.

Main Level Floor Plan

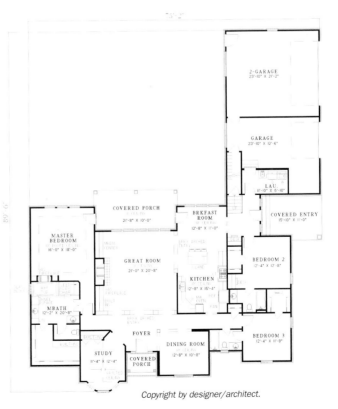

Upper Level Floor Plan

Copyright by designer/architect.

Masonry Design

Although asphalt is used more than other materials for driveways, there are appealing masonry options, including concrete, pavers, brick, and stone. The choice is important because driveways (and main entry walks) are a prominent feature of today's houses. Driveways are often the main access route into the house. To make a design statement, use an attractive masonry product.

Most walks are narrow enough for you to install flat without having to worry about runoff. But driveways, which are wider, generally need a slope to encourage runoff. A slight rise along the center of a wide drive won't be noticeable.

As a general guide, size the main part of a driveway between 10 and 12 feet wide for a one-car garage, and 16 to 24 feet wide for a two-car garage. (If the drive will form part of a walkway, add another 2 feet.)

An apron that tapers out to meet the street makes it easier to back your car in or out. Extra parking that doesn't obstruct normal activities is extremely useful; allow 12 feet per vehicle for cars, more for trucks and RVs.

Take the time to lay out drives and walks with stakes and string (or a hose for curves) so that you can visualize the overall space and see how your vehicles fit before starting work.

CREATIVE HOMEOWNER ULTIMATE GUIDE TO

Masonry & Concrete

DESIGN · BUILD · MAINTAIN

60 STEP-BY-STEP PROJECTS
- CONCRETE
- BLOCK
- STUCCO
- BRICK
- STONE
- TILE

The following article was reprinted from *Ultimate Guide to Masonry and Concrete* (Creative Homeowner 2006).

You can lay basic end-to-end patterns of mortarless brick to make a transition from narrow walks to wide patios.

Walkway and Driveway Materials

Concrete slabs make strong, long-lasting driveways as long as the ground underneath is relatively stable and the pour is reinforced with welded wire. This rugged material can appear slightly commercial looking, however. You can improve its appearance by imprinting patterns (a process called pattern stamping) on the surface before the mix hardens. One drawback: light-colored concrete will show oil stains.

Concrete pavers have the same durability as poured concrete; some blocks can withstand up to 2,000 psi of pressure, which is more than enough for driveways. The many seams are weak links in the system. Pavers come in a wide range of colors and styles, so it is easy to complement the look of your home. While fairly simple to lay yourself, professional installations cost more than poured concrete.

Stone and brick can make durable drives, but they're not a good choice for steep driveways; they tend to get slippery when wet and collect ice in cold climates. In terms of installation, if you're looking to save money, brick that is set on a sand bed costs less than brick with mortared joints set on a concrete slab. Stones can be set in a mortar or sand bed, or placed directly on well-compacted ground.

Stone Gallery

Stone is one of the most durable building materials. It's also available in a natural state in more sizes, shapes, textures, and colors than any other material. To create a natural-looking design, use stone to build sweeping walks and drives, and unique garden and retaining walls that blend beautifully with the existing landscape.

With formwork providing support during construction, you can build expansive arched openings with stone.

Different shapes and sizes form unique walls.

Stone works well for house and garden walls.

You can fit together a variety of shapes to form a patio.

Stones embedded in sand over a layer of gravel form durable walks and drives.

Brick Gallery

Brick is the one of the most versatile masonry materials. It is used for house walls to provide great strength and resistance to fire, rot, and other elements that can gradually erode wood-frame buildings. But the versatility does not stop there. There are also many varieties that you can use for walks, drives, and garden walls.

Carefully laid brickwork with a classic arched opening provides a durable garden wall.

Brick presents a traditional wall surface, even when exposed inside the house.

Brick pavers blend with any landscaping.

Modular brickwork makes an elegant set of steps.

Plan #321031

Dimensions: 79'4" W x 59'6' D

Levels: 1

Square Footage: 3,200

Bedrooms: 3

Bathrooms: 2½

Foundation: Daylight basement

Materials List Available: Yes

Price Category: G

Images provided by designer/architect.

Copyright by designer/architect.

Optional Basement Level Floor Plan

Plan #271100

Dimensions: 69'10" W x 66'5" D

Levels: 2

Square Footage: 3,263

Main Level Sq. Ft.: 2,017

Upper Level Sq. Ft.: 1,246

Bedrooms: 4

Bathrooms: 2½

Foundation: Basement

Material List Available: No

Price Category: G

Images provided by designer/architect.

CAD FILE AVAILABLE

Main Level Floor Plan

Upper Level Floor Plan

Copyright by designer/architect.

Plan #161094

Dimensions: 68'8" W x 56'8" D
Levels: 2
Square Footage: 3,366
Main Level Sq. Ft.: 1,759
Upper Level Sq. Ft.: 1,607
Bedrooms: 5
Bathrooms: 4
Foundation: Walkout basement
Material List Available: No
Price Category: G

This home, as shown in the photograph, may differ from the actual blueprints. For more detailed information, please check the floor plans carefully.

CAD FILE AVAILABLE

Images provided by designer/architect.

This luxurious two-story home combines a stately exterior style with a large, functional floor plan.

Features:

• Great Room: The volume ceiling in this room is decorated with wood beams and reaches a two-story height, while 9-ft. ceiling heights prevail throughout the rest of the first floor.

• Bright and Open: Split stairs lead to the second-floor balcony, which offers a dramatic view of the great room. Light radiates through the multiple rear windows

to flood the great room, breakfast area, and kitchen with natural daylight.

• Master Suite: Built-in bookshelves flank the entrance to this lavish retreat, with its large sitting area, which is surrounded by windows, and deluxe master bath, which sports spacious closets, dual vanities, and an oversized whirlpool tub.

• Bedrooms: Three more bedrooms, each with large closets and private access to the bathroom, complete this family-friendly home.

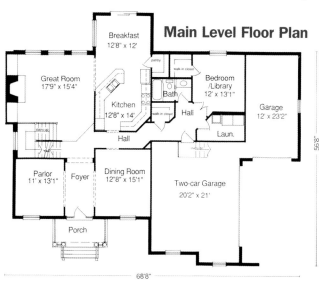

Main Level Floor Plan

Upper Level Floor Plan

Copyright by designer/architect.

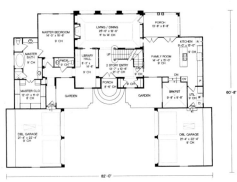

Main Level Floor Plan

Images provided by designer/architect.

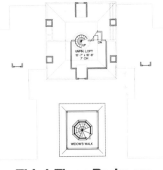

Third Floor Bedroom Floor Plan

Copyright by designer/ architect.

Upper Level Floor Plan

Plan #121049

Dimensions: 82' W x 60'8" D

Levels: 2

Square Footage: 3,335

Main Level Sq. Ft.: 2,054

Upper Level Sq. Ft.: 1,281

Bedrooms: 4

Bathrooms: 3½

Foundation: Slab

Materials List Available: Yes

Price Category: G

Upper Level Floor Plan

Copyright by designer/architect.

Plan #221054

Dimensions: 63'8" W x 75'4" D

Levels: 2

Square Footage: 3,206

Main Level Sq. Ft.: 2,064

Upper Level Sq. Ft.: 1,142

Bedrooms: 4

Bathrooms: 3½

Foundation: Basement

Materials List Available: No

Price Category: G

Images provided by designer/architect.

Rear Elevation

Main Level Floor Plan

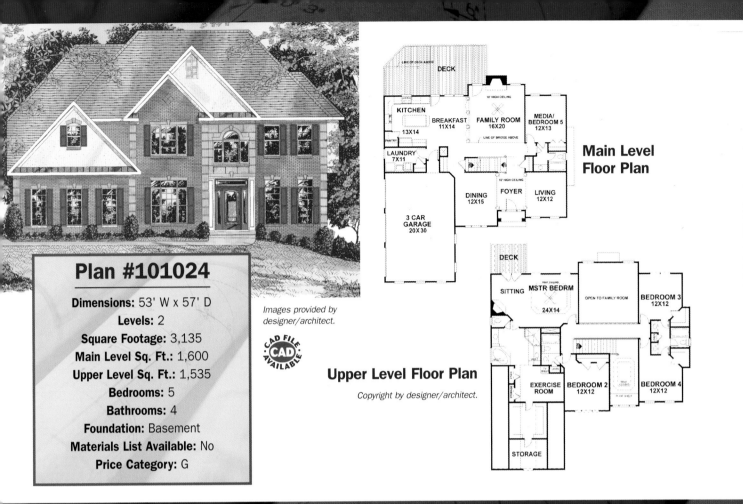

Plan #101024

Dimensions: 53' W x 57' D
Levels: 2
Square Footage: 3,135
Main Level Sq. Ft.: 1,600
Upper Level Sq. Ft.: 1,535
Bedrooms: 5
Bathrooms: 4
Foundation: Basement
Materials List Available: No
Price Category: G

Images provided by designer/architect.

Main Level Floor Plan

Upper Level Floor Plan

Copyright by designer/architect.

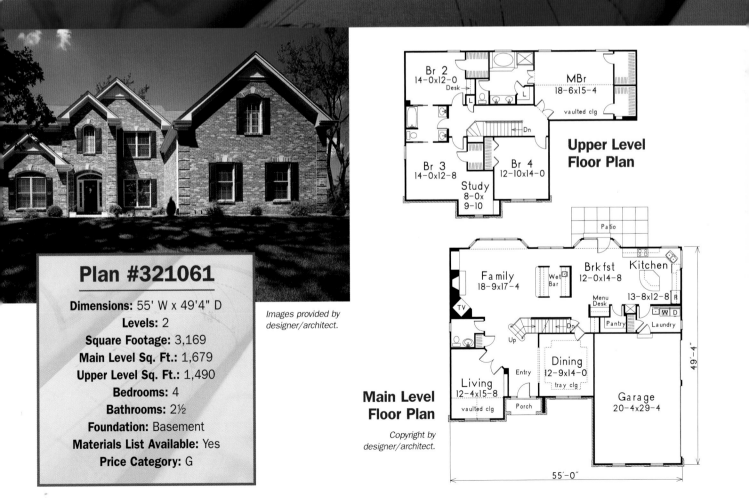

Plan #321061

Dimensions: 55' W x 49'4" D
Levels: 2
Square Footage: 3,169
Main Level Sq. Ft.: 1,679
Upper Level Sq. Ft.: 1,490
Bedrooms: 4
Bathrooms: 2½
Foundation: Basement
Materials List Available: Yes
Price Category: G

Images provided by designer/architect.

Upper Level Floor Plan

Main Level Floor Plan

Copyright by designer/architect.

Plan #101119

Dimensions: 60' W x 99' D

Levels: 2

Square Footage: 3,264

Main Level Sq. Ft.: 2,082

Upper Level Sq. Ft.: 1,182

Bedrooms: 4

Bathrooms: 4½

Foundation: Crawl space or basement

Material List Available: No

Price Category: G

Images provided by designer/architect.

Upper Level Floor Plan

Main Level Floor Plan

Copyright by designer/architect.

Plan #151126

Dimensions: 89' W x 86'4" D

Levels: 1.5

Square Footage: 3,474

Bedrooms: 4

Bathrooms: 5

Foundation: Crawl space or slab; walkout or basement for fee

CompleteCost List Available: Yes

Price Category: E

Images provided by designer/architect.

Main Level Floor Plan

Upper Level Floor Plan

Copyright by designer/architect.

Plan #441013

Dimensions: 69' W x 59' D
Levels: 2
Square Footage: 3,317
Main Level Sq. Ft.: 2,657
Lower Level Sq. Ft.: 660
Bedrooms: 4
Bathrooms: 3½
Foundation: Slab
Materials List Available: No
Price Category: G

Images provided by designer/architect.

Take best advantage of views with this unique luxury residence. The contemporary façade dresses up the two-level home, which puts its main living areas on the upper level.

CAD FILE AVAILABLE

Features:

• **Foyer:** Double doors on the lower floor open to this two-story welcoming space, which leads to the curved staircase to the main level or to the office (or bedroom) with full bathroom on the lower level. If you prefer, take the elevator to the main floor upstairs.

• **Common Areas:** Living and dining areas on the main level are open and include the great room, with fireplace and built-in media center; the formal dining area, defined by

decorative columns; and the breakfast nook, which is attached to the island kitchen.

• **Master Suite:** This suite is on the right side of the main level. It has a bay window, and the mater bath area has a spa bathtub with dual vanities and walk-in closet.

• **Bedrooms:** The two additional bedrooms are located on the main level and share the compartmented bathroom there. Each has a walk-in closet.

Lower Level Floor Plan

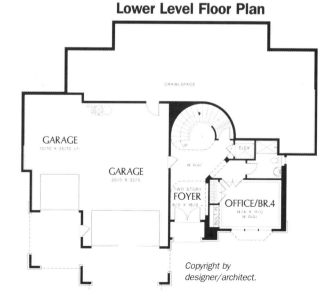

Copyright by designer/architect.

Main Level Floor Plan

Plan #121062

Dimensions: 70' W x 62' D

Levels: 2

Square Footage: 3,448

Main Level Sq. Ft.: 2,375

Upper Level Sq. Ft.: 1,073

Bedrooms: 4

Bathrooms: 3½

Foundation: Basement

Materials List Available: Yes

Price Category: G

Images provided by designer/architect.

You'll love this design if you're looking for a comfortable home with dimensions and details that create a sense of grandeur.

Features:

• Entry: A soaring ceiling, curved staircase, and balcony that overlooks a tall plant shelf combine to create your first impression of grandeur in this home.

• Great Room: A transom-topped bowed window highlights this room, with its 11-ft., beamed ceiling, built-in wet bar, and see-through fireplace.

• Kitchen: Designed for the gourmet cook, this kitchen has every amenity you could desire.

• Breakfast Room: Adjacent to the great room and the kitchen, this gazebo-shaped breakfast area lights both the kitchen and hearth room.

Main Level Floor Plan

Upper Level Floor Plan

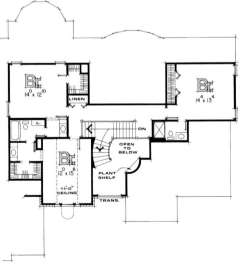

Copyright by designer/architect.

Plan #151024

Dimensions: 60' W x 73'8" D
Levels: 2
Square Footage: 3,623
Main Level Sq. Ft.: 2,391
Upper Level Sq. Ft.: 1,232
Bedrooms: 3
Bathrooms: 3½
Foundation: Crawl space, slab; optional full basement plan available for extra fee
CompleteCost List Available: Yes
Price Category: H

Images provided by designer/architect.

The 2-story foyer gives elegance to this traditional home with four fireplaces, 10-ft. ceilings, and multiple pairs of French doors.

Features:

• Great Room: With French doors leading to the covered porch, the study, and the master suite, this room is a natural hub for guests and family.

• Study: Off the great room, this impressive study features an 11-ft. ceiling and gas fireplace.

• Master Suite: Enter from the great room, and enjoy the fireplace, two walk-in closets, the whirlpool tub, and a private patio.

• Kitchen/Hearth Room: Always the traditional center of activity, this area includes a computer area, an island, ample storage, a butler's pantry, and a separate laundry/hobby room with a sink.

• Game Room: Upstairs, the game room is just the place for hosting large groups.

Main Level Floor Plan

Copyright by designer/architect.

Upper Level Floor Plan

Plan #181221

Dimensions: 60' W x 44' D

Levels: 2

Square Footage: 3,411

Main Level Sq. Ft.: 1,488

Upper Level Sq. Ft.: 603

Basement Level Sq. Ft.: 1,321

Bedrooms: 3

Bathrooms: 2½

Foundation: Basement

Materials List Available: Yes

Price Category: G

This stone- and wood-sided home will be a joy to come home to.

Features:

- Living Room: This large entertaining area features a fireplace and large windows.

- Kitchen: Any cook would feel at home in this island kitchen, which has an abundance of cabinets and counter space.

- Master Bedroom: Located on the main level for privacy, this room features a walk-in closet and access to the main-level full bathroom.

- Bedrooms: One bedroom is located on the upper level and the other is located on the main level. Each has a large closet.

CAD FILE AVAILABLE

Study

Living Room

Main Level Floor Plan

44'-0"
13,2 m

60'-0"
18.0 m

Upper Level Floor Plan

Copyright by designer/architect.

Basement Level Floor Plan

Dining Room/ Kitchen

Foyer

Main Level Floor Plan

Images provided by designer/architect.

CAD FILE AVAILABLE

Plan #151180

Dimensions: 67'3" W x 68'6" D

Levels: 2

Square Footage: 3,167

Main Level Sq. Ft.: 2,486

Upper Level Sq. Ft.: 681

Bedrooms: 4

Bathrooms: 3

Foundation: Crawl space or slab; basement or walkout available for fee

CompleteCost List Available: Yes

Price Category: G

Upper Level Floor Plan

Copyright by designer/architect.

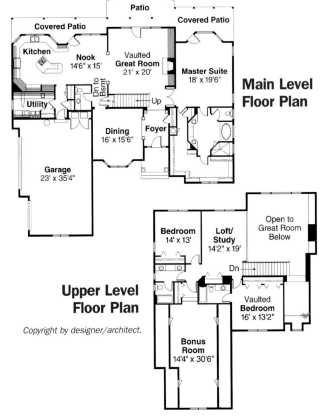

Images provided by designer/architect.

CAD FILE AVAILABLE

Plan #361036

Dimensions: 71' W x 70' D

Levels: 2

Square Footage: 3,541

Main Level Sq. Ft.: 2,551

Upper Level Sq. Ft.: 990

Bedrooms: 3

Bathrooms: 3½

Foundation: Crawl space or basement

Material List Available: No

Price Category: H

Main Level Floor Plan

Upper Level Floor Plan

Copyright by designer/architect.

Plan #451005

Dimensions: 71'10" W x 56'6" D

Levels: 2

Square Footage: 2,355

Bedrooms: 4

Bathrooms: 2½

Foundation: Walkout basement

Material List Available: No

Price Category: E

Images provided by designer/architect.

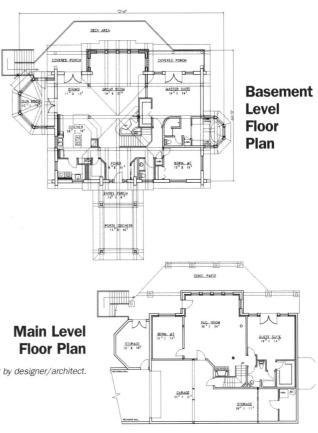

Basement Level Floor Plan

Main Level Floor Plan

Copyright by designer/architect.

Plan #151106

Dimensions: 70' W x 81' D

Levels: 1.5

Square Footage: 3,568

Main Level Sq. Ft.: 3,051

Upper Level Sq. Ft.: 517

Bedrooms: 3

Bathrooms: 3 full, 2 half

Foundation: Crawl space or slab; basement or walkout for fee

CompleteCost List Available: Yes

Price Category: F

Images provided by designer/architect.

Main Level Floor Plan

Upper Level Floor Plan

Copyright by designer/architect.

Plan #441024

Dimensions: 90'6" W x 84' D
Levels: 2
Square Footage: 3,517
Main Level Sq. Ft.: 2,698
Upper Level Sq. Ft.: 819
Bedrooms: 3
Bathrooms: 3½
Foundation: Crawl space; slab or basement available for fee
Materials List Available: No
Price Category: H

Images provided by designer/architect.

You'll feel like royalty every time you pull into the driveway of this European-styled manor house.

Features:

- Kitchen: This gourmet chef's center hosts an island with a vegetable sink. The arched opening above the primary sink provides a view of the fireplace and entertainment center in the great room. A walk-in food pantry and a butler's pantry are situated between this space and the dining room.

- Master Suite: Located on the main level, this private retreat boasts a large sleeping area and a sitting area. The grand master bath features a large walk-in closet, dual vanities, a large tub, and a shower.

- Bedrooms: Two secondary bedrooms are located on the upper level, and each has its own bathroom.

- Laundry Room: This utility room houses cabinets, a folding counter, and an ironing board.

- Garage: This large three-car garage has room for storage. Family members entering the home from this area will find a coat closet and a place to stash briefcases and backpacks.

Rear View

**Main Level
Floor Plan**

◄90'-6"►

84'

**Upper Level
Floor Plan**

Copyright by designer/architect.

Kitchen

Great Room

Master bath

Master Bedroom

Main Level Floor Plan

Plan #151112

Dimensions: 67'8" W x 49' D

Levels: 2

Square Footage: 3,661

Main Level Sq. Ft.: 2,018

Upper Level Sq. Ft.: 1,643

Bedrooms: 4

Bathrooms: 2½

Foundation: Crawl space or slab; basement or walkout available for fee

CompleteCost List Available: Yes

Price Category: F

Images provided by designer/architect.

Front View

Upper Level Floor Plan

Copyright by designer/architect.

Main Level Floor Plan

Plan #151011

Dimensions: 59'6" W x 74'4" D

Levels: 2

Square Footage: 3,437

Main Level Sq. Ft.: 2,184

Upper Level Sq. Ft.: 1,253

Bedrooms: 5

Bathrooms: 4

Foundation: Crawl space or slab; basement or daylight basement for fee

CompleteCost List Available: Yes

Price Category: G

Images provided by designer/architect.

Copyright by designer/architect.

Upper Level Floor Plan

Plan #441025

Dimensions: 70' W x 101'6" D
Levels: 2
Square Footage: 3,457
Main Level Sq. Ft.: 2,222
Upper Level Sq. Ft.: 1,235
Bedrooms: 4
Bathrooms: 3 full, 2 half
Foundation: Crawl space;
slab or basement available for fee
Materials List Available: No
Price Category: G

Images provided by designer/architect.

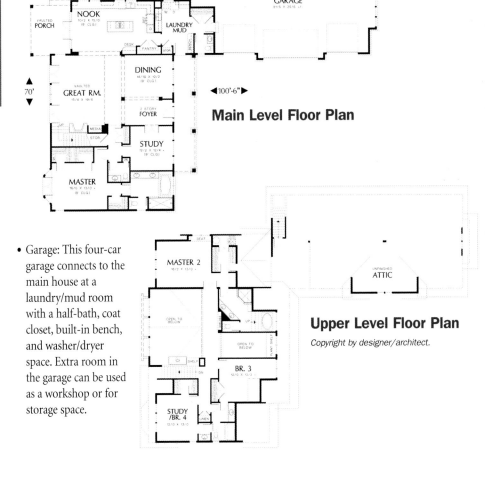

Main Level Floor Plan

Upper Level Floor Plan

Copyright by designer/architect.

Classic Craftsman tradition shines through in this spectacular two-story home.

Features:

- **Great Room:** This open room features two sets of double doors to the rear yard, a fireplace, and a built-in media center.

- **Kitchen:** Casual dining takes place in the breakfast nook, which is open to this island kitchen and leads to a vaulted porch.

- **Master Suites:** One master suite is found on the first floor. It glows with appointments, from double-door access to the rear yard to a fine bath with spa tub, separate shower, and double sinks. The second master suite, on the second floor, holds a window seat and a private bath with spa tub.

- **Bedrooms:** Two additional bedrooms (or a bedroom and a study) share a full compartmented bathroom with private vanities for each room.

- **Garage:** This four-car garage connects to the main house at a laundry/mud room with a half-bath, coat closet, built-in bench, and washer/dryer space. Extra room in the garage can be used as a workshop or for storage space.

Plan #121063

Dimensions: 84' W x 52' D
Levels: 2
Square Footage: 3,473
Main Level Sq. Ft.: 2,500
Upper Level Sq. Ft.: 973
Bedrooms: 4
Bathrooms: 3½
Foundation: Basement
Materials List Available: Yes
Price Category: G

Images provided by designer/architect.

Enjoy the many amenities in this well-designed and gracious home.

Features:

- Entry: A large sparkling window and a tapering split staircase distinguish this lovely entryway.

- Great Room: This spacious great room will be the heart of your new home. It has a 14-ft. spider-beamed window that serves to highlight its built-in bookcase, built-in entertainment center, raised hearth fireplace,

wet bar, and lovely arched windows topped with transoms.

- Kitchen: Anyone who walks into this kitchen will realize that it's designed for both convenience and efficiency.

- Master Suite: The tiered ceiling in the bedroom gives an elegant touch, and the bay window adds to it. The two large walk-in closets and the spacious bath, with columns setting off the whirlpool tub and two vanities, complete this dream of a suite.

Main Level Floor Plan

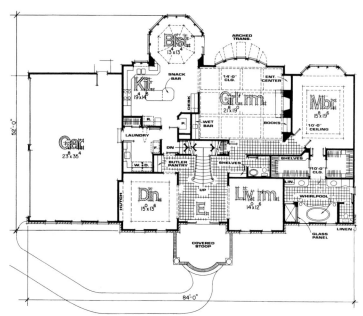

Upper Level Floor Plan

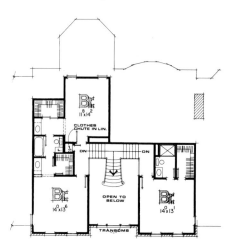

Copyright by designer/architect.

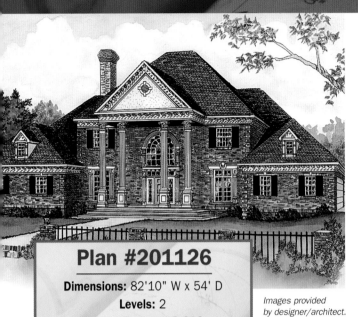

Upper Level Floor Plan

childrens den 18⁸ x 12
br 3 14 x 12
br 4 14⁴ x 12
open to foy
br 2 16⁴ x 12

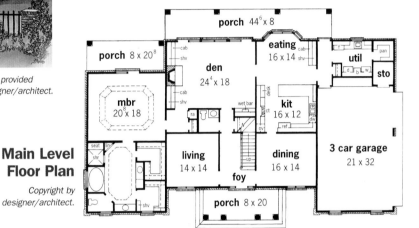

Main Level Floor Plan

Copyright by designer/architect.

porch 44⁶ x 8
porch 8 x 20⁸
eating 16 x 14
util
den 24⁴ x 18
mbr 20⁸ x 18
wet bar
kit 16 x 12
sto
living 14 x 14
dining 16 x 14
3 car garage 21 x 32
foy
porch 8 x 20

Plan #201126

Dimensions: 82'10" W x 54' D
Levels: 2
Square Footage: 3,813
Main Level Sq. Ft.: 2,553
Upper Level Sq. Ft.: 1,260
Bedrooms: 4
Bathrooms: 3½
Foundation: Crawl space, slab
Materials List Available: Yes
Price Category: H

Images provided by designer/architect.

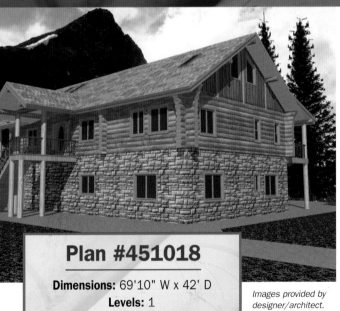

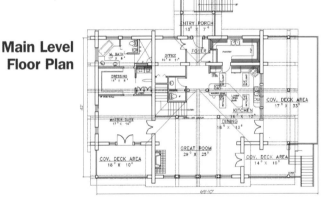

Main Level Floor Plan

Basement Level Floor Plan

Copyright by designer/architect.

Plan #451018

Dimensions: 69'10" W x 42' D
Levels: 1
Square Footage: 3,755
Main Level Sq. Ft.: 1,944
Basement Level Sq. Ft.: 1,811
Bedrooms: 2
Bathrooms: 2½
Foundation: Basement or walkout
Material List Available: No
Price Category: H

Images provided by designer/architect.

CAD FILE AVAILABLE

Rear Elevation

Plan #121019

Dimensions: 70' W x 60' D
Levels: 2
Square Footage: 3,775
Main Level Sq. Ft.: 1,923
Upper Level Sq. Ft.: 1,852
Bedrooms: 4
Bathrooms: 3
Foundation: Basement
Materials List Available: Yes
Price Category: H

Images provided by designer/architect.

The grand exterior presence is carried inside, beginning with the dramatic curved staircase.

Features:

• Ceiling Height: 8 ft.

• Den: French doors lead to the sophisticated den, with its bayed windows and wall of bookcases.

• Living Room: A curved wall and a series of arched windows highlight this large space.

• Formal Dining Room: The living room shares the curved wall and arched windows found in the living room.

• Screened Porch: This huge space features skylights and is accessible by another French door from the dining room.

• Family Room: Family and guests alike will be drawn to this room, with its trio of arched windows and fireplace flanked by bookcases.

• Kitchen: An island adds convenience and distinction to this large, functional kitchen.

• Garage: This spacious three-bay garage provides plenty of space for cars and storage.

Main Level Floor Plan

Upper Level Floor Plan

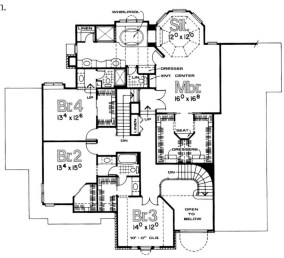

Copyright by designer/architect.

Plan #161096

Dimensions: 67'6" W x 75'6" D
Levels: 2
Square Footage: 3,435
Main Level Sq. Ft.: 2,479
Upper Level Sq. Ft.: 956
Bedrooms: 4
Bathrooms: 3½
Foundation: Walkout basement;
basement for fee
Material List Available: No
Price Category: G

A stone-and-brick exterior is excellently coordinated to create a warm and charming showplace.

Features:

- Great Room: The spacious foyer leads directly into this room, which visually opens to the rear yard, providing natural light and outdoor charm.

- Kitchen: This fully equipped kitchen is located to provide the utmost convenience in serving the formal dining room and the breakfast area, which is surrounded by windows and has a double-soffit ceiling treatment. The combination of breakfast room, hearth room, and kitchen creatively forms a comfortable family gathering place.

- Master Suite: A tray ceiling tops this suite and its luxurious dressing area, which will pamper you after a hard day.

- Balcony: Wood rails decorate the stairs leading to this balcony, which offers a dramatic view of the great room and foyer below.

- Bedrooms: A secondary private bedroom suite with personal bath, plus two bedrooms that share a Jack-and-Jill bathroom, complete the exciting home.

Images provided by designer/architect.

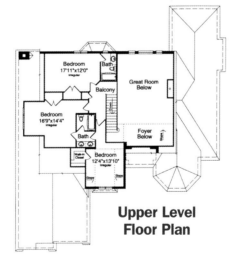

**Upper Level
Floor Plan**

Rear Elevation

Hearth Room

**Main Level
Floor Plan**

*Copyright by
designer/architect.*

www.ultimateplans.com   305

Plan #161086

Dimensions: 65'8" W x 52'8" D

Levels: 2

Square Footage: 3,610

Main Level Sq. Ft.: 1,838

Upper Level Sq. Ft.: 1,772

Bedrooms: 4

Bathrooms: 3½

Foundation: Walkout; crawl space, slab or basement for fee

Materials List Available: Yes

Price Category: H

Images provided by designer/architect.

Main Level Floor Plan

Upper Level Floor Plan

Optional Basement Level Floor Plan

Copyright by designer/architect.

Plan #361034

Images provided by designer/architect.

Dimensions: 115' W x 84' D

Levels: 1

Square Footage: 3,926

Bedrooms: 3

Bathrooms: 3½

Foundation: Slab

Material List Available: No

Price Category: H

Copyright by designer/architect.

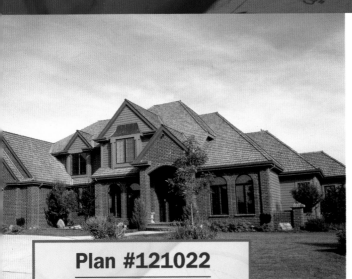

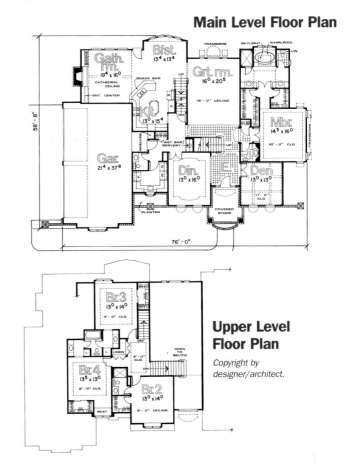

Main Level Floor Plan

Images provided by designer/architect.

Upper Level Floor Plan

Copyright by designer/architect.

Plan #121022

Dimensions: 76' W x 58'8" D
Levels: 2
Square Footage: 3,556
Main Level Sq. Ft.: 2,555
Upper Level Sq. Ft.: 1,001
Bedrooms: 4
Bathrooms: 3 full, 2 half
Foundation: Basement
Materials List Available: Yes
Price Category: H

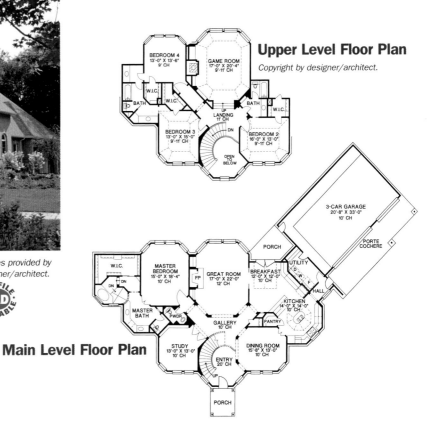

Upper Level Floor Plan

Copyright by designer/architect.

Images provided by designer/architect.

Main Level Floor Plan

Plan #121100

Dimensions: 100'10" W x 80'5" D
Levels: 2
Square Footage: 3,750
Main Level Sq. Ft.: 2,274
Upper Level Sq. Ft.: 1,476
Bedrooms: 4
Bathrooms: 3½
Foundation: Slab
Materials List Available: No
Price Category: G

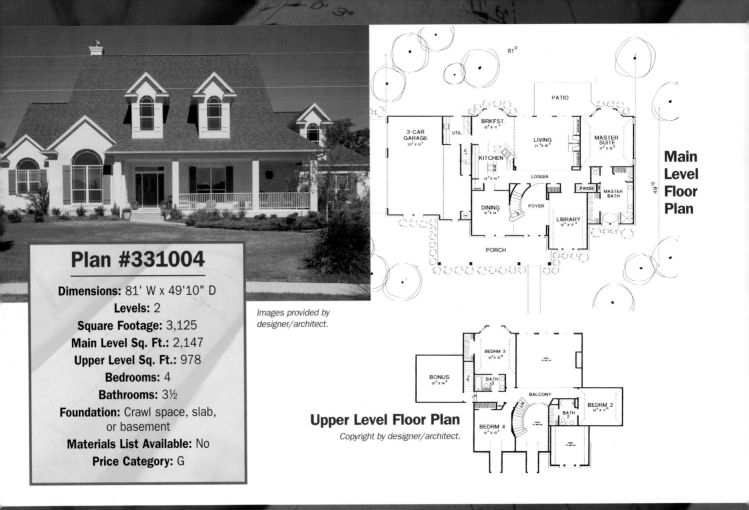

Plan #331004

Dimensions: 81' W x 49'10" D
Levels: 2
Square Footage: 3,125
Main Level Sq. Ft.: 2,147
Upper Level Sq. Ft.: 978
Bedrooms: 4
Bathrooms: 3½
Foundation: Crawl space, slab, or basement
Materials List Available: No
Price Category: G

Images provided by designer/architect.

Main Level Floor Plan

Upper Level Floor Plan

Copyright by designer/architect.

Plan #151055

Dimensions: 82'4" W x 81'6" D
Levels: 1
Square Footage: 3,183
Bedrooms: 4
Bathrooms: 2½
Foundation: Crawl space or slab; basement or walkout available for fee
CompleteCost List Available: Yes
Price Category: E

Images provided by designer/architect.

CAD FILE AVAILABLE

Copyright by designer/architect.

Front View

Plan #441029

Dimensions: 70' W x 71' D
Levels: 2
Square Footage: 3,217
Main Level Sq. Ft.: 2,292
Upper Level Sq. Ft.: 925
Bedrooms: 3
Bathrooms: 3½
Foundation: Crawl space;
slab or basement available for fee
Material List Available: No
Price Category: G

Images provided by designer/architect.

Influenced by the Modernist movement, this California contemporary design is grand in façade and comfortable to live in.

Features:

• Entry: The two-story foyer opens to the formal dining room (also two-story) and the great room. Decorative columns help define these spaces. The curved wall of glass overlooking the rear patio brightens the great room.

• Master Suite: This suite, which has a salon with curved window wall, features a private bath with spa tub and walk-in closet.

• Bedrooms: The two family bedrooms share the upper level with the library, which has built-ins. Each upper-level bedroom has its own bathroom and walk-in closet.

• Home Office: The left wing of the main level contains this space, which features a curved window wall.

Upper Level Floor Plan

Copyright by designer/architect.

Main Level Floor Plan

Rear View

Plan #151232

Dimensions: 79'6" W x 71'4" D
Levels: 1.5
Square Footage: 3,901
Main Level Sq. Ft.: 3,185
Upper Level Sq. Ft.: 716
Bedrooms: 3
Bathrooms: 4
Foundation: Crawl space or slab
CompleteCost List Available: Yes
Price Category: H

This elegant brick home has something for everyone

Features:

• **Great Room:** This large gathering area has a fireplace and access to the rear grilling porch.

• **Hearth Room:** Relaxing and casual, this cozy area has a fireplace and is open to the kitchen.

• **Kitchen:** This large island kitchen has a built-in pantry and is open to the breakfast nook.

• **Master Suite:** A private bathroom with a corner whirlpool tub and a large walk-in closet turn this area into a spacious retreat.

• **Bonus Room:** This large space located upstairs near the two secondary bedrooms can be turned into a media room.

Images provided by designer/architect.

Main Level Floor Plan

Copyright by designer/architect.

Upper Level Floor Plan

Kitchen

Great Room

Plan #121023

Dimensions: 85'5" W x 74'8" D
Levels: 2
Square Footage: 3,904
Main Level Sq. Ft.: 2,813
Upper Level Sq. Ft.: 1,091
Bedrooms: 4
Bathrooms: 3½
Foundation: Basement
Materials List Available: Yes
Price Category: H

Images provided by designer/architect.

Spacious and gracious, here are all the amenities you expect in a fine home.

Features:

- Ceiling Height: 8 ft. except as noted.
- Foyer: This magnificent entry features a graceful curved staircase with balcony above.
- Sunken Living Room: This sunken room is filled with light from a row of bowed windows. It's the perfect place for social gatherings both large and small.
- Den: French doors open into this truly distinctive den with its 11-ft. ceiling and built-in bookcases.
- Formal Dining Room: Entertain guests with style and grace in this dining room with corner column.
- Master Suite: Another set of French doors leads to this suite that features two walk-in closets, a whirlpool flanked by vanities, and a private sitting room with built-in bookcases.

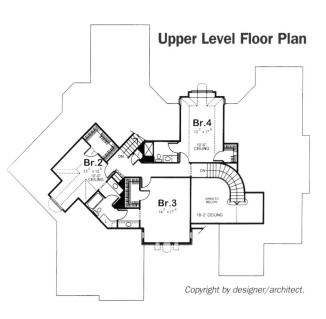

Copyright by designer/architect.

Plan #161035

Dimensions: 75' W x 64'11" D
Levels: 2
Square Footage: 3,688
Main Level Sq. Ft.: 2,702
Upper Level Sq. Ft.: 986
Bedrooms: 4
Bathrooms: 3½
Foundation: Basement
Materials List Available: No
Price Category: H

Images provided by designer/architect.

You'll appreciate the style of the stone, brick, and cedar shake exterior of this contemporary home.

Features:

- Hearth Room: Positioned for an easy flow for guests and family, this hearth room features a bank of windows that integrate it with the yard.

- Breakfast Room: Move through the sliding doors here to the rear porch on sunny days.

- Kitchen: Outfitted for a gourmet cook, this kitchen is also ideal for friends and family who can perch at the island or serve themselves at the bar.

- Master Suite: A stepped ceiling, crown moldings, and boxed window make the bedroom easy to decorate, while the two walk-in closets, lavish dressing area, and whirlpool tub in the bath make this area comfortable and luxurious.

Main Level Floor Plan

Upper Level Floor Plan

Copyright by designer/architect.

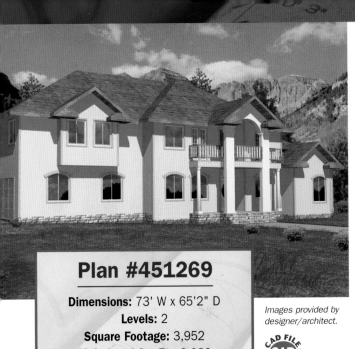

Main Level Floor Plan

Plan #451269

Dimensions: 73' W x 65'2" D
Levels: 2
Square Footage: 3,952
Main Level Sq. Ft.: 2,080
Upper Level Sq. Ft.: 1,872
Bedrooms: 3
Bathrooms: 3
Foundation: Crawl space
Material List Available: No
Price Category: H

Images provided by designer/architect.

CAD FILE AVAILABLE

Rear Elevation

Upper Level Floor Plan

Copyright by designer/architect.

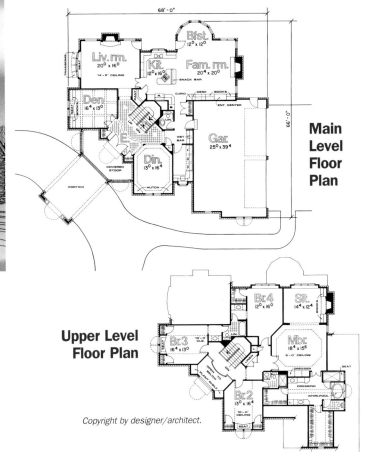

Main Level Floor Plan

Plan #121103

Dimensions: 68' W x 66' D
Levels: 2
Square Footage: 3,992
Main Level Sq. Ft.: 2,040
Upper Level Sq. Ft.: 1,952
Bedrooms: 4
Bathrooms: 3½
Foundation: Basement
Material List Available: Yes
Price Category: H

Images provided by designer/architect.

CAD FILE AVAILABLE

Upper Level Floor Plan

Copyright by designer/architect.

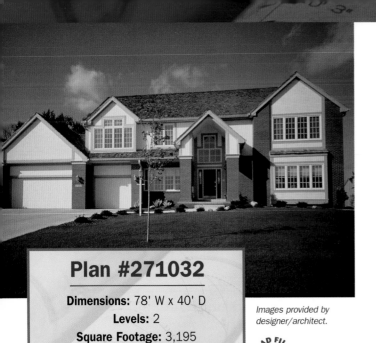

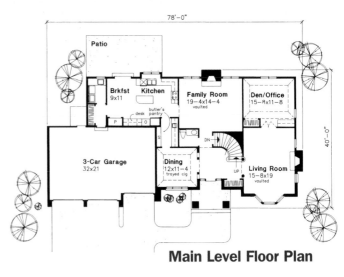

Main Level Floor Plan

Plan #271032

Dimensions: 78' W x 40' D

Levels: 2

Square Footage: 3,195

Main Level Sq. Ft.: 1,758

Upper Level Sq. Ft.: 1,437

Bedrooms: 4

Bathrooms: 2½

Foundation: Basement

Materials List Available: No

Price Category: E

Upper Level Floor Plan

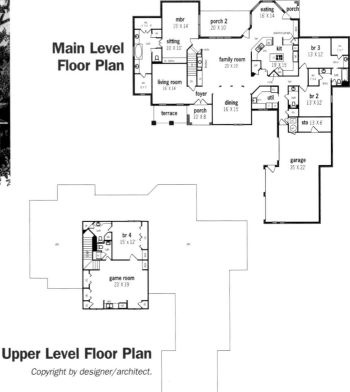

Main Level Floor Plan

Plan #211150

Dimensions: 86' W x 86' D

Levels: 2

Square Footage: 3,970

Main Level Sq. Ft.: 3,086

Upper Level Sq. Ft.: 884

Bedrooms: 4

Bathrooms: 3 full, 2 half

Foundation: Slab

Materials List Available: No

Price Category: H

Upper Level Floor Plan

**Main Level
Floor Plan**

Plan #121026

Dimensions: 66'8" W x 76' D

Levels: 2

Square Footage: 3,926

Main Level Sq. Ft.: 2,351

Upper Level Sq. Ft.: 1,575

Bedrooms: 4

Bathrooms: 3 full, 2 half

Foundation: Basement

Materials List Available: Yes

Price Category: H

*Images provided by
designer/architect.*

**Upper Level
Floor Plan**

*Copyright by
designer/architect.*

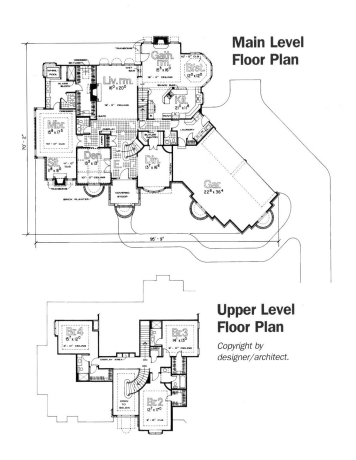

**Main Level
Floor Plan**

Plan #121018

Dimensions: 95'9" W x 70'2" D

Levels: 2

Square Footage: 3,950

Main Level Sq. Ft.: 2,839

Upper Level Sq. Ft.: 1,111

Bedrooms: 4

Bathrooms: 4 full, 2 half

Foundation: Basement

Materials List Available: Yes

Price Category: H

*Images provided by
designer/architect.*

**Upper Level
Floor Plan**

*Copyright by
designer/architect.*

Plan #441026

Dimensions: 60' W x 52' D

Levels: 2

Square Footage: 3,623

Main Level Sq. Ft.: 1,835

Upper Level Sq. Ft.: 1,788

Bedrooms: 4

Bathrooms: 2½

Foundation: Crawl space

Materials List Available: No

Price Category: H

CAD FILE AVAILABLE · CAD

Images provided by designer/architect.

Crazy about Craftsman styling? This exquisite plan has it in abundance and doesn't skimp on the floor plan, either. Massive stone bases support the Arts and Crafts columns at the entry porch.

Features:

- Living Room: This large gathering area features a cozy fireplace.
- Dining Room: This formal room is connected to the island kitchen via a butler's pantry.

- Master Suite: Located upstairs, this suite features a walk-in closet and luxury bath.
- Bedrooms: The three family bedrooms share a centrally located compartmented bathroom.

Rear Elevation

Main Level Floor Plan

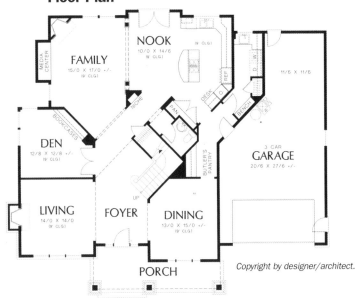

Copyright by designer/architect.

Upper Level Floor Plan

Plan #371092

Dimensions: 71'6" W x 70'8" D
Levels: 2
Square Footage: 3,836
Main Level Sq. Ft.: 2,981
Upper Level Sq. Ft.: 855
Bedrooms: 5
Bathrooms: 4
Foundation: Slab
Materials List Available: No
Price Category: H

Images provided by designer/architect.

This grand home has an arched covered entry and great styling that would make this home a focal point of the neighborhood.

Features:

- Family Room: This large gathering area boasts a fireplace flanked by a built-in media center. Large windows flood the room with natural light, and there is access to the rear porch.

- Kitchen: This large island kitchen has a raised bar and is open to the family room. Its walk-in pantry has plenty of room for supplies.

- Master Suite: This retreat features a stepped ceiling and a see-through fireplace to the master bath, which has a large walk-in closet, dual vanities, a glass shower, and a marble tub.

- Secondary Bedrooms: Bedrooms 2 and 3 are located on the main level and share a common bathroom. Bedrooms 4 and 5 are located on the upper level and share a Jack-and-Jill bathroom.

Main Level Floor Plan

Upper Level Floor Plan

Plan #441012

Dimensions: 65' W x 55' D
Levels: 1
Square Footage: 3,682
Main Level Sq. Ft.: 2,192
Basement Level Sq. Ft.: 1,490
Bedrooms: 4
Bathrooms: 4
Foundation: Slab
Materials List Available: No
Price Category: H

Images provided by designer/architect.

Accommodating a site that slopes to the rear, this home is not only good-looking but practical.

Features:

• **Den:** Just off the foyer is this cozy space, complete with built-ins.

• **Great Room:** This vaulted gathering area features a lovely fireplace, a built-in media center, and a view of the back yard.

• **Kitchen:** This island kitchen is ready to handle the daily needs of your family or aid in entertaining your guests.

• **Lower Level:** Adding even more livability to the home, this floor contains the games room with media center and corner fireplace, two more bedrooms (each with a full bathroom), and the wide covered patio.

CAD FILE AVAILABLE

Main Level Floor Plan

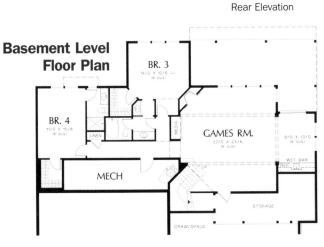

Rear Elevation

Basement Level Floor Plan

Copyright by designer/architect.

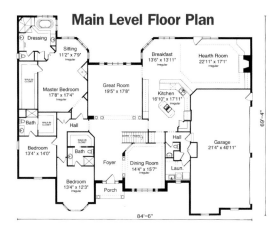

Copyright by designer/architect.

Images provided by designer/architect.

Optional Basement Level Floor Plan

Plan #321034

Dimensions: 75'8" W x 52'6" D

Levels: 1

Square Footage: 3,508

Bedrooms: 4

Bathrooms: 3

Foundation: Basement, walkout

Materials List Available: Yes

Price Category: H

Main Level Floor Plan

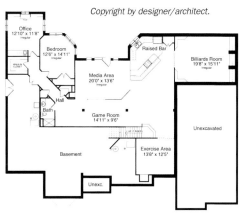

Copyright by designer/architect.

Images provided by designer/architect.

Optional Basement Level Floor Plan

Plan #161028

Dimensions: 84'6" W x 69'4" D

Levels: 1

Square Footage: 3,570

Optional Finished Basement Sq. Ft.: 2,367

Bedrooms: 3

Bathrooms: 3½

Foundation: Basement

Materials List Available: Yes

Price Category: H

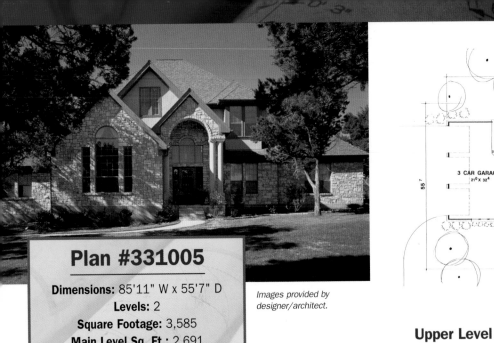
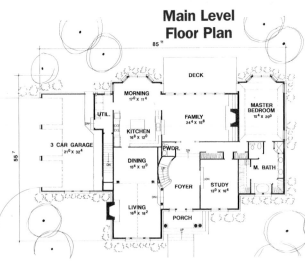

Main Level Floor Plan

Plan #331005

Dimensions: 85'11" W x 55'7" D
Levels: 2
Square Footage: 3,585
Main Level Sq. Ft.: 2,691
Upper Level Sq. Ft.: 894
Bedrooms: 4
Bathrooms: 3½
Foundation: Crawl space, slab, or basement
Materials List Available: No
Price Category: H

Upper Level Floor Plan

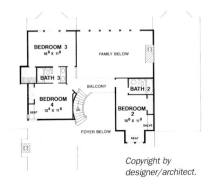

Rear View

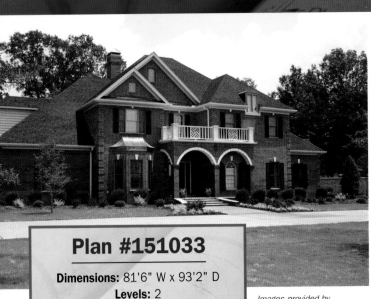

Main Level Floor Plan

Plan #151033

Dimensions: 81'6" W x 93'2" D
Levels: 2
Square Footage: 5,548
Main Level Sq. Ft.: 3,276
Upper Level Sq. Ft.: 2,272
Bedrooms: 5
Bathrooms: 4½
Foundation: Crawl space or slab; basement for fee
CompleteCost List Available: Yes
Price Category: J

CAD FILE AVAILABLE

Upper Level Floor Plan

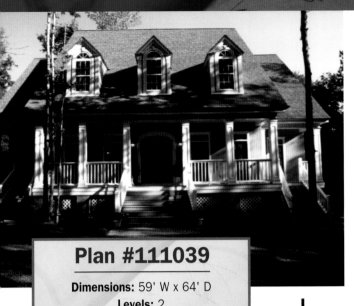

Main Level Floor Plan

Wood Deck 30'10"x 13'

Porch 30'5"x 8'

Master Bedroom 16'4"x 16'4"

Breakfast 11'4"x 13'

Living 21'6"x 17'2"

Util.

WIC WIC

Kitchen 11'4" 18'4"

Bath WIC Ma. Bath

Dining 13'6"x 13'10"

Study 13'8"x 12'

Foyer

Porch

Porch

Porch 36'x 7'

Plan #111039

Dimensions: 59' W x 64' D
Levels: 2
Square Footage: 3,335
Main Level Sq. Ft.: 2,129
Upper Level Sq. Ft.: 1,206
Bedrooms: 4
Bathrooms: 4
Foundation: Basement
Materials List Available: No
Price Category: G

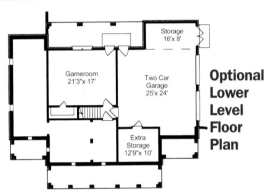

Storage 16'x 8'

Gameroom 21'3"x 17'

Two Car Garage 25'x 24'

Extra Storage 12'9"x 10'

Optional Lower Level Floor Plan

Upper Level Floor Plan

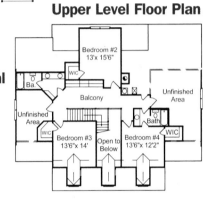

Bedroom #2 13'x 15'6"

Ba. WIC

Balcony

Unfinished Area

Unfinished Area

Bath WIC

Bedroom #3 13'6"x 14'

Open to Below

Bedroom #4 13'6"x 12'2"

Main Level Floor Plan

SUNROOM 12'0" X 13'0"

NK. 11'0" X 8'0"

KIT. 15'0" X 14'0"

FAM. RM. 2-STORY CLG. 20'0" X 15'0"

VAULTED CLG.

MBR. 19'0" X 14'0"

4 CAR GAR. 21'0" X 38'0"

DIN. 13'0" X 13'0"

SIT. AREA 10'0" X 8'0"

STUDY 12'0" X 12'0"

E. 2-STORY CLG.

Plan #221022

Dimensions: 79' W x 55' D
Levels: 2
Square Footage: 3,382
Main Level Sq. Ft.: 2,376
Upper Level Sq. Ft.: 1,006
Bedrooms: 4
Bathrooms: 3½
Foundation: Basement
Materials List Available: No
Price Category: G

CAD FILE AVAILABLE

OPEN TO FAM. RM.

BR. #4 11'8" X 12'4"

BR. #2 13'4" X 12'8"

OPEN TO E.

BR. #3 11'8" X 12'6"

Upper Level Floor Plan

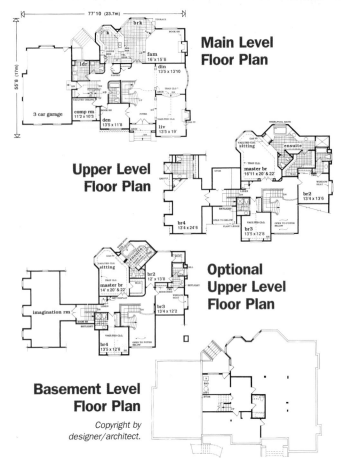

Plan #401049

Dimensions: 77'10" W x 55'8" D

Levels: 2

Square Footage: 4,087

Main Level Sq. Ft.: 2,403

Upper Level Sq. Ft.: 1,684

Bedrooms: 4

Bathrooms: 4½

Foundation: Basement

Materials List Available: Yes

Price Category: I

Images provided by designer/architect.

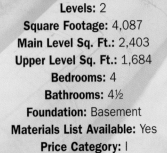

Main Level Floor Plan

Upper Level Floor Plan

Optional Upper Level Floor Plan

Basement Level Floor Plan

Copyright by designer/architect.

Plan #161056

Dimensions: 86'2" W x 63'8" D

Levels: 1

Square Footage: 5,068

Main Level Sq. Ft.: 3,171

Basement Level Sq. Ft.: 1,897

Bedrooms: 4

Bathrooms: 3½

Foundation: Basement or walkout

Material List Available: Yes

Price Category: J

Images provided by designer/architect.

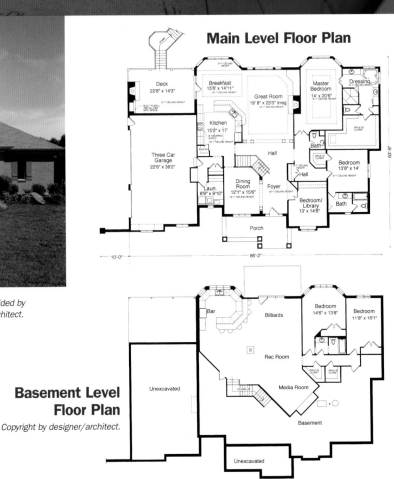

Main Level Floor Plan

Basement Level Floor Plan

Copyright by designer/architect.

Plan #161103

Dimensions: 113'10" W x 60'6" D
Levels: 2
Square Footage: 5,633
Main Level Sq. Ft.: 3,850
Upper Level Sq. Ft.: 1,783
Bedrooms: 4
Bathrooms: 3½
Foundation: Walkout; basement for fee
Material List Available: No
Price Category: J

Images provided by designer/architect.

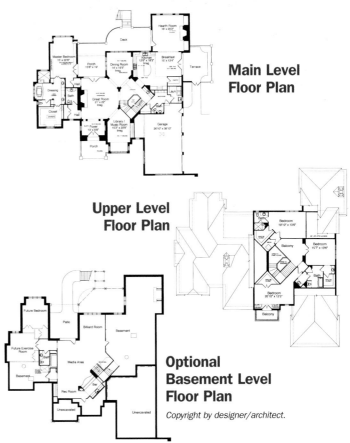

Main Level Floor Plan

Upper Level Floor Plan

Optional Basement Level Floor Plan

Copyright by designer/architect.

Plan #131031

Dimensions: 69'8" W x 48'4" D
Levels: 2
Square Footage: 4,027
Main Level Sq. Ft.: 2,198
Upper Level Sq. Ft.: 1,829
Bedrooms: 5
Bathrooms: 4½
Foundation: Crawl space, slab, or basement
Materials List Available: Yes
Price Category: I

Images provided by designer/architect.

Main Level Floor Plan

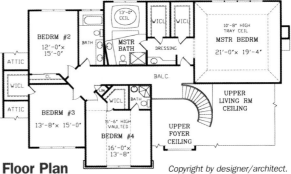

Upper Level Floor Plan

Copyright by designer/architect.

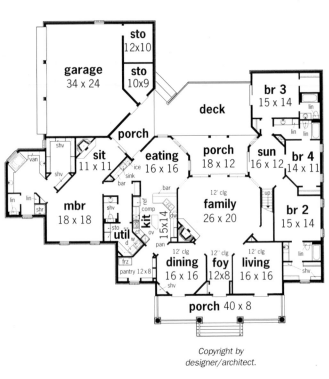

Plan #211067

Dimensions: 96' W x 90' D

Levels: 1

Square Footage: 4,038

Bedrooms: 4

Bathrooms: 4½

Foundation: Crawl space

Materials List Available: Yes

Price Category: I

Images provided by designer/architect.

Copyright by designer/architect.

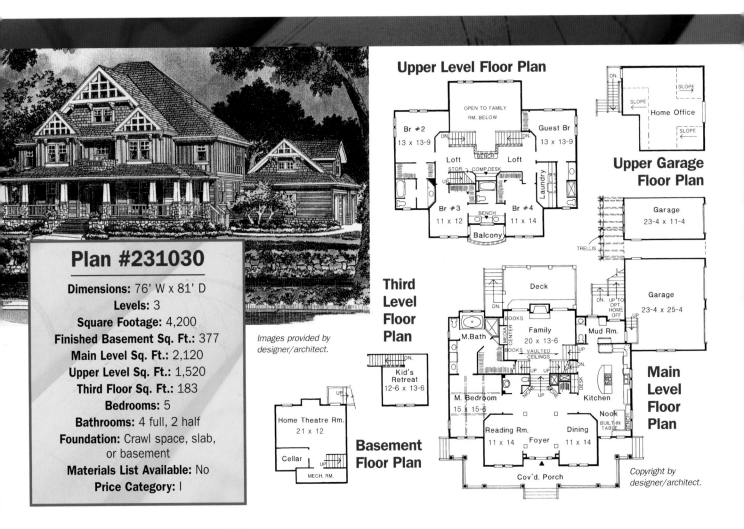

Plan #231030

Dimensions: 76' W x 81' D

Levels: 3

Square Footage: 4,200

Finished Basement Sq. Ft.: 377

Main Level Sq. Ft.: 2,120

Upper Level Sq. Ft.: 1,520

Third Floor Sq. Ft.: 183

Bedrooms: 5

Bathrooms: 4 full, 2 half

Foundation: Crawl space, slab, or basement

Materials List Available: No

Price Category: I

Images provided by designer/architect.

Copyright by designer/architect.

Upper Level Floor Plan

Plan #151020

Dimensions: 96'10" W x 75'10" D
Levels: 2
Square Footage: 4,532
Main Level Sq. Ft.: 3,732
Upper Level Sq. Ft.: 800
Bedrooms: 3
Bathrooms: 3½
Foundation: Crawl space or slab; basement available for fee
CompleteCost List Available: Yes
Price Category: I

Images provided by designer/architect.

Main Level Floor Plan

Copyright by designer/architect.

Plan #261006

Dimensions: 73'10" W x 60' D
Levels: 2
Square Footage: 4,583
Main Level Sq. Ft.: 2,575
Upper Level Sq. Ft.: 2,008
Bedrooms: 4
Bathrooms: 3 full, 2 half
Foundation: Basement
Materials List Available: No
Price Category: I

Images provided by designer/architect.

Main Level Floor Plan

Upper Level Floor Plan

Copyright by designer/architect.

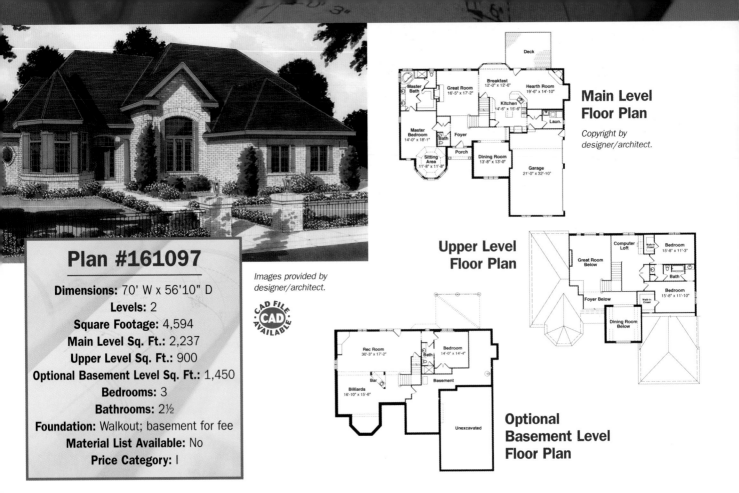

Plan #161097

Dimensions: 70' W x 56'10" D

Levels: 2

Square Footage: 4,594

Main Level Sq. Ft.: 2,237

Upper Level Sq. Ft.: 900

Optional Basement Level Sq. Ft.: 1,450

Bedrooms: 3

Bathrooms: 2½

Foundation: Walkout; basement for fee

Material List Available: No

Price Category: I

Images provided by designer/architect.

Main Level Floor Plan

Copyright by designer/architect.

Upper Level Floor Plan

Optional Basement Level Floor Plan

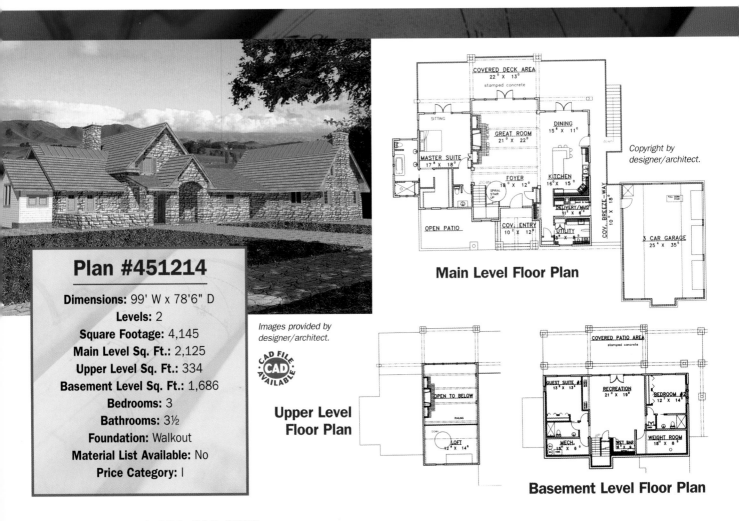

Plan #451214

Dimensions: 99' W x 78'6" D

Levels: 2

Square Footage: 4,145

Main Level Sq. Ft.: 2,125

Upper Level Sq. Ft.: 334

Basement Level Sq. Ft.: 1,686

Bedrooms: 3

Bathrooms: 3½

Foundation: Walkout

Material List Available: No

Price Category: I

Images provided by designer/architect.

Copyright by designer/architect.

Main Level Floor Plan

Upper Level Floor Plan

Basement Level Floor Plan

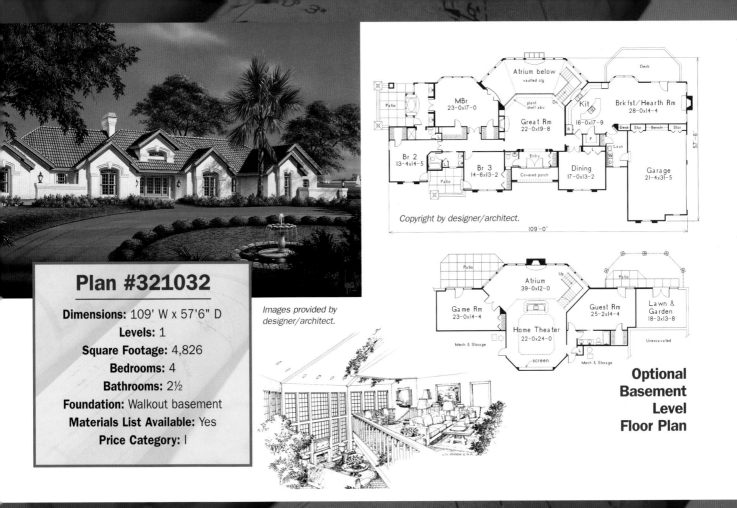

Plan #321032

Dimensions: 109' W x 57'6" D
Levels: 1
Square Footage: 4,826
Bedrooms: 4
Bathrooms: 2½
Foundation: Walkout basement
Materials List Available: Yes
Price Category: I

Images provided by designer/architect.

Optional Basement Level Floor Plan

Plan #211077

Dimensions: 94' W x 68' D
Levels: 2
Square Footage: 5,560
Main Level Sq. Ft.: 4,208
Upper Level Sq. Ft.: 1,352
Bedrooms: 4
Bathrooms: 4 full, 2 half
Foundation: Crawl space or slab
Materials List Available: Yes
Price Category: J

Images provided by designer/architect.

Main Level Floor Plan

Upper Level Floor Plan
Copyright by designer/architect.

Main Level Floor Plan

Plan #151524

Dimensions: 79'10" W x 60'6" D

Levels: 2

Square Footage: 4,461

Main Level Sq. Ft.: 2,861

Upper Level Sq. Ft.: 1,600

Bedrooms: 5

Bathrooms: 4½

Foundation: Crawl space or slab; basement or walkout available for fee

CompleteCost List Available: Yes

Price Category: I

Images provided by designer/architect.

CAD FILE AVAILABLE

Upper Level Floor Plan

Copyright by designer/architect.

Main Level Floor Plan

Plan #161044

Dimensions: 90'6" W x 78'9" D

Levels: 2

Square Footage: 4,652

Main Level Sq. Ft.: 3,414

Upper Level Sq. Ft.: 1,238

Bedrooms: 4

Bathrooms: 3½

Foundation: Basement

Materials List Available: Yes

Price Category: I

Images provided by designer/architect.

CAD FILE AVAILABLE

Rear Elevation

Upper Level Floor Plan

Copyright by designer/architect.

Plan #161100

Dimensions: 89' W x 59'2" D

Levels: 1

Square Footage: 5,377

Main Level Sq. Ft.: 2,961

Basement Level Sq. Ft.: 2,416

Bedrooms: 3

Bathrooms: 2 full, 2 half

Foundation: Walkout; basement for fee

Material List Available: No

Price Category: I

CAD File Available: Yes

This luxury home is perfect for you and your family.

Images provided by designer/architect.

Features:

- Foyer: This beautiful foyer showcases the two-sided fireplace, which warms its space, as well as that of the great room.

- Gathering Areas: The kitchen, breakfast area, and hearth room will quickly become a favorite gathering area, what with the warmth of the fireplace and easy access to a covered porch. Expansive windows with transoms create a light and airy atmosphere.

- Master Suite: This suite makes the most of its circular sitting area and deluxe dressing room with platform whirlpool tub, dual vanities, commode room with closet, and two-person shower.

- Lower Level: This lower level is finished with additional bedrooms and areas dedicated to entertaining, such as the wet bar, billiards area, media room, and exercise room

Rear View

Main Level Floor Plan

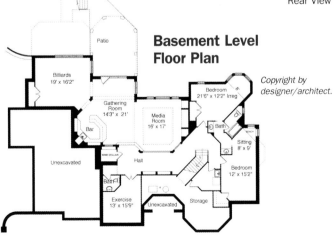

Basement Level Floor Plan

Copyright by designer/architect.

Plan #441015

Dimensions: 130'3" W x 79'3" D
Levels: 1
Square Footage: 4,732
Bedrooms: 4
Bathrooms: 3 full, 2 half
Foundation: Walkout basement
Materials List Available: No
Price Category: I

An artful use of stone was employed on the exterior of this rustic hillside home to complement other architectural elements, such as the angled, oversize four-car garage and the substantial roofline.

Features:

- **Great Room:** This massive vaulted room features a large stone fireplace at one end and a formal dining area at the other. A built-in media center and double doors separate the great room from a home office with its own hearth and built-ins.

- **Kitchen:** This kitchen features a walk-in pantry and snack counter and opens to a skylighted outdoor kitchen. Its appointments include a cooktop and a corner fireplace.

- **Home Theatre:** This space has a built-in viewing screen, a fireplace, and double terrace access.

- **Master Suite:** This private space is found at the other side of the home. Look closely for expansive his and her walk-in closets, a spa tub, a skylighted double vanity area, and a corner fireplace in the salon.

- **Bedrooms:** Three family bedrooms are on the lower level; bedroom 4 has a private bathroom and walk-in closet.

- **Garage:** This large garage has room for four cars; don't miss the dog shower and grooming station just off the garage.

Images provided by designer/architect.

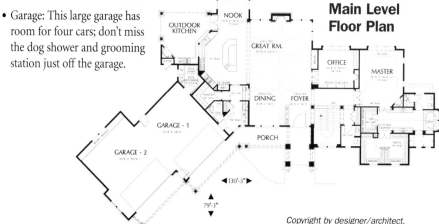

Main Level Floor Plan

Copyright by designer/architect.

Entry

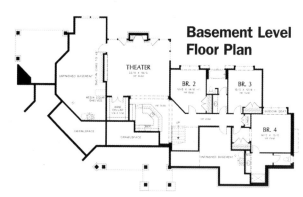

Basement Level Floor Plan

Master Bath

Rear View

Foyer

Dining Room

Great Room

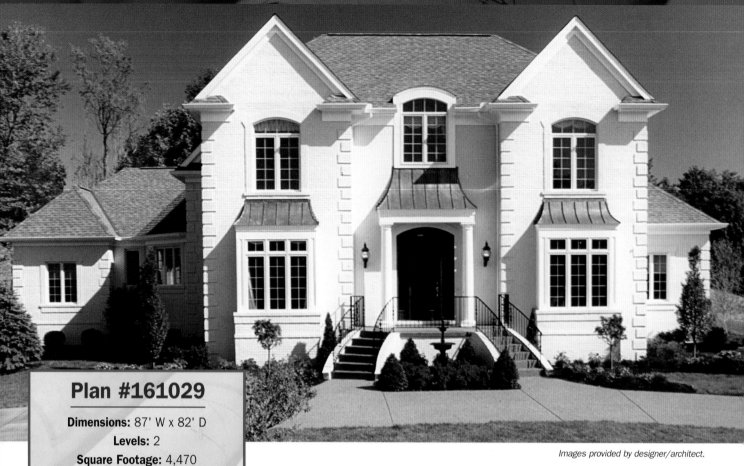

Plan #161029

Dimensions: 87' W x 82' D
Levels: 2
Square Footage: 4,470
Main Level Sq. Ft.: 3,300
Upper Level Sq. Ft.: 1,170
Bedrooms: 4
Bathrooms: 3 full, 2 half
Foundation: Basement
Materials List Available: Yes
Price Category: I

Images provided by designer/architect.

This gracious home is so impressive — inside and out — that it suits the most discriminating tastes.

Features:

- Foyer: A balcony overlooks this gracious area decorated by tall columns.

- Hearth Room: Visually open to the kitchen and the breakfast area, this room is ideal for any sort of gathering.

- Great Room: Colonial columns also form the entry here, and a magnificent window treatment that includes French doors leads to the terrace.

- Library: Built-in shelving adds practicality to this quiet retreat.

- Kitchen: Spread out on the oversized island with a cooktop and seating.

- Additional Bedrooms: Walk-in closets and private access to a bath define each bedroom.

CAD FILE AVAILABLE

Main Level Floor Plan

Upper Level Floor Plan

Copyright by designer/architect.

Plan #161105

Dimensions: 90'2" W x 104'5" D
Levels: 2
Square Footage: 6,806
Main Level Sq. Ft.: 4,511
Upper Level Sq. Ft.: 2,295
Bedrooms: 4
Bathrooms: 4 full, 2 half
Foundation: Walkout basement
Material List Available: No
Price Category: K

The opulence and drama of this European-inspired home features a solid brick exterior with limestone detail, arched dormers, and a parapet.

CAD FILE AVAILABLE

Features:

- **Foyer:** A large octagonal skylight tops a water fountain feature displayed in this exquisite entryway. The formal dining room and library flank the entry and enjoy a 10-ft. ceiling height.

- **Family Living Area:** The gourmet kitchen, breakfast area, and cozy hearth room comprise this family activity center of the home. Wonderful amenities such as a magnificent counter with seating, a celestial ceiling over the dining table, an alcove for an entertainment center, a stone-faced wood-burning fireplace, and access to the rear porch enhance the informal area.

- **Master Suite:** This luxurious suite enjoys a raised ceiling, a seating area with bay window, and access to the terrace. The dressing room pampers the homeowner with a whirlpool tub, a ceramic tile shower enclosure, two vanities, and a spacious walk-in closet.

- **Upper Level:** Elegant stairs lead to the second-floor study loft and two additional bedrooms, each with a private bathroom and large walk-in closet. On the same level, and located for privacy, the third bedroom serves as a guest suite, showcasing a cozy sitting area and private bathroom.

Upper Level Floor Plan

Main Level Floor Plan

Optional Basement Level Floor Plan

Plan #161093

Dimensions: 56' W x 53' D
Levels: 1
Square Footage: 4,328
Main Level Sq. Ft.: 2,582
Basement Sq. Ft.: 1,746
Bedrooms: 3
Bathrooms: 3½
Foundation: Walkout
Materials List Available: No
Price Category: I

Images provided by designer/architect.

Features:

- **Great Room:** This gathering room, which features a fireplace and a decorative ceiling, offers an extensive view of the rear yard.

- **Kitchen:** Spacious and up-to-date, this extra-large combination gourmet kitchen and breakfast room is an ideal area for doing chores and hosting family gatherings.

- **Main Level:** The extravagant master suite, with its private bathroom and dressing area, the library with built-in shelves, and the formal dining room round out the

main floor. Accented by a wood rail, the extra-wide main stairway leads to the lavish lower level.

- **Lower Level:** The two additional bedrooms, adjoining bathroom, media room, billiard room, and exercise room comprise this fantastic finished lower level.

Detailed stucco and stone accents impart warmth and character to the exterior of this one level home.

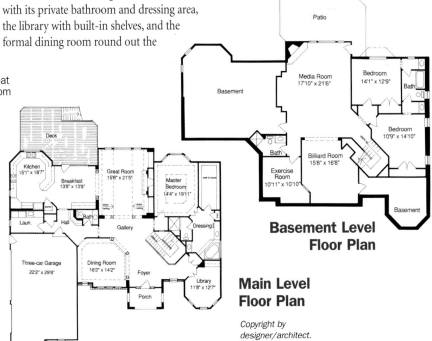

Basement Level Floor Plan

Main Level Floor Plan

Copyright by designer/architect.

Master Bedroom

Dining Room

Great Room

Foyer

Plan #161060

Dimensions: 113'10" W x 60'6" D
Levels: 2
Square Footage: 5,143
Main Level Sq. Ft.: 3,323
Upper Level Sq. Ft.: 1,820
Bedrooms: 4
Bathrooms: 3½
Foundation: Basement, walkout basement
Materials List Available: No
Price Category: J

Images provided by designer/architect.

Luxury, comfort, beauty, spaciousness — this home has everything you've been wanting, including space for every possible activity.

CAD FILE AVAILABLE

Features:

- **Courtyard:** Enjoy the privacy here before entering this spacious home.
- **Great Room:** Open to the foyer, dining area, and kitchen, this great room has a fireplace flanked by windows and leads to the open rear deck.
- **Dining Room:** Situated between the foyer and the kitchen, this room is ideal for formal dining.
- **Library:** Located just off the foyer, this library offers a calm retreat from activities in the great room.
- **Utility Area:** The mudroom, pantry, half-bath and laundry room add up to household convenience.
- **Master Suite:** You'll love the huge walk-in closet, extensive window feature, and bath with a dressing room and two vanities.

Upper Level Floor Plan

Copyright by designer/architect.

Rear Elevation

Main Level Floor Plan

Basement Level Floor Plan

Plan #401048

Dimensions: 57'8" W x 103'6" D
Levels: 2
Square Footage: 5,159
Main Level Sq. Ft.: 2,473
Upper Level Sq. Ft.: 2,686
Bedrooms: 4
Bathrooms: 4½
Foundation: Basement
Materials List Available: Yes
Price Category: I

Images provided by designer/architect.

This unusual stucco-and-siding design opens with a grand portico to a foyer that extends to the living room with fireplace.

CAD FILE AVAILABLE · CAD

Features:

- **Dining Room:** Step up a few steps to this dining room, with its coffered ceiling and butler's pantry, which connects to the gourmet kitchen.

- **Hearth Room:** Attached to the kitchen, this hearth room has the requisite fireplace and three sets of French doors that lead to the covered porch.

- **Family Room:** This room features a coffered ceiling and a fireplace flanked by French doors.

- **Master Suite:** This area includes a tray ceiling, covered deck, and lavish bath.

- **Bedrooms:** All bedrooms are located on the second floor. Two full bathrooms serve the family bedrooms and a bonus room that might be used as an additional bedroom or hobby space.

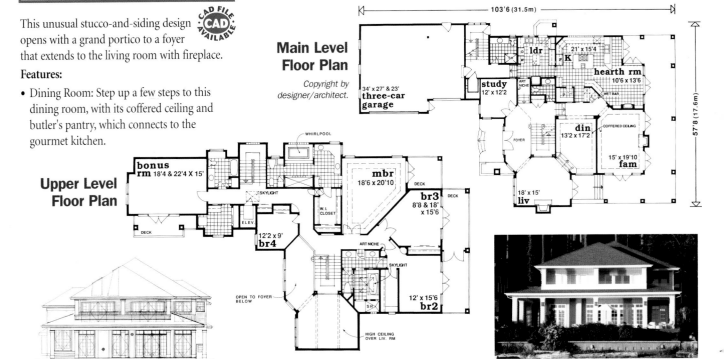

Main Level Floor Plan

Copyright by designer/architect.

Upper Level Floor Plan

Rear Elevation

Rear View

Plan #401050

Dimensions: 81' W x 61' D
Levels: 2
Square Footage: 6,841
Main Level Sq. Ft.: 2,596
Upper Level Sq. Ft.: 2,233
Finished Basement Sq. Ft.: 2,012
Bedrooms: 4
Bathrooms: 3 full, 2 half
Foundation: Basement
Materials List Available: Yes
Price Category: I

This grand two-story European home is adorned with a facade of stucco and brick, meticulously appointed with details for gracious living.

CAD FILE AVAILABLE

Features:

- **Foyer:** Guests enter through a portico to find this stately two-story foyer.

- **Living Room:** This formal area features a tray ceiling and a fireplace and is joined by a charming dining room with a large bay window.

- **Kitchen:** A butler's pantry joins the dining room to this gourmet kitchen, which holds a separate wok kitchen, an island work center, and a breakfast room with double doors that lead to the rear patio.

- **Family Room:** Located near the kitchen, this room enjoys a built-in aquarium, media center, and fireplace.

- **Den:** This room with a tray ceiling, window seat, and built-in computer center is tucked in a corner for privacy.

- **Master Suite:** The second floor features this spectacular space, which has a separate sitting room, an oversized closet, and a bath with a spa tub.

Upper Level Floor Plan

Main Level Floor Plan

Basement Level Floor Plan

Rear Elevation

Plan #161104

Dimensions: 130' W x 84'6" D
Levels: 2
Square Footage: 8,088
Main Level Sq. Ft.: 5,418
Upper Level Sq. Ft.: 2,670
Bedrooms: 4
Bathrooms: 4 full, 2 half
Foundation: Basement
Material List Available: No
Price Category: L

Images provided by designer/architect.

Spectacular exterior with solid brick, limestone trim, and custom wood door reflects an authentic European manor.

CAD FILE AVAILABLE

Features:

- Kitchen: A 17-ft. high ceiling with arched timber beams, wall oven, island with vegetable sink, and second island with seating all create a true gourmet working space that overlooks the breakfast room and the cozy hearth room.

- Master Suite: This palatial suite with curved ceilings, fireplace-side whirlpool tub, large shower, sunken solarium, dressing room with two vanities and dressing table will pamper you. Four closets, including a compartmented double-entry master and secondary laundry area provide unmatched convenience.

- Bedrooms: Two sets of stairs lead to the second floor bedrooms—two with private sitting areas. Each bedroom enjoys a private bath and walk-in closet.

- Additional Space: A sunken covered porch, enhances the rear-yard enjoyment, while a finished lower level creates additional rooms for fun and entertainment.

Rear View

Copyright by designer/architect.

Main Level Floor Plan

Upper Level Floor Plan

Basement Level Floor Plan

Plan #161101

Dimensions: 136'3" W x 69' D
Levels: 2
Square Footage: 8,414
Main Level Sq. Ft.: 4,011
Upper Level Sq. Ft.: 2,198
Optional Lower Level Sq. Ft.: 2,205
Bedrooms: 4
Bathrooms: 4 full, 2 half
Foundation: Walkout; basement for fee
Material List Available: Yes
Price Category: L

Images provided by designer/architect.

The grandeur of this mansion-style home boasts period stone, two-story columns, an angular turret, a second-floor balcony, and a gated courtyard.

(CAD FILE AVAILABLE)

Features:

- **Formal Living:** Formal areas consist of the charming living room and adjacent music room, which continues to the library, with its sloped ceilings and glass surround. Various ceiling treatments, with 10-ft. ceiling heights, and 8-ft.-tall doors add luxury and artistry to the first floor.

- **Hearth Room:** This large room, with false wood-beamed ceiling, adds a casual yet rich atmosphere to the family gathering space. Dual French doors on each side of the fireplace create a pleasurable indoor-outdoor relationship.

- **Kitchen:** This space is an enviable work place for the gourmet cook. Multiple cabinets and expansive counter space create a room that may find you spending a surprisingly enjoyable amount of time on food preparation. The built-in grill on the porch makes outdoor entertaining convenient and fun.

- **Master Suite:** This suite offers a vaulted ceiling, dual walk-in closets, and his and her vanities. The whirlpool tub is showcased on a platform and surrounded by windows for a relaxing view of the side yard. Private access to the deck is an enchanting surprise.

Rear View

Copyright by designer/architect.

Main Level Floor Plan

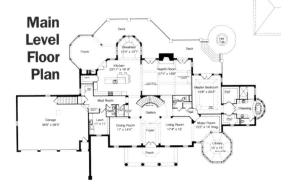

Upper Level Floor Plan

Basement Level Floor Plan

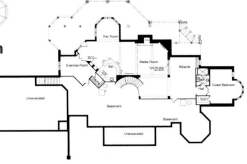

Let Us Help You Plan Your Dream Home

Whether you've always dreamed of building your own home or you can't find the right house from among the dozens you've toured, our collection of ultimate home plans can help you achieve the home of your dreams. You could have an architect create a one-of-a-kind home for you, but the design services alone could end up costing up to 15 percent of the cost of construction—a hefty premium for any building project. Isn't it a better idea to select from among the hundreds of unique designs shown in our collection for a fraction of the cost?

What does Creative Homeowner® Offer?

In this book, Creative Homeowner® provides hundreds of home plans from the country's best architects and designers. Our designs are among the most popular available. Whether your taste runs from traditional to contemporary, Victorian to early American, you are sure to find the best house design for you and your family. Our plans packages include detailed drawings to help you or your builder construct your dream house. **(See page 342.)**

Can I Make Changes to the Plans?

Creative Homeowner® offers three ways to help you achieve a truly unique home design. Our customizing service allows for extensive changes to our designs. **(See page 343.)** We also provide reverse images of our plans, or we can give you and your builder the tools for making minor changes on your own. **(See page 344.)**

Can You Help Me Stay on Budget?

Building a house is a large financial investment. To help you stay within your budget, Creative Homeowner® can provide you with general construction costs based on your zip code. **(See page 344.)** Also, many of our plans come with the option of buying detailed materials lists to help you price out construction costs.

Is There Anything I Missed?

A typical construction crew consists of a number of skilled professionals. If you plan on doing all or part of the work yourself, or you want to keep tabs on your builder, we offer best-selling building and design books at attractive prices. (See our company Web site at www.creativehomeowner.com.) Our home-building book package covers all phases of home construction, from framing and drywalling to wiring and plumbing. **(See page 352.)**

Our Plans Packages Offer:

All of our home plans are the result of many hours of work by leading architects and professional designers. Most of our home plans include each of the following.

Frontal Sheet

This artist's rendering of the front of the house gives you an idea of how the house will look once it is completed and the property landscaped.

Detailed Floor Plans

These plans show the size and layout of the rooms. They also provide the locations of doors, windows, fireplaces, closets, stairs, and electrical outlets and switches.

Foundation Plan

A foundation plan gives the dimensions of basements, walk-out basements, crawl spaces, pier foundations, and slab construction. Each house design lists the type of foundation included. If the plan you choose does not have the foundation type you require, our customer service department can help you customize the plan to meet your needs.

Roof Plan

In addition to providing the pitch of the roof, these plans also show the locations of dormers, skylights, and other elements.

Exterior Elevations

These drawings show the front, rear, and sides of the house as if you were looking at it head on. Elevations also provide information about architectural features and finish materials.

Interior Elevations and Details

Interior elevations show specific details of such elements as fireplaces, kitchen and bathroom cabinets, built-ins, and other unique features of the design.

Cross Sections

These show the structure as if it were sliced to reveal construction requirements, such as insulation, flooring, and roofing details.

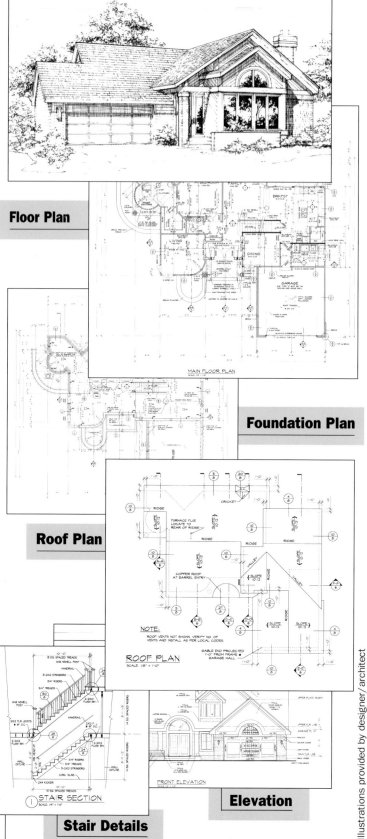

Frontal Sheet

Floor Plan

Foundation Plan

Roof Plan

Elevation

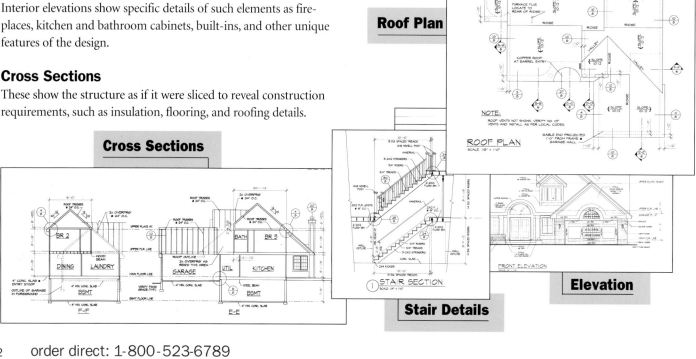

Cross Sections

Stair Details

Illustrations provided by designer/architect

Customize Your Plans in 4 Easy Steps

1 **Select the home plan** that most closely meets your needs. Purchase of a reproducible master is necessary in order to make changes to a plan.

2 **Call 1-800-523-6789 to place your order.** Tell our sales representative you are interested in customizing your plan. To receive your customization cost estimate, we will send you a checklist (via fax or email) for you to complete indicating the changes you would like to make to your plan. There is a $50 nonrefundable consultation fee for this service. If you decide to continue with the custom changes, the $50 fee is credited to the total amount charged.

3 **Fax the completed checklist** to 1-201-760-2431 or email it to us at customize@creativehomeowner.com. Within three business days of receipt of your checklist, a detailed cost estimate will be provided to you.

4 **Once you approve the estimate,** a 75% retainer fee is collected and customization work begins. Preliminary drawings typically take 10 to 15 business days. After approval, we will collect the balance of your customization order cost before shipping the completed plans. You will receive five sets of blueprints or a reproducible master, plus a customized materials list if desired.

Terms & Copyright

These home plans are protected under the terms of United States Copyright Law and may not be copied or reproduced in any way, by any means, unless you have purchased reproducible masters, which clearly indicate your right to copy or reproduce. We authorize the use of your chosen home plan as an aid in the construction of one single-family home only. You may not use this home plan to build a second or multiple dwellings without purchasing another blueprint or blueprints, or paying additional home plan fees.

Architectural Seals

Because of differences in building codes, some cities and states now require an architect or engineer licensed in that state to review and "seal" a blueprint, or officially approve it, prior to construction. Delaware, Nevada, New Jersey, and New York require that all plans for houses built in those states be redrawn by an architect licensed in the state in which the home will be built. We strongly advise you to consult with your local building official for information regarding architectural seals.

Modification Pricing Guide

Categories	Average Cost For Modification
Add or remove living space	Quote required
Bathroom layout redesign	Starting at $120
Kitchen layout redesign	Starting at $120
Garage: add or remove	Starting at $400
Garage: front entry to side load or vice versa	Starting at $300
Foundation changes	Starting at $220
Exterior building materials change	Starting at $200
Exterior openings: add, move, or remove	$65 per opening
Roof line changes	Starting at $360
Ceiling height adjustments	Starting at $280
Fireplace: add or remove	Starting at $90
Screened porch: add	Starting at $280
Wall framing change from 2x4 to 2x6	Starting at $200
Bearing and/or exterior walls changes	Quote required
Non-bearing wall or room changes	$65 per room
Metric conversion of home plan	Starting at $400
Adjust plan for handicapped accessibility	Quote required
Adapt plans for local building code requirements	Quote required
Engineering stamping only	Quote required
Any other engineering services	Quote required
Interactive illustrations (choices of exterior materials)	Quote required

Note: *Any home plan can be customized to accommodate your desired changes. The average prices above are provided only as examples of the most commonly requested changes, and are subject to change without notice. Prices for changes will vary according to the number of modifications requested, plan size, style, and method of design used by the original designer. To obtain a detailed cost estimate, please contact us.*

Before Customization

After

Decide What Type of Plan Package You Need

How many Plans Should You Order?

Standard 8-Set Package. We've found that our 8-set package is the best value for someone who is ready to start building. Once the process begins, a number of people will require their own set of blueprints. The 8-set package provides plans for you, your builder, the subcontractors, mortgage lender, and the building department.

Minimum 5-Set Package. If you are in the bidding process, you may want to order only four sets for the bidding round and reorder additional sets as needed.

1-Set Study Package. The 1-set package allows you to review your home plan in detail. The plan will be marked as a study print, and it is illegal to build a house from a study print alone. It is a violation of copyright law to reproduce a blueprint without permission.

Buying Additional Sets

If you require additional copies of blueprints for your home construction, you can order additional sets within 60 days of the original order date at a reduced price. The cost is $45.00 for each additional set. For more information, contact customer service.

Reproducible Masters

If you plan to make minor changes to one of our home plans, you can purchase reproducible masters. Printed on vellum paper, an erasable paper that you can reproduce in a copying machine, reproducible masters allow an architect, designer, or builder to alter our plans to give you a customized home design. This package also allows you to print as many copies of the modified plans as you need for construction.

Mirror-Reverse Sets/Right-Reading Reverse

Plans can be printed in mirror-reverse—we can "flip" plans to create a mirror image of the design. This is useful when the house would fit your site or personal preferences if all the rooms were on the opposite side than shown. As the image is reversed, the lettering and dimensions will also be reversed, meaning they will read backwards. Therefore, when ordering mirror-reverse drawings, you must order at least one set of right-reading plans. A $50.00 fee per plan order will be charged for mirror-reverse (regardless of the number of mirror-reverse sets ordered). Some plans are available in right-reading reverse, this feature will show the plan in reverse, but the writing on the plan will be readable. A $150.00 fee per plan order will be charged for right-reading reverse (regardless of the number of right-reading reverse sets ordered). Please contact our order department at or visit our website to check the availibility of this feature for your chosen plan.

EZ Quote: Home Cost Estimator

EZ Quote is our response to one of the most frequently asked questions we hear from customers: "How much will the house cost me to build?" EZ Quote: Home Cost Estimator will enable you to obtain a calculated building cost to construct your new home, based on labor rates and building material costs within your zip code area. This summary is useful for those who want to know the total construction costs before purchasing sets of home plans. It will also provide a level of comfort when you begin soliciting bids from builders. The cost is $29.95 for the first EZ Quote and $14.95 for each additional one. Available only in the U.S. and Canada.

CompleteCost Estimator

CompleteCost Estimator is a valuable tool for use in planning and constructing your new home. It combines the detail of a materials list with line-by-line cost estimating. The result is a complete, detailed estimate—similar to a bid—that will act as a checklist for all the items you will need to select or coordinate during our building process. CompleteCost Estimator is only available for certain plans (please see Plan Index) and may only be ordered with the purchase of at least five sets of home plans. The cost is $125.00 for CompleteCost Estimator.

Materials List

Available for most of our plans, the Materials List provides you an invaluable resource in planning and estimating the cost of your home. Each Materials List outlines the quantity, dimensions, and type of materials needed to build your home (with the exception of mechanical systems). You will get faster, more-accurate bids from your contractors and building suppliers—and avoid paying for unused materials. A Materials List may only be ordered with the purchase of at least five sets of home plans.

Order Toll Free by Phone
1-800-523-6789
By Fax: 201-760-2431

Regular office hours are
8:30AM–7:30PM ET, Mon–Fri

Orders received 3PM ET, will be
processed and shipped within two
business days.

Order Online
www.ultimateplans.com

Mail Your Order
Creative Homeowner
Attn: Home Plans
24 Park Way
Upper Saddle River, NJ 07458

Canadian Customers
Order Toll Free 1-800-393-1883

Mail Your Order (Canada)
Creative Homeowner Canada
Attn: Home Plans
113-437 Martin St., Ste. 215
Penticton, BC V2A 5L1

Before You Order

Our Exchange Policy

Blueprints are nonrefundable. However, should you find that the plan you have purchased does not fit your needs, you may exchange that plan for another plan in our collection within 60 days from the date of your original order. The entire content of your original order must be returned before an exchange will be processed. You will be charged a processing fee of 20% of the amount of the original order, the cost difference between the new plan set and the original plan set (if applicable), and all related shipping costs for the new plans. Contact our order department for more information. Please note: reproducible masters may only be exchanged if the package is unopened.

Building Codes and Requirements

At the time of creation, our plans meet the building code requirements published by the Building Officials and Code Administrators International, the Southern Building Code Congress International, the International Conference of Building Officials, or the Council of American Building Officials. Because building codes vary from area to area, some drawing modifications and/or the assistance of a professional designer or architect may be necessary to comply with your local codes or to accommodate specific building site conditions. We strongly advise you to consult with your local building official for information regarding codes governing your area.

Blueprint Price Schedule

Price Code	1 Set	5 Sets	8 Sets	Reproducible Masters	CAD	Materials List
A	$300	$345	$395	$530	$950	$85
B	$375	$435	$480	$600	$1,100	$85
C	$435	$500	$550	$650	$1,200	$85
D	$490	$560	$610	$710	$1,300	$95
E	$550	$620	$660	$770	$1,400	$95
F	$610	$680	$720	$830	$1,500	$95
G	$670	$740	$780	$890	$1,600	$95
H	$760	$830	$870	$980	$1,700	$95
I	$860	$930	$970	$1,080	$1,800	$105
J	$960	$1,030	$1,070	$1,190	$1,900	$105
K	$1,070	$1,150	$1,190	$1,320	$2,030	$105
L	$1,180	$1,270	$1,310	$1,460	$2,170	$105

Note: All prices subject to change

Shipping & Handling

Shipping & Handling	1-4 Sets	5-7 Sets	8+ Sets or Reproducibles	CAD
US Regular (7–10 business days)	$18	$20	$25	$25
US Priority (3–5 business days)	$25	$30	$35	$35
US Express (1–2 business days)	$40	$45	$50	$50
Canada Express (1–2 business days)	$60	$70	$80	$80
Worldwide Express (3–5 business days)	$80	$80	$80	$80

Note: All delivery times are from date the blueprint package is shipped (typically within 1-2 days of placing order).

Order Form Please send me the following:

Plan Number: _____ **Price Code:** _____ (See Plan Index.)

Indicate Foundation Type: (Select ONE. See plan page for availability.)

❏ Slab ❏ Crawl space ❏ Basement ❏ Walk-out basement

❏ Optional Foundation for Fee _____ $_____
(Please enter foundation here)

Please call all our order department or visit our website for optional foundation fee

Basic Blueprint Package
Cost

❏ CAD File $_____
❏ Reproducible Masters $_____
❏ 8-Set Plan Package $_____
❏ 5-Set Plan Package $_____
❏ 1-Set Study Package $_____
❏ Additional plan sets:
___ sets at $45.00 per set $_____
❏ Print in mirror-reverse: $50.00 per order $_____
Please call all our order department or visit our website for availibility
❏ Print in right-reading reverse: $150.00 per order $_____
Please call all our order department or visit our website for availibility

Important Extras

❏ Materials List $_____
❏ CompleteCost Materials Report at $125.00 $_____
Zip Code of Home/Building Site _____
❏ EZ Quote for Plan #_____ at $29.95 $_____
❏ Additional EZ Quotes for Plan #s_____ $_____
at $14.95 each
Shipping (see chart above) $_____
SUBTOTAL $_____
Sales Tax (NJ residents only, add 6%) $_____
TOTAL $_____

Order Toll Free: 1-800-523-6789   By Fax: 201-760-2431
Creative Homeowner
24 Park Way
Upper Saddle River, NJ 07458

Name _____
(Please print or type)

Street _____
(Please do not use a P.O. Box)

City _____ State _____

Country _____ Zip _____

Daytime telephone ( ) _____

Fax ( ) _____
(Required for reproducible orders)

E-Mail _____

Payment ❏ Check/money order *Make checks payable to Creative Homeowner*

❏ VISA   ❏ MasterCard   ❏ American Express Cards   ❏ DISCOVER

Credit card number _____

Expiration date (mm/yy) _____

Signature _____

Please check the appropriate box:
❏ Licensed builder/contractor   ❏ Homeowner   ❏ Renter

SOURCE CODE **CA450**   www.ultimateplans.com

Copyright Notice

All home plans sold through this publication are protected by copyright. Reproduction of these home plans, either in whole or in part, including any form and/or preparation of derivative works thereof, for any reason without prior written permission is strictly prohibited. The purchase of a set of home plans in no way transfers any copyright or other ownership interest in it to the buyer except for a limited license to use that set of home plans for the construction of one, and only one, dwelling unit. The purchase of additional sets of the home plans at a reduced price from the original set or as a part of a multiple-set package does not convey to the buyer a license to construct more than one dwelling.

Similarly, the purchase of reproducible home plans (sepias, mylars) carries the same copyright protection as mentioned above. It is generally allowed to make up to a maximum of 10 copies for the construction of a single dwelling only. To use any plans more than once, and to avoid any copyright license infringement, it is necessary to contact the plan designer to receive a release and license for any extended use. Whereas a purchaser of reproducible plans is granted a license to make copies, it should be noted that because blueprints are copyrighted, making photocopies from them is illegal.

Copyright and licensing of home plans for construction exist to protect all parties. Copyright respects and supports the intellectual property of the original architect or designer. Copyright law has been reinforced over the past few years. Willful infringement could cause settlements for statutory damages to $150,000.00 plus attorney fees, damages, and loss of profits.

Index

For pricing, see page 345.

Plan #	Price Code	Page	Total Finished Sq. Ft.	Materials List	CompleteCost
101002	B	34	1,296	N	N
101003	C	33	1,593	Y	N
101004	C	18	1,787	Y	N
101004	C	19	1,787	Y	N
101005	D	94	1,992	Y	N
101008	D	136	2,088	Y	N
101010	D	150	2,187	Y	N
101011	D	153	2,184	Y	N
101012	E	180	2,288	N	N
101012	E	181	2,288	N	N
101013	E	252	2,564	Y	N
101013	E	253	2,564	Y	N
101017	E	152	2,253	N	N
101022	D	128	1,992	Y	N
101022	D	129	1,992	Y	N
101024	G	289	3,135	N	N
101028	D	136	1,963	N	N
101030	D	135	2,071	N	N
101031	D	84	1,932	N	N
101033	E	169	2,260	N	N
101034	E	171	2,470	N	N
101035	E	176	2,461	N	N
101036	B	50	1,343	N	N
101087	D	148	2,197	Y	N
101091	E	167	2,270	N	N
101098	E	162	2,398	Y	N
101100	E	188	2,479	Y	N
101119	G	290	3,264	N	N
111004	F	249	2,968	N	N
111006	E	198	2,241	N	N
111015	E	214	2,208	N	N
111016	E	214	2,240	N	N
111017	E	172	2,323	N	N
111018	F	234	2,745	N	N
111031	F	264	2,869	N	N
111039	G	321	3,335	N	N
121001	D	91	1,911	Y	N
121002	B	35	1,347	Y	N
121003	E	213	2,498	Y	N
121006	C	69	1,762	Y	N
121007	E	267	2,512	Y	N
121008	C	52	1,651	Y	N
121015	D	119	1,999	Y	N
121017	E	173	2,353	Y	N
121018	H	315	3,950	Y	N
121019	H	304	3,775	Y	N
121022	H	307	3,556	Y	N
121023	H	311	3,904	Y	N
121024	G	251	3,057	Y	N
121025	E	248	2,562	Y	N
121026	H	315	3,926	Y	N
121029	E	244	2,576	Y	N
121030	F	255	2,613	Y	N
121031	C	30	1,772	Y	N
121046	F	245	2,655	Y	N
121047	G	271	3,072	Y	N
121049	G	288	3,335	Y	N
121050	D	101	1,996	Y	N
121051	D	87	1,808	Y	N
121056	B	12	1,479	Y	N
121057	E	166	2,311	Y	N
121061	G	243	3,025	Y	N
121062	G	292	3,448	Y	N
121063	G	302	3,473	Y	N
121067	F	230	2,708	Y	N
121068	E	190	2,391	Y	N
121073	E	257	2,579	Y	N
121074	E	184	2,486	Y	N
121079	F	229	2,688	Y	N
121080	E	196	2,384	Y	N
121082	F	246	2,932	Y	N
121083	F	242	2,695	Y	N
121084	C	33	1,728	Y	N
121085	D	144	1,948	Y	N
121086	D	105	1,998	Y	N
121088	E	189	2,340	Y	N
121090	F	245	2,645	Y	N
121091	F	254	2,689	Y	N
121092	D	102	1,887	Y	N
121094	C	77	1,768	Y	N
121095	E	201	2,282	Y	N
121097	E	195	2,417	Y	N
121100	G	307	3,750	Y	N
121103	H	313	3,992	Y	N
121110	D	89	1,855	Y	N
131006	E	148	2,193	Y	N
131014	B	24	1,380	Y	N
131015	E	97	1,860	Y	N
131031	I	323	4,027	Y	N
131036	F	266	2,585	Y	N
131039	C	26	1,029	Y	N
131041	D	58	1,679	Y	N
131045	E	168	2,347	Y	N
131050	G	236	2,874	Y	N
141011	D	139	1,869	Y	N
141022	F	239	2,911	Y	N
141029	E	175	2,289	Y	N
141031	E	212	2,367	Y	N
151002	E	273	3,124	N	Y
151004	D	146	2,107	N	Y
151005	D	112	1,940	N	Y
151007	C	44	1,787	N	Y
151008	D	106	1,892	N	Y
151009	C	48	1,601	N	Y
151010	B	14	1,379	N	Y
151011	G	300	3,437	N	Y
151015	F	238	2,789	N	Y
151016	C	22	1,783	N	Y
151018	F	259	2,755	N	Y
151019	F	228	2,642	N	Y
151020	I	325	4,532	N	Y
151021	G	279	3,385	N	Y
151024	H	293	3,623	N	Y
151026	C	42	1,574	N	Y
151028	E	167	2,252	N	Y
151032	F	267	2,824	N	Y
151033	J	320	5,548	N	Y
151037	C	68	1,538	N	Y
151039	B	56	1,353	N	Y
151050	D	121	2,096	N	Y
151054	C	37	1,746	N	Y
151055	E	308	3,183	N	Y
151057	F	228	2,951	N	Y
151063	D	221	2,554	N	Y
151068	D	92	1,880	N	Y
151081	E	277	3,394	N	Y
151104	D	99	1,860	N	Y
151106	F	297	3,568	N	Y
151112	F	300	3,661	N	Y
151117	D	111	1,957	N	Y
151126	E	290	3,474	N	Y
151144	F	262	2,624	N	Y
151170	D	95	1,965	N	Y
151180	G	296	3,167	N	Y
151232	H	310	3,901	N	Y
151281	B	25	1,461	N	Y
151336	B	16	1,480	N	Y
151383	E	232	2,534	N	Y
151384	F	218	2,742	N	Y
151386	D	110	1,989	N	Y
151447	D	160	2,147	N	Y

Index

For pricing, see page 345.

Index

For pricing, see page 345.

Plan #111031

Dimensions: 56' W x 53' D

Levels: 2

Square Footage: 2,869

Main Level Sq. Ft.: 2,152

Upper Level Sq. Ft.: 717

Bedrooms: 4

Bathrooms: 3

Foundation: Crawl space, slab

Materials List Available: No

Price Category: F

Images provided by designer/architect.

Features:

- Ceiling Height: 9 ft.
- Front Porch: The middle of the three French doors with circle tops here opens to the foyer.
- Living Room: Archways from the foyer open to both this room and the equally large dining room.
- Family Room: Also open to the foyer, this room features a two-story sloped ceiling and a balcony from the upper level. You'll love the fireplace, with its raised brick hearth and the

two French doors with circle tops, which open to the rear porch.

- Kitchen: A center island, range with microwave, built-in desk, and dining bar that's open to the breakfast room add up to comfort and efficiency.
- Master Suite: A Palladian window and linen closet grace this suite's bedroom, and the bath has an oversized garden tub, standing shower, two walk-in closets, and double vanity.

This home is ideal for any family, thanks to its spaciousness, beauty, and versatility.

Copyright by designer/architect.

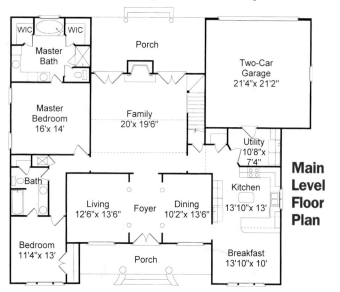

Main Level Floor Plan

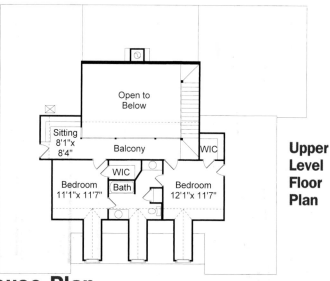

Upper Level Floor Plan

Featured House Plan

See page 264

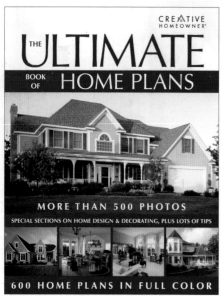
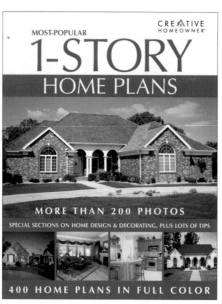
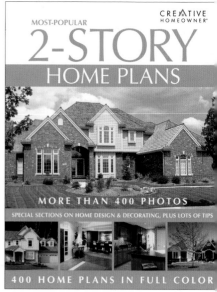
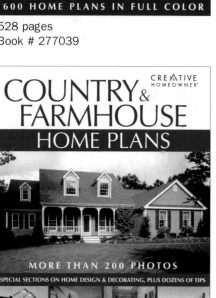
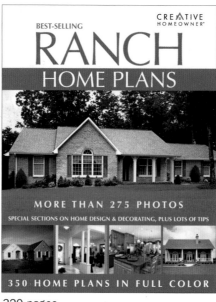